IMAGES
of America

HISTORIC LIGHTHOUSES OF THE FLORIDA KEYS

On the Cover: Sarasota photographer Joseph Steinmetz and his wife, Lois Foley Steinmetz, are pictured in front of the harbor light at Fort Jefferson on Garden Key in the Dry Tortugas. (Courtesy of the State Archives of Florida.)

IMAGES
of America

Historic Lighthouses of the Florida Keys

Laura Albritton and Jerry Wilkinson

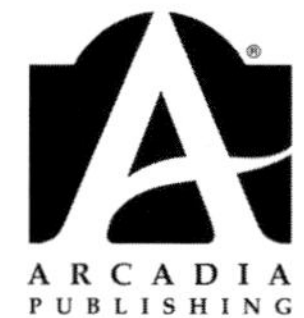

ARCADIA
PUBLISHING

ISBN 978-1-4671-0782-2

Published by Arcadia Publishing
Charleston, South Carolina

Printed in the United States of America

Library of Congress Control Number: 2021946143

For all general information, please contact Arcadia Publishing:
Telephone 843-853-2070
Fax 843-853-0044
E-mail sales@arcadiapublishing.com
For customer service and orders:
Toll-Free 1-888-313-2665

Visit us on the Internet at www.arcadiapublishing.com

Dedicated to Mary Lou Wilkinson and Zickie and Iris Allgrove

Contents

ACKNOWLEDGMENTS

We would like to thank Eric Martin, president of the Florida Keys Reef Lights Foundation, for generously sharing his expertise and making helpful suggestions. His foundation does important work regarding the research into and preservation of many of the lighthouses pictured in this book. The exhibitions at the Key West Lighthouse and Keeper's Quarters Museum provided additional insight into the lives of the keepers and their families. Thanks also go to Monroe County historian Tom Hambright for clarifying certain facts, Gail Swanson for her book on the Sombrero Key light, and the Florida Keys History & Discovery Center for a useful post about Mary "Eliza" Bethel. We wish to acknowledge the late Love Dean and the late Tom Taylor, both friends of Jerry, whose work on Florida Reef lighthouses remains so valuable to anyone researching this subject. We are grateful to the following institutions for the use of their images: the Monroe County Public Library at Key West, the State Archives of Florida, the US Lighthouse Society Archives, the US Coast Guard Historian's Office, the Library of Congress, and the National Archives. Once again, Arcadia Publishing has been a pleasure to work with, especially Angel Prohaska, Katelyn Jenkins, Sara Miller, and Stacia Bannerman. Credit goes to Iris Allgrove for her wonderful sketch of Sand Key based on William Whitehead's original. Last but never least, we wish to thank Mary Lou Wilkinson and Zickie Allgrove for their help, patience, and good humor.

Introduction

The first mariners to ply the Florida Reef did not need navigational aids such as lighthouses or lightships. The Matecumbes from the Florida Keys, the Taino from nearby Cuba, and the Tequesta of South Florida plied the waters in canoes with the shallowest of drafts, and as a result, did not fear the corals or shoals that, in some places, rested only three to five feet below the surface. Their vessels were well suited to the region. By day they could differentiate depth by the colors of the ocean and by night navigate by the stars. Even if they did run aground, the worst that might happen was a scrape to a sturdy hull or a momentary foundering.

Once Europeans arrived in the Americas, the Spanish brought ships with ample holds to bring back plunder from the New World, as well as tropical fruit trees, tobacco, mined silver, and sugar. Setting out from Vera Cruz or Havana, vessels sailed through the Straits of Florida, where the Florida Current originates, and along the Florida Reef, the third largest reef system on our planet. Over the next few centuries, many colonial vessels that ventured to the Americas wrecked here, and the Florida Reef became something of a ship graveyard. Yet, without any significant settlements in southern Florida, the Spanish Crown had little reason to invest in the difficult task of constructing lighthouses to prevent such wrecks. Instead, sailors charted the waters as best they could—and prayed.

When the United States took possession of Florida, the Americans had ambitious plans for expansion. They saw the Florida Straits as one great shipping lane to connect regions and domestic trade; they recognized the military and strategic significance of the Florida Territory, including the Florida Keys. Lt. Comdr. Matthew Perry (later a famed commodore) planted the US flag on the island of Key West in 1822. Tasked with assessing the region, he found an urgent need for navigational aids along the Florida Reef. Perry recommended that the US government undertake to build four lighthouses, starting at Cape Florida (in today's Miami-Dade County).

Although the federal government did not follow Perry's recommendations to the letter, at least in regards to their location, four early lighthouses were indeed constructed. The settlement of Key West at the time consisted of fewer than 500 people, and conditions for the laborers constructing the lighthouses at Cape Florida, Key West, Garden Key, and Sand Key were highly challenging. Despite the victory in completing four lighthouses as of 1827, complaints about these lights commenced almost immediately. One captain grumbled that a ship might easily run aground vainly searching for the beacon emitting from Cape Florida. (Although Cape Florida, on Key Biscayne, is not part of the Florida Keys, that lighthouse did illuminate the Florida Reef and for a time lay within the boundaries of Monroe County.)

By the end of 1846, only one of the four original masonry lights remained. Two were rebuilt with brick, while the third, at Sand Key, utilized what was—at the time—state-of-the-art engineering. Two men in particular, engineers Isaiah Lewis and George Gordon Meade, brought innovation and new technology to Florida Keys lighthouses. The next reef lights would be constructed of iron, and their appearance would be quite radically different from that of the conical towers at Key West and Garden Key. Secured by iron piles and, in some cases, foot plates, these reef lights survived all the intense weather that the subtropics managed to hurl at them. Some lighthouse keepers even had the hair-raising experience of riding out hurricanes in lighthouse towers miles from shore.

These lighthouses also played a role in America's Civil War. After Florida seceded from the United States and joined the Confederacy in 1861, the Florida Reef lighthouses became highly important to each side's war effort. A group of Confederates attacked the Cape Florida light on Key Biscayne and succeeded in disabling it for the duration of the war. But the Union held onto the lighthouses at Carysfort Reef, Sombrero Key, Sand Key, Key West, the Northwest Passage, the Tortugas Lighthouse on Loggerhead Key, and the Tortugas harbor light (at Fort Jefferson) on Garden Key. In fact, Union troops secured the island of Key West immediately after Florida's secession, and Fort Jefferson served as a prison for Confederates, including the doctor who assisted President Lincoln's assassin, John Wilkes Booth.

At one time, the Florida Keys lights numbered 11: Fowey Rocks, Carysfort Reef, Alligator Reef, Sombrero Key, American Shoal, Sand Key, Key West, Northwest Passage, Rebecca Shoal, the Tortugas Lighthouse on Loggerhead Key, and the Tortugas harbor light at Fort Jefferson. Yet as much as they might appear massive, immutable monuments, the lighthouses changed almost every decade. Some were raised several feet; the system of lighting the lamps themselves evolved multiple times.

Lighthouse keepers came and others retired. Some died in accidents during the course of their duties. In 1939, the US Coast Guard took over administration and maintenance of the lighthouses; civilians were no longer eligible to keep the Florida Keys lights. Two lighthouses disappeared off the map entirely. Automation in the 20th century seemed to transform everything, and then the ubiquity of GPS, Global Positioning Systems, revolutionized even more. Lighthouses were born of necessity; now they were no longer needed. Sailors had other means to avoid the Florida Reef. But by now, many of the lighthouses were beloved, and people in the Florida Keys and those who simply loved lighthouses began to plan their preservation. In the case of Key West, the conical brick light underwent a major restoration and serves as part of a museum and major island attraction. The Tortugas harbor light at Fort Jefferson on Garden Key has been folded into the National Park Service and was recently restored off-island. Others have not been so fortunate.

Sand Key suffered serious damage in a mysterious fire. Then most of the lighthouses began to go dark, as they were decommissioned. George Gordon Meade predicted that his lights might last 200 years but had not counted on them being left—without maintenance—to deteriorate. Sea, salt air, and sun have taken a constant toll, and without scraping, repainting, and repair, the condition of iron lights such as Carysfort Reef and Sombrero Key worsens every year. The US government offers several for sale. The National Park Service awarded Alligator Reef lighthouse to an Islamorada nonprofit, Friends of the Pool; one organization, the Florida Keys Reef Lights Foundation, hopes to acquire others. Lighthouse enthusiasts travel from all over to make the pilgrimage to these distinguished examples of American maritime heritage. Although lighthouses are secular, practical constructions, it is easy to feel, in their shadows, a sense of awe. They remind us of humankind's ingenuity, as well as the forces of nature.

We feel privileged to share the following images and history of the historic lighthouses of the Florida Keys.

One

The Perilous Reef and the First Lights

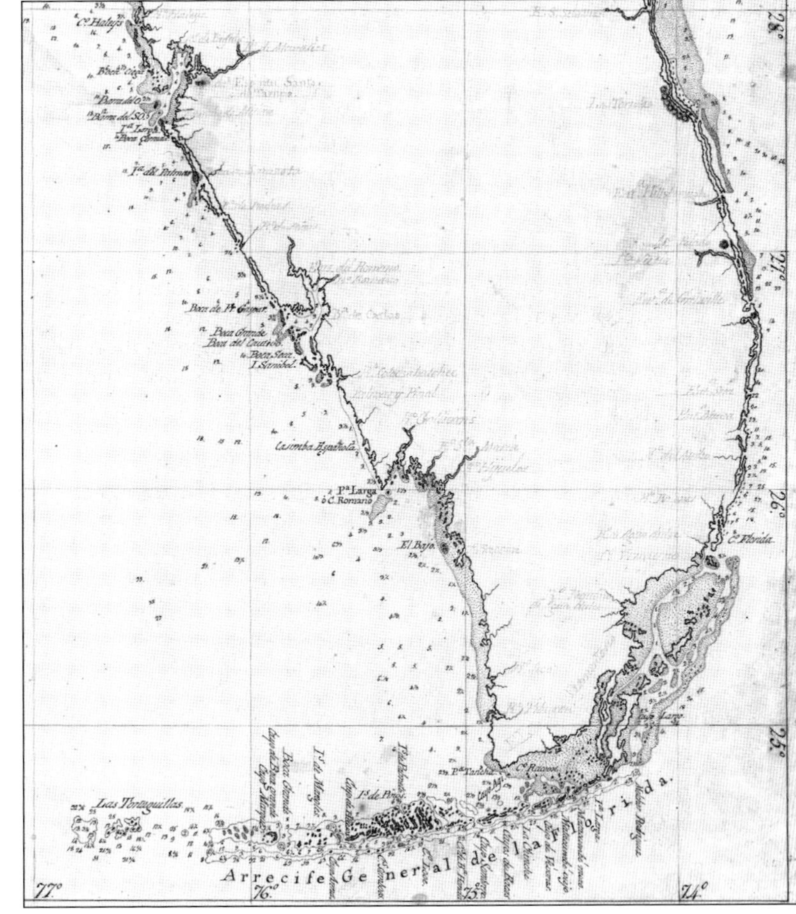

This 1810 Spanish map depicts lower Florida, the Florida Keys, and "Areceife General de Florida," the Florida Reef. Surveyor Vicente Pintado intended that depth findings would help vessels avoid the coral reefs. Spaniards knew from grim experience the loss of life and property that occurred in these waters. After the US government took possession of Florida, it began to consider the necessity of lighthouses. (Courtesy of the Library of Congress.)

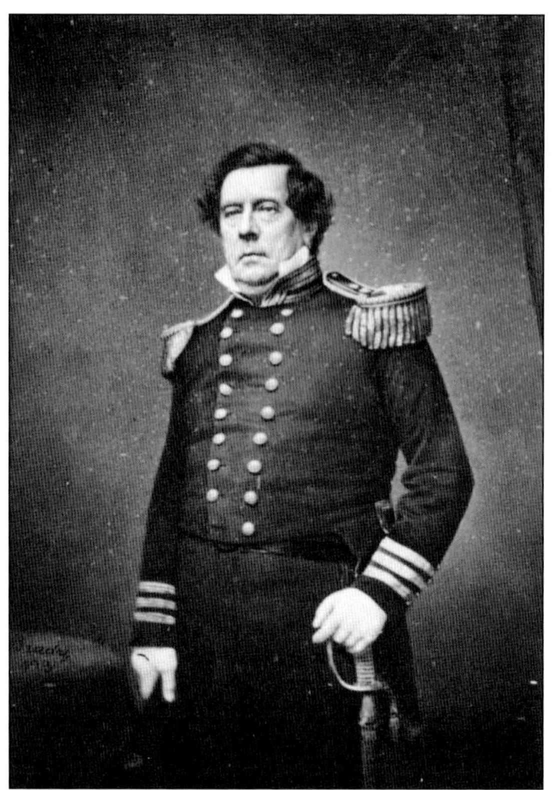

In February 1822, Secretary of the Navy Smith Thompson directed Lt. Comdr. Matthew C. Perry (later commodore) of USS *Shark* to inspect Key West, "a small Island on the edge of the Florida Stream . . . midway between the Dry Tortugas and Cape Florida," as "a [potential] port of Rendezvous & for Commerce." In March, Perry wrote Thompson that "the difficulties of Navigation" in the Florida Keys were "numerous." (Courtesy of the National Archives.)

Aboard the schooner USS *Shark*, Perry examined the routes past these strategically and commercially important islands. He reported that "so Common are Ship wrecks in the neighborhood, that many Vessels are employed Solely for the purpose of rescueing property from destruction." He recommended constructing four lighthouses "on each extreme of the Florida Reef:" Cape Florida, Key Largo, Sand Key, and the Dry Tortugas. (Courtesy of the Naval History and Heritage Command.)

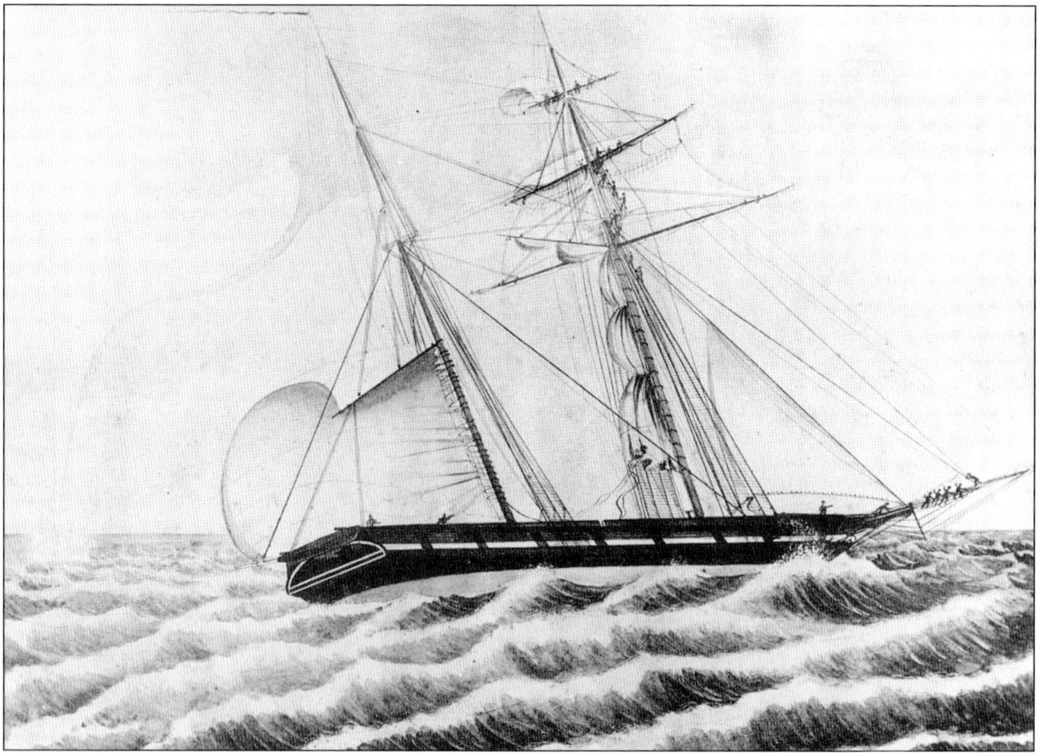

Wreckers were the beneficiaries of what Perry called "the intricate coast" where "the Gulf Stream Sweeps the Florida Reef, with incredible velocity." By rescuing ships that foundered, the wreckers saved lives, sometimes vessels, and usually the valuable cargoes. Starting in the 1820s, wrecking became the principal industry of the Keys. With few navigational aids, the reef became a veritable ship graveyard. (Courtesy of Jerry Wilkinson.)

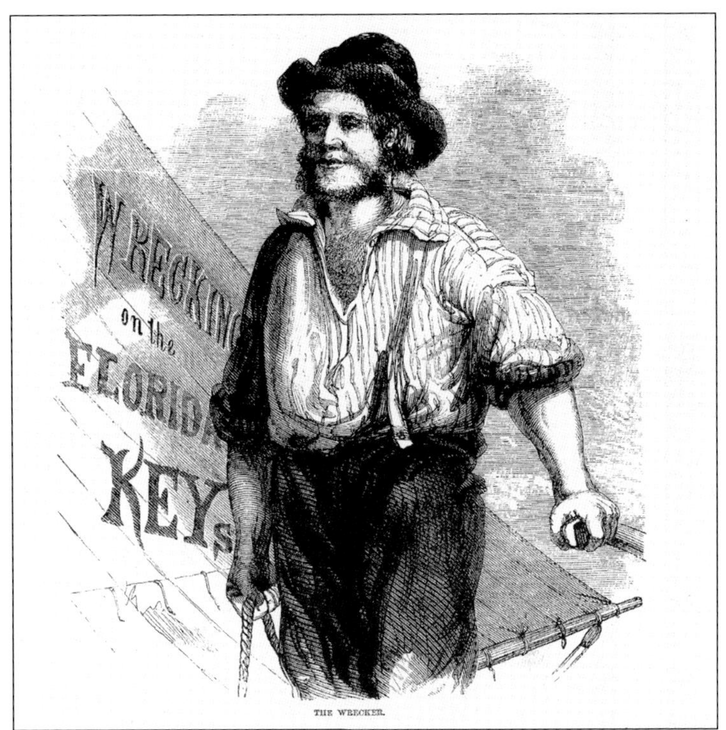

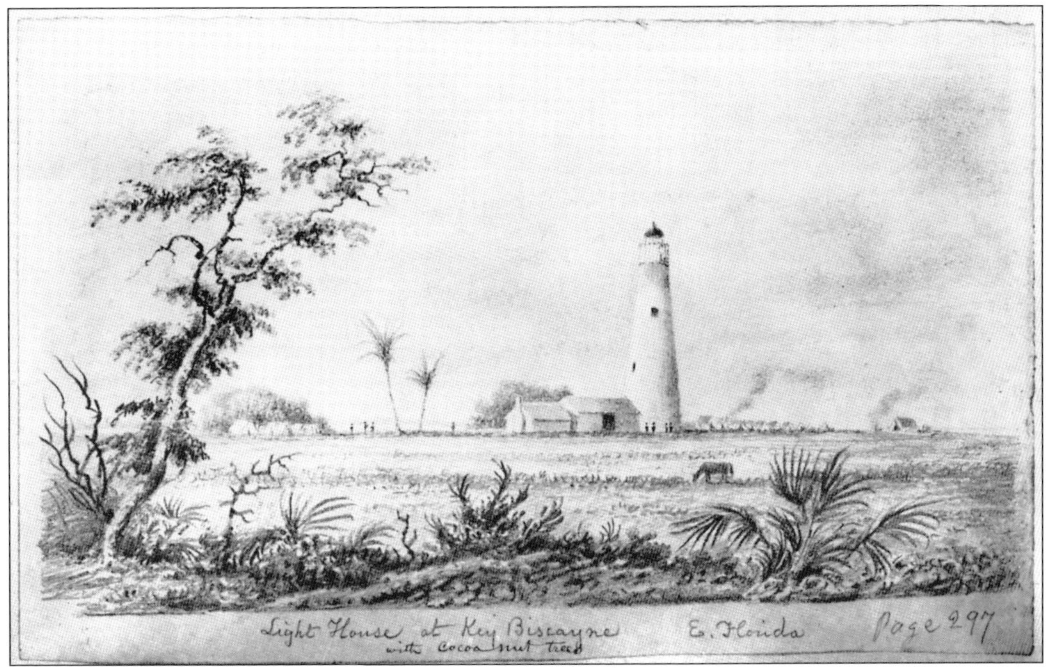

Following Perry's recommendation, the first lighthouse constructed on the Florida Reef stood at Cape Florida on Key Biscayne. Built of brick brought from Boston, the light rose 65 feet and was completed by the end of 1825. The next lights, at Key West, Garden Key in the Dry Tortugas, and Sand Key, followed the essential design of Cape Florida: conical brick structures. (Courtesy of the State Archives of Florida.)

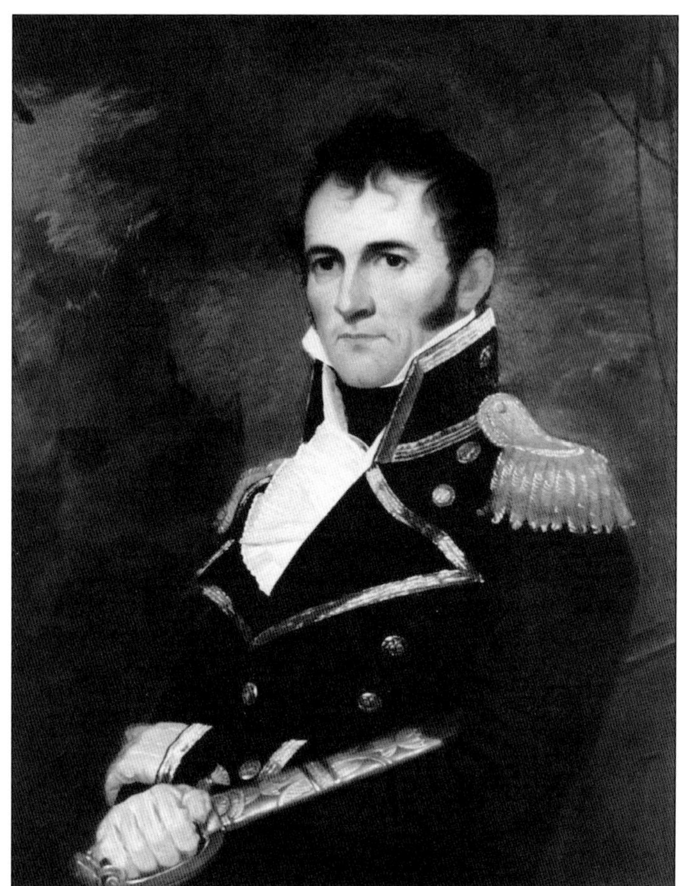

Capt. David Porter (later commodore) overrode a plan to build a lighthouse in the tiny Sambo Keys—which were often below sea level—in favor of Key West. After its lighting in early 1826, Michael Mabrity took charge of the 15-lamp, fixed-light lighthouse as principal keeper, with his wife, Barbara, as assistant keeper. (Courtesy of the Naval History and Heritage Command.)

As William Whitehead's 1838 sketch shows, the original, 65-foot Key West lighthouse stood on the southwestern shore, not on Whitehead Street (center, numbered 8). After her husband's death from yellow fever, Barbara Mabrity took over as its principal keeper. With no assistant (until 1854) and six children, she faithfully maintained the lighthouse from 1832 to 1864. (Courtesy of Monroe County Library, Key West.)

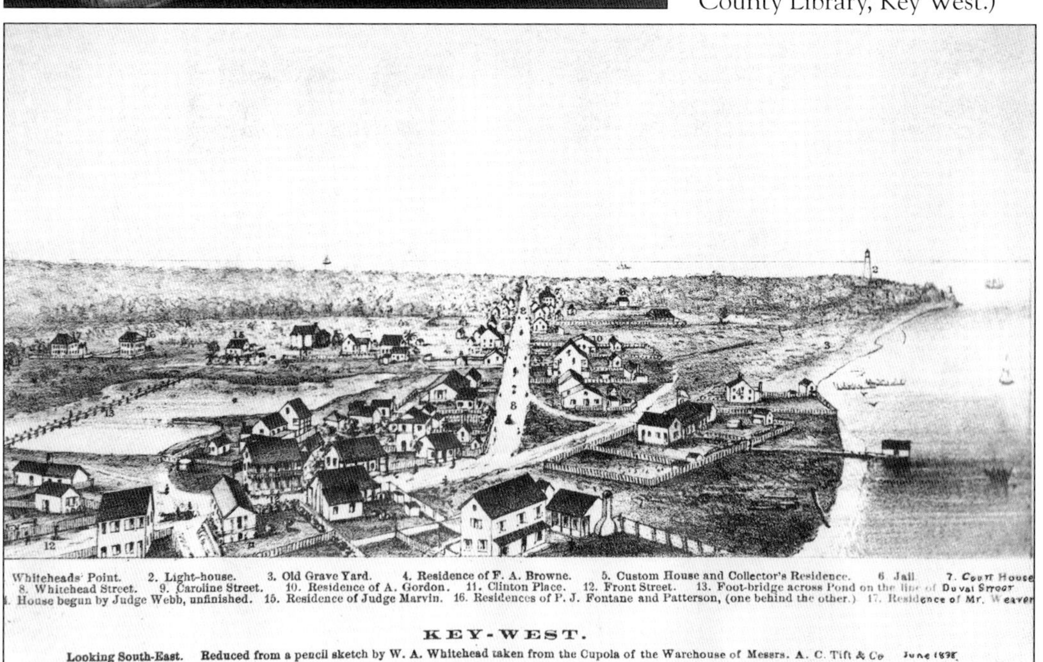

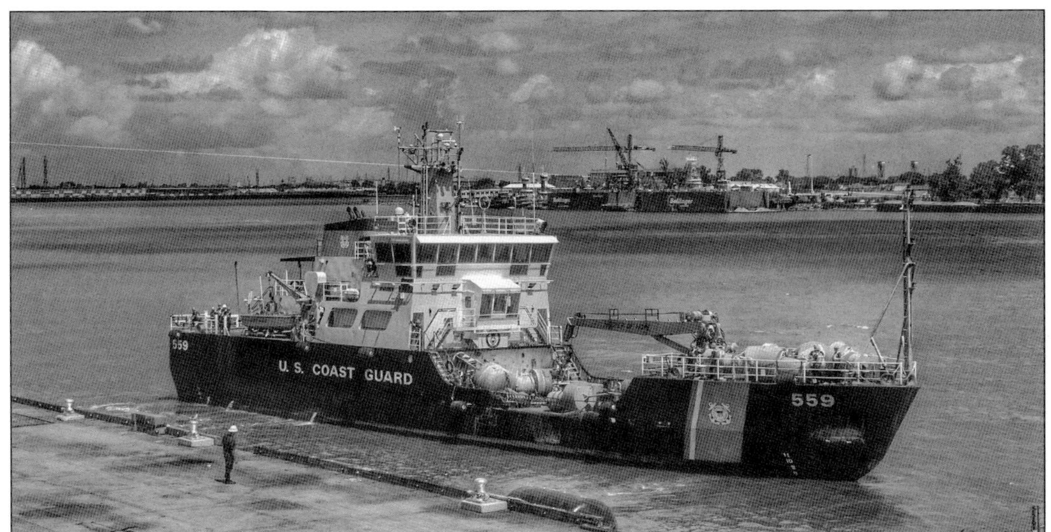

In 1999, the US Coast Guard named this 175-foot Keeper-class buoy tender for the courageous Barbara Mabrity. During three hurricanes (1835, 1841, 1842), she managed to keep the Key West light lit. In 1846, a hurricane destroyed the lighthouse, but Mabrity survived. One story suggests that 14 people died within the lighthouse, although historian Tom Hambright has noted this may be erroneous. (Photograph by Bernard Spragg via Flickr.)

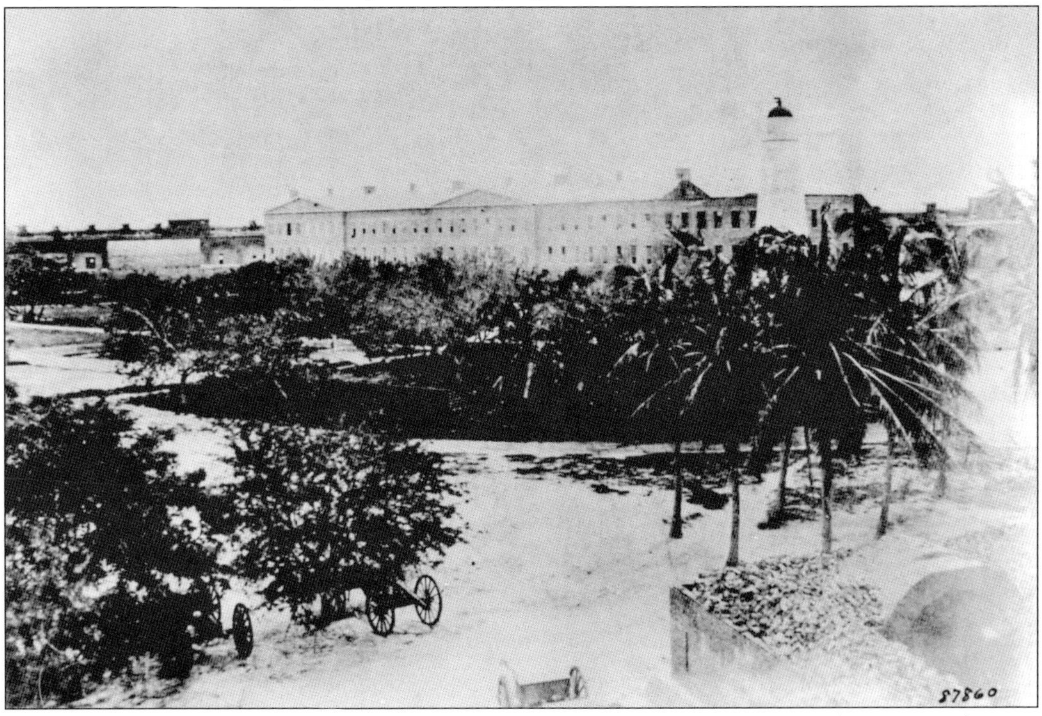

Yet more Boston brick was used to construct a third lighthouse, this at Garden Key in the Dry Tortugas, almost 70 miles west of Key West. Although workers finished the 65-foot tower in March 1826, keeper John Flaherty did not light the lamp until July. He and his wife, Rebecca, lived in great isolation; the fort in this photograph did not exist at the time. (Courtesy of the US Coast Guard Historian's Office.)

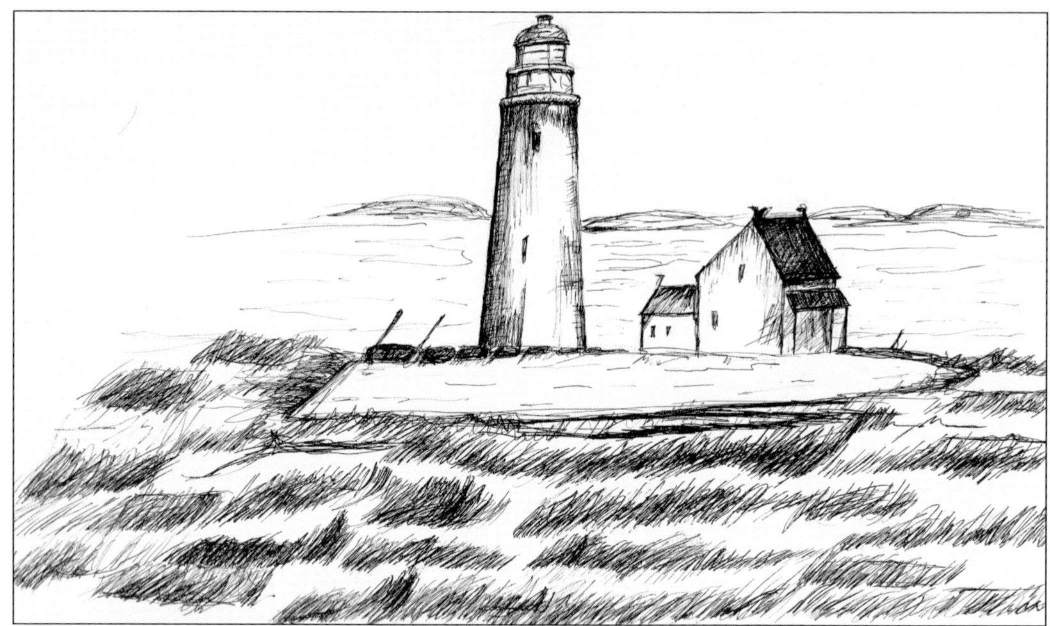

Although Perry expressed concern that Sand Key was unstable, its 63-foot brick tower (70 feet with lantern) was completed in 1827. The Flahertys left Garden Key for the Sand Key post. After John Flaherty died in 1830, Rebecca became keeper. Rebecca remarried in 1834 and remained at the light with her husband until 1836. Capt. Francis Watlington then briefly kept the light. (Illustration by Iris Allgrove, from William Whitehead's sketch.)

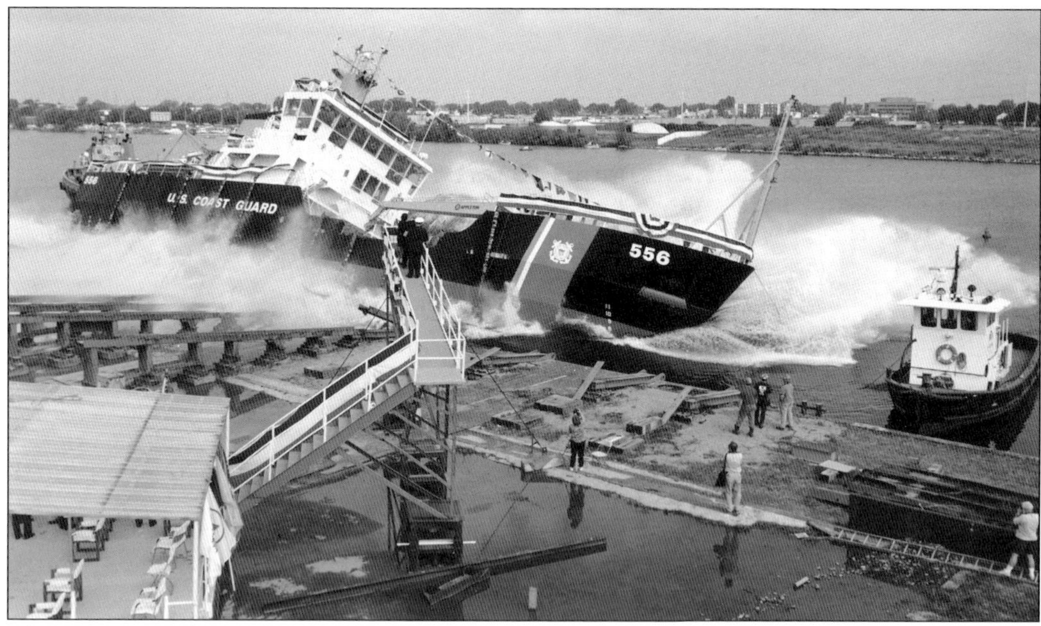

The Coast Guard named another cutter (shown launching in this photograph) after Florida Keys lighthouse keeper Joshua Appleby. Appleby took over the revolving Sand Key light in 1837. The traumatic 1846 hurricane washed the lighthouse and keeper's quarters completely away, along with Appleby, his daughter Eliza, his grandson, and two visitors. (Courtesy of Monroe County Library, Key West.)

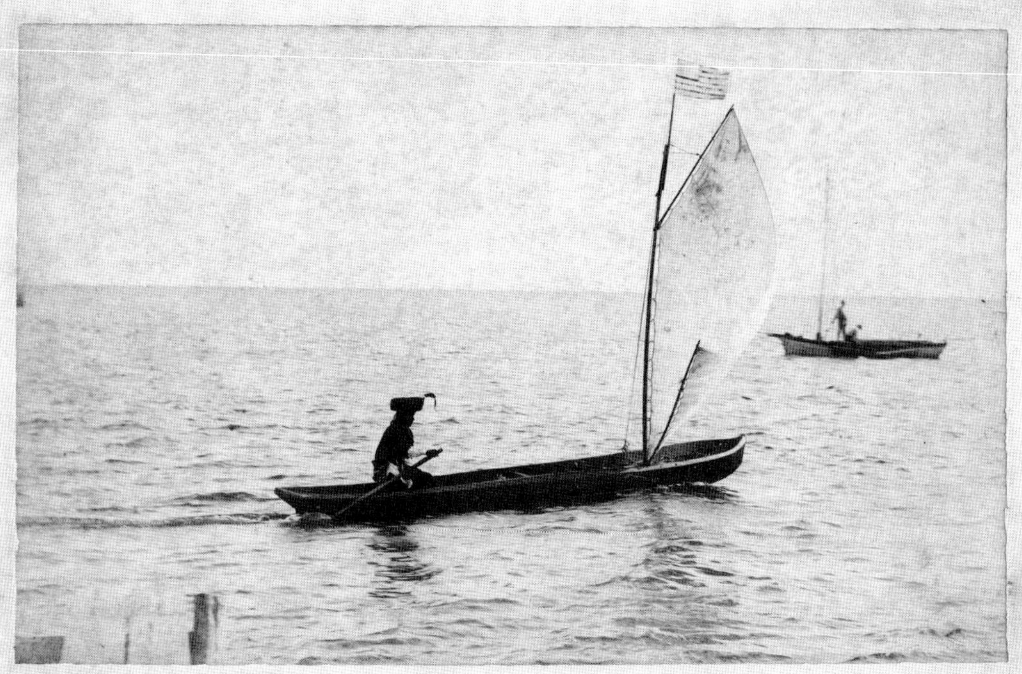

Indigenous peoples often mistrusted the new lighthouses, construing them as the white man's moon or all-seeing eye and thus a means of surveillance. Starting in the mid-1700s, the Seminole tribe had begun to form in Florida and consisted of mainly Georgia Creeks, Mikasuki, Yuchis (descendants of the Calusa), Yamasees, and Black people who escaped bondage. Once white settlers began migrating into the Florida territory in the 1820s, they pressured the US government to remove the Seminoles. Three wars followed. The Cape Florida light, in particular, caused Seminoles grave concern, because Key Biscayne had been a stop on the Underground Railroad. Over time, sympathetic Bahamian captains carried around 300 refugees to freedom at Andros Island, but the construction of the lighthouse ended this escape route. The light also overlooked the Seminoles' Little Hunting Grounds across Biscayne Bay. On July 23, 1836, warriors attacked the Cape Florida light, killed one man, Aaron Carter (probably a slave), and seriously wounded the assistant keeper, John Thompson. Fire and explosion destroyed most of the lighthouse. (Photograph by Ralph Middleton Munroe, courtesy of the University of Miami Library.)

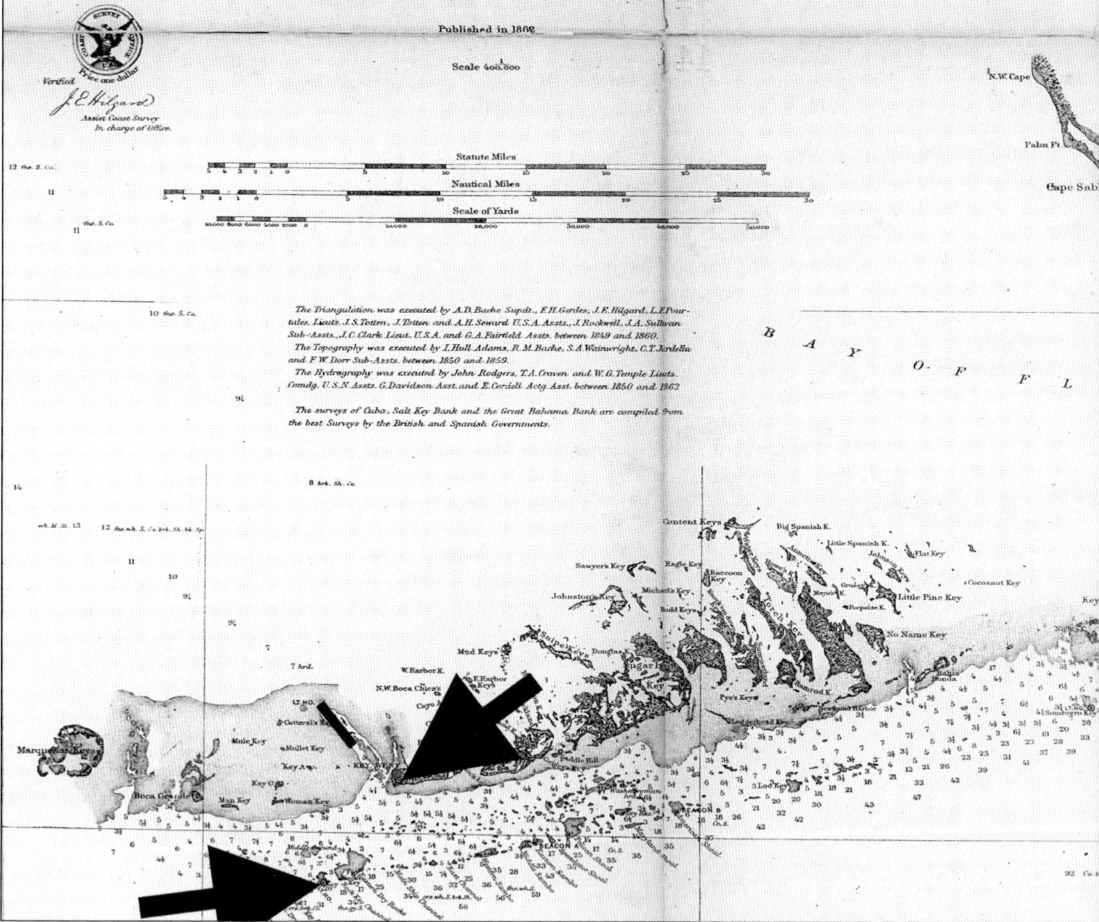

This map of the Florida Reef shows the location of three of the four masonry lighthouses that had been built by 1827 (arrows, left to right): Sand Key, Key West, and Cape Florida. Not pictured is the Garden Key light. Obviously, long stretches of the reef were not illuminated by lighthouses, although lightships provided some assistance to navigators. A black line (left) indicates the

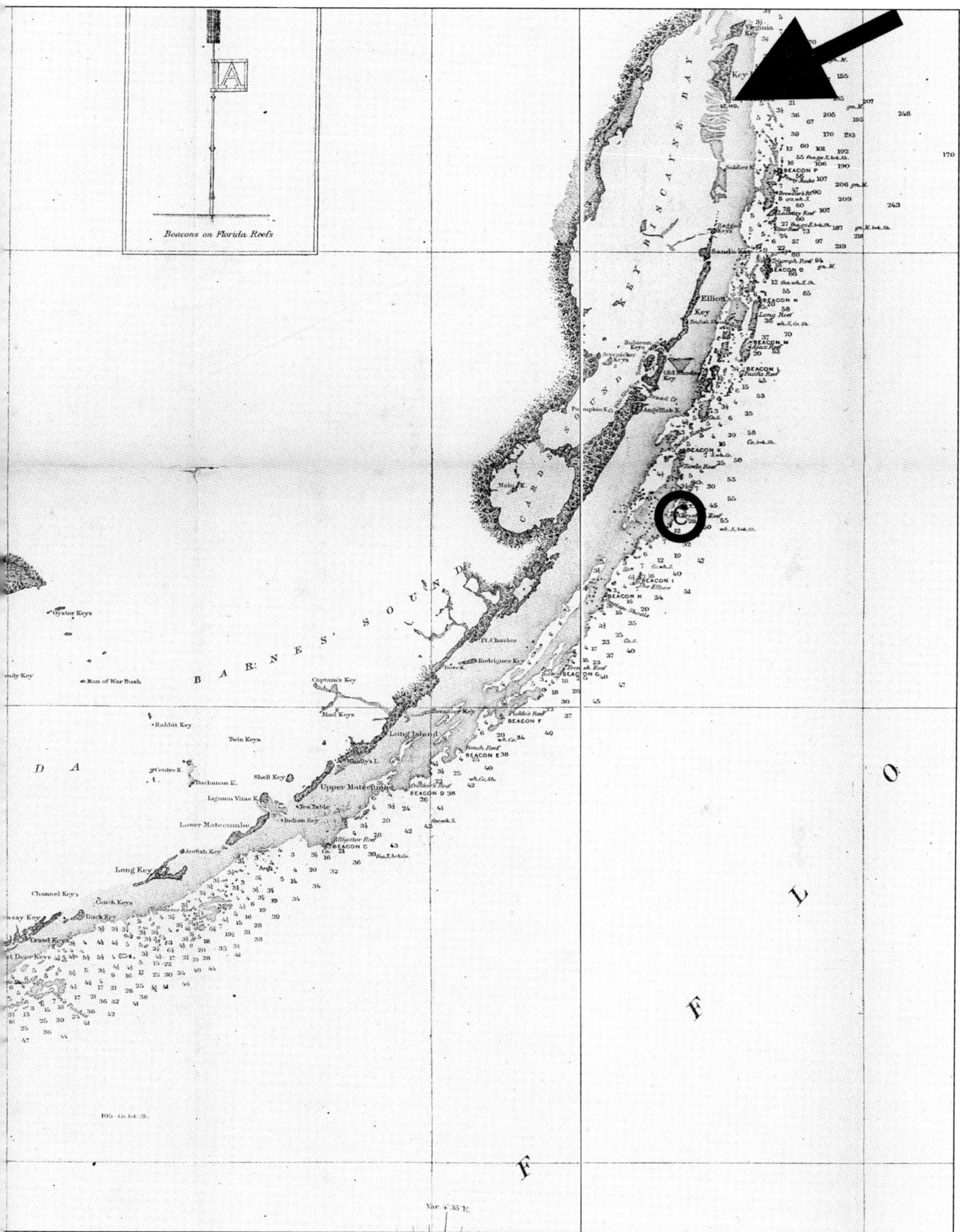

Northwest Passage, northwest of Key West, where a lightship called *Key West* was stationed; a circle (right) shows where the lightship *Caesar* was stationed at Carysfort Reef off north Key Largo. After the 1846 hurricane, the lightship *Honey* was stationed at Sand Key. (Courtesy of the Library of Congress.)

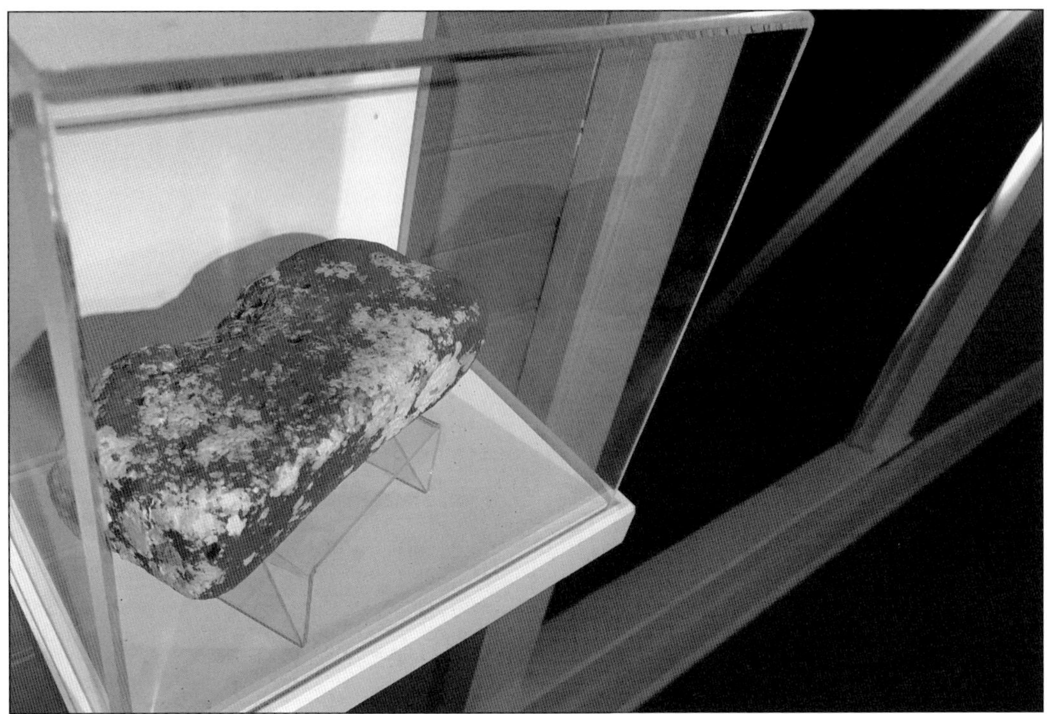

Divers occasionally have found bricks from the 1827 Sand Key lighthouse on the ocean floor. The Florida History Department at the Key West library has one; the Key West Lighthouse and Keeper's Quarters Museum displays another (pictured here). These much-eroded bricks remind one of the risks of being a keeper. (Courtesy of Laura Albritton.)

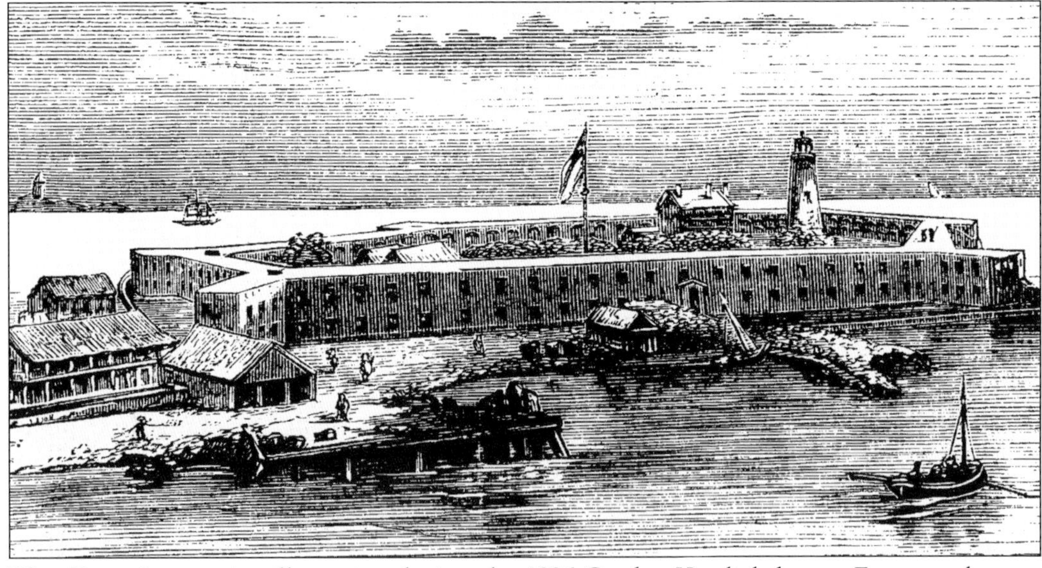

This *Harper's* magazine illustration depicts the 1826 Garden Key lighthouse. For several years, there was little on the island besides the light and its outbuildings. (Construction on the fort started in 1846 and continued intermittently for three decades.) While two Florida Reef lights were destroyed by hurricane and another by fire, the brick lighthouse on Garden Key survived. However, many mariners found the light frustratingly inadequate. (Courtesy of Laura Albritton.)

Two

Two Brick Lights

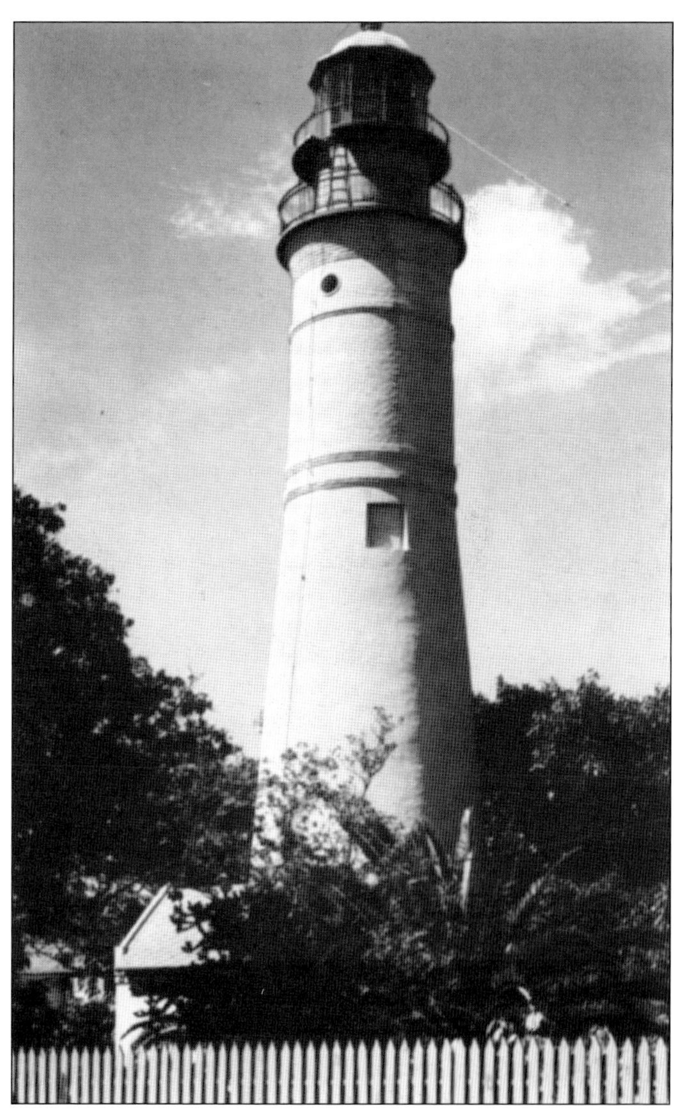

In 1846, a hurricane obliterated the two brick lighthouses on Key West and Sand Key; the brick light at Cape Florida had been destroyed by fire and an explosion in 1836. Brick remained the building material of choice when the Key West and Cape Florida lights were reconstructed. Both Florida Reef lighthouses would undergo further improvements in the 19th century. (Courtesy of Laura Albritton.)

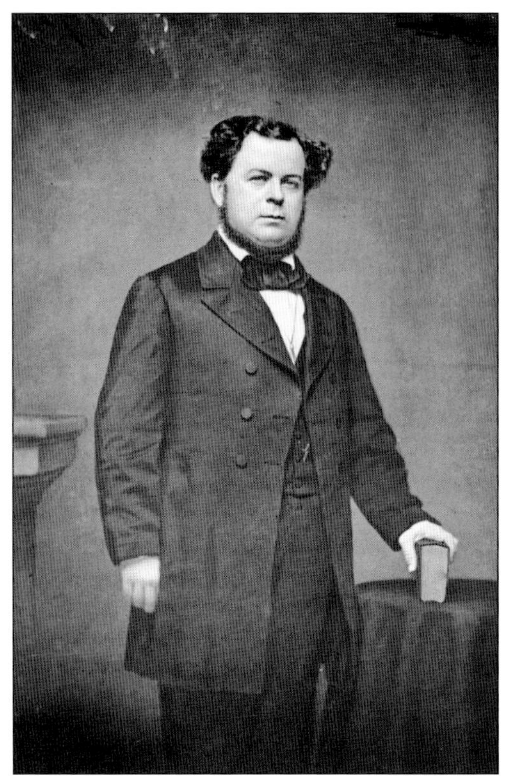

Collector of customs Stephen Mallory (left) chose the new position for the second Key West lighthouse. Mallory witnessed firsthand the destruction of the 1846 hurricane, writing that "slates from roofs, boards, and even heavy pieces of timber were driven through the air like straws" and water "high as my breast . . . the entire town at that time (4 o'clock P.M.) being underwater." Cognizant of the structural failure of the previous light, he selected a location that appeared to be (and indeed was) more secure due to its elevation. Key West pioneer John Simonton (below) sold a plot of land 13 to 14 feet above sea level and received $200. Built in two months, the lighthouse had solid, four-and-a-half-foot-thick walls at ground level and 15 reflective lanterns. (Both, courtesy of Monroe County Library, Key West.)

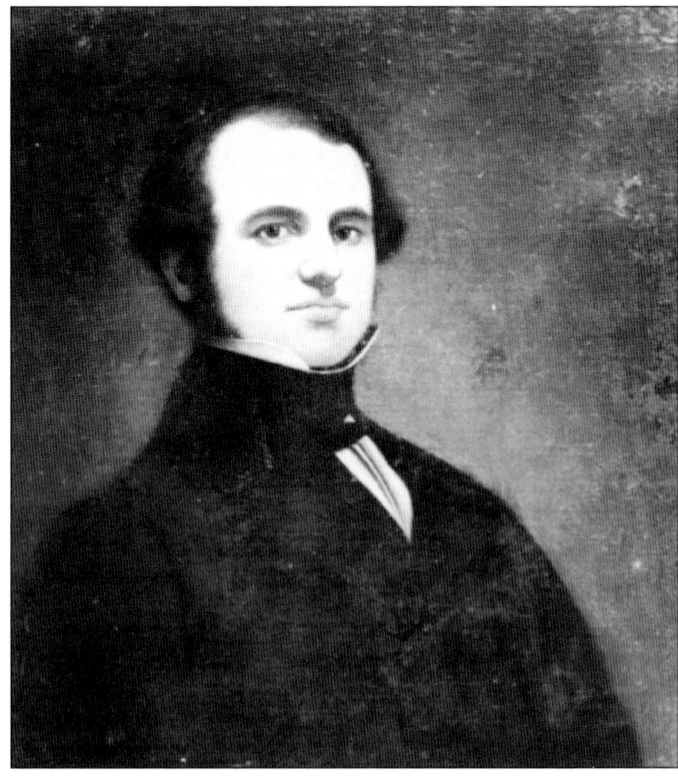

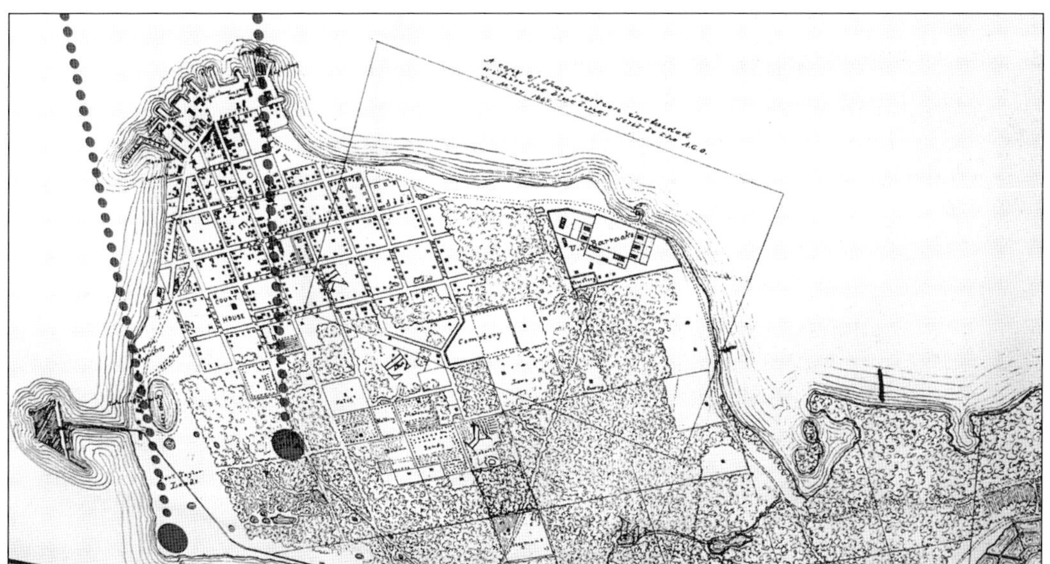

This illustration on display in the lighthouse museum indicates the location of the first Key West lighthouse (left) and the second (right, on Whitehead Street). Completed in 1848, the conical brick structure rose 50 feet, with a seven-foot-tall lantern. According to science writer Steve Mirsky, "a circular hole several feet deep and 25 feet in diameter was chiseled out of the solid coral bedrock to form the foundation." (Photograph by Laura Albritton.)

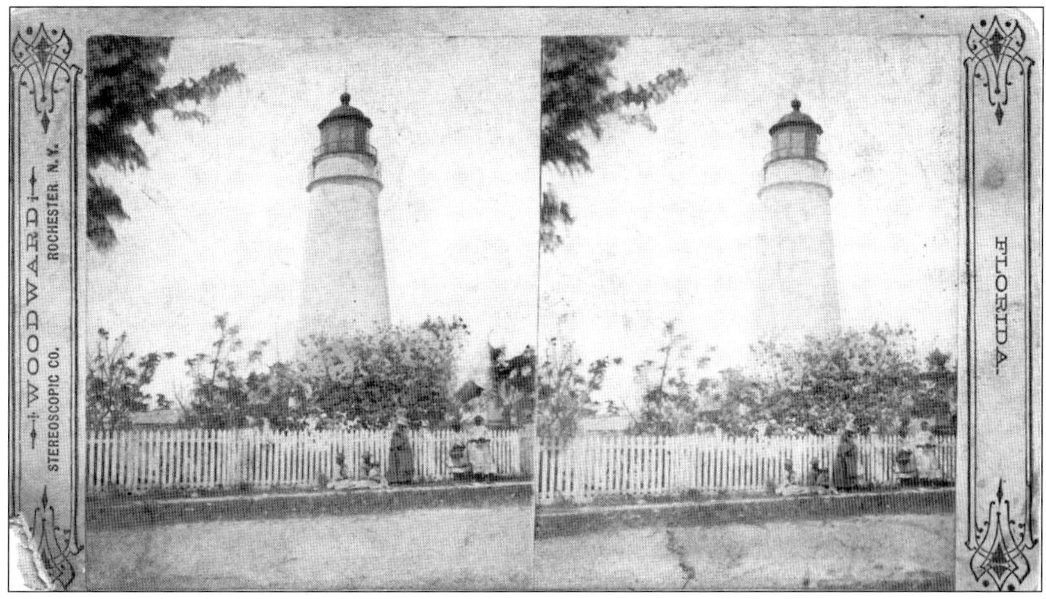

Although the US Congress had deemed $12,000 appropriate for the Key West lighthouse construction, the project came in under budget at $7,247. Workers completed the keeper's quarters in 1849. Barbara Mabrity, who had survived the 1846 hurricane, subsequently took up residence as the principal keeper. In this stereoscopic photograph, a group of women and children poses before the picket fence. (Courtesy of Monroe County Library, Key West.)

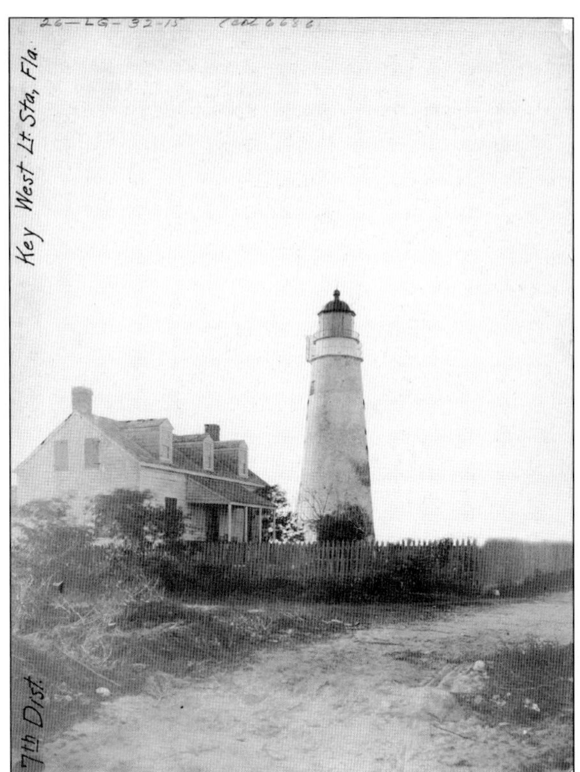

The second Key West light was constructed of brick. Bricks exhibit the most strength when compressed and primarily rely on gravity. By the very nature of the form of construction, the overall structure will be significantly heavier than a comparable wooden or steel structure. As a result, better ground and soil conditions are needed. Clearly, relocating the lighthouse inland was a wise decision. (Courtesy of the National Archives.)

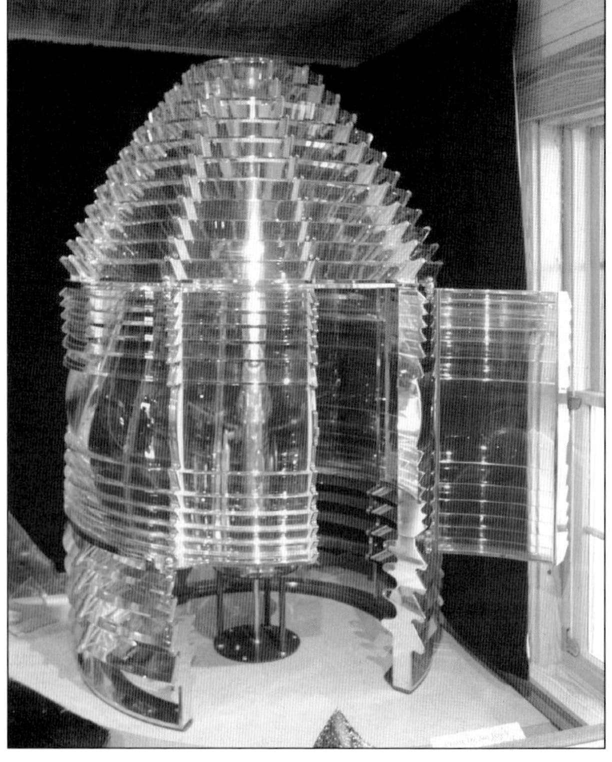

Superintendent of lighthouses Stephen Pleasanton did not embrace the new Fresnel lens technology. Key West only received its first Fresnel lens in 1858. It was a third-order (or third largest) lens, similar in size to the one pictured here. (Photograph by Ralph Eshelman, courtesy of the US Lighthouse Society Archives.)

Barbara Mabrity wrote these instructions for keeping the Key West lighthouse. Instruction number three reads, "In order to maintain the greatest degree of light during the night, the wicks are to be trimmed every three hours, and often as necessary, taking care that they are exactly even on the top, and the flame must be maintained at its full height." (Photograph by Laura Albritton.)

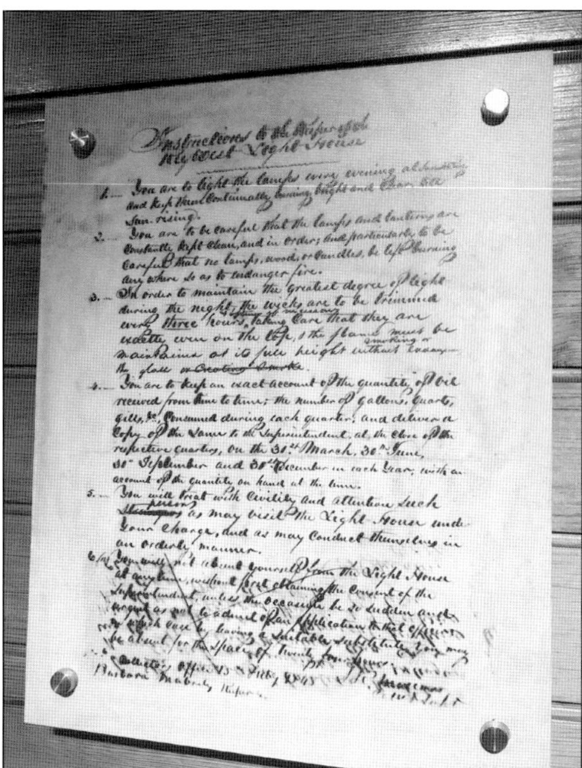

Instructions to the Keeper of the
Key West Light House

1.— You are to light the lamps every evening at [illegible] and keep them continually burning bright and clear till Sun-rising.

2.— You are to be careful that the lamps and lanterns are constantly kept clean, and in order; and particularly to be careful that no lamps, wood, or Candles, be left burning any where so as to endanger fire.

3.— In order to maintain the greatest degree of light during the night, the wicks are to be trimmed every three hours, taking care that they are exactly even on the top, & the flame must be maintained at its full height without smoking or [illegible] the glass or creating smoke.

4.— You are to keep an exact account of the quantity of Oil received from time to time; the number of gallons, quarts, gills, &c., consumed during each quarter; and deliver a copy of the same to the Superintendent, at the close of the respective quarters, on the 31st March, 30th June, 30th September and 31st December in each year, with an account of the quantity on hand at the time.

5.— You will treat with civility and attention such persons as may visit the Light House under your charge, and as may conduct themselves in an orderly manner.

6.— You will not absent yourself from the Light House at any time, without first obtaining the consent of the Superintendent, unless the occasion be so sudden and urgent as not to admit of an application to that officer [illegible]

[illegible] Barbara Mabrity Keeper [illegible]

This photograph shows the Key West lighthouse's spiral staircase. After keeper Barbara Mabrity retired, the keepers who served from 1864 until 1870 kept the light for an average of one to two years. They included Frederick W. Anderson (1864–1865), James Ingraham (1865–1867), Henry M. Crane (1867–1868), and Peter Crocker (1868–1870). John Carroll, married to Barbara Mabrity's granddaughter, had the position from 1870 to 1889. (Photograph by Laura Albritton.)

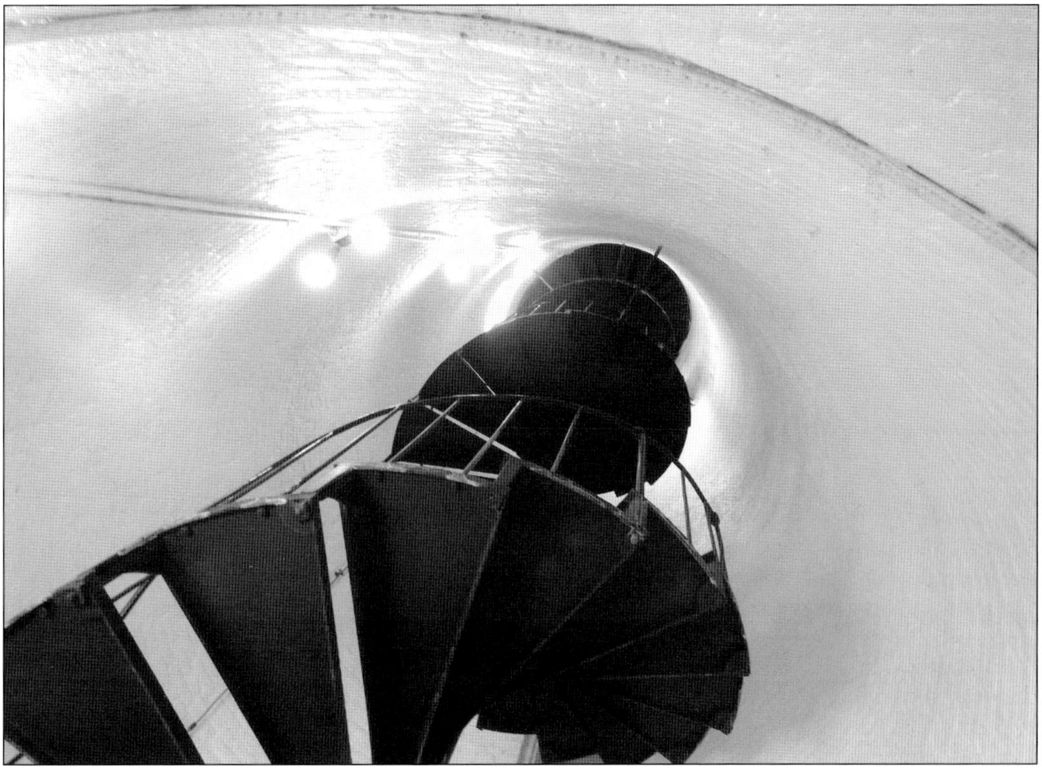

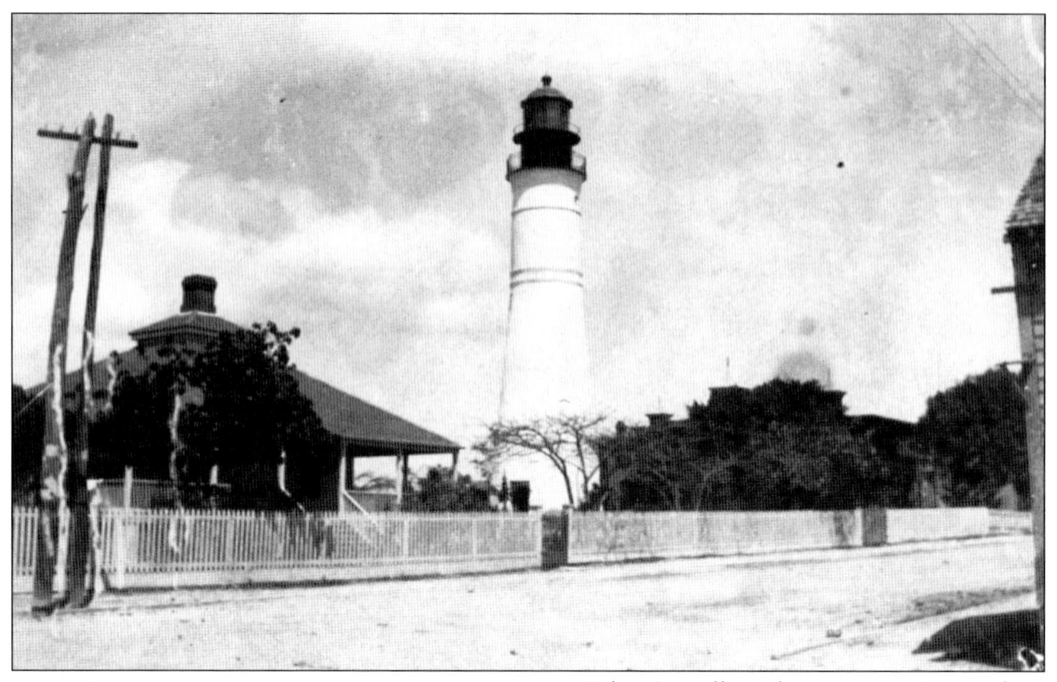

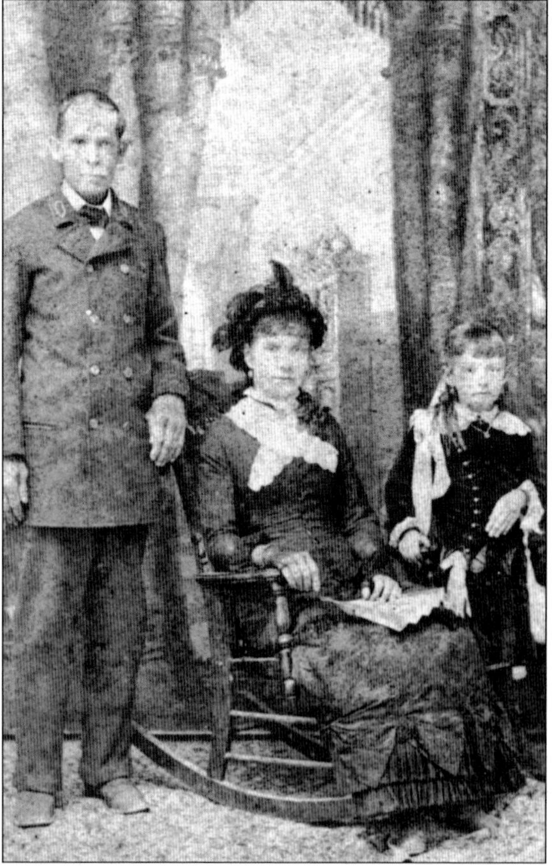

John Carroll's wife, née Mary Armanda Fletcher, served as assistant keeper (1876–1889) and, following his death, principal keeper. Mary's father was also a lighthouse keeper. During the Carrolls' tenure, the lantern height was raised five feet (1873) and a new keepers' quarters built to house multiple families (1887). Later, in 1895, the tower was raised 20 feet, as shown here. (Courtesy of Monroe County Library, Key West.)

In 1889, William Bethel, Michael and Barbara Mabrity's grandson, became keeper at Key West after serving at four other lighthouses, three in the Florida Keys. He is pictured here with his wife, Mary Elizabeth Bethel, and their daughter Lorena. William kept the light until he died in 1908 following an accident during a hurricane. Mary would serve as both assistant and principal keeper. (Courtesy of Monroe County Library, Key West.)

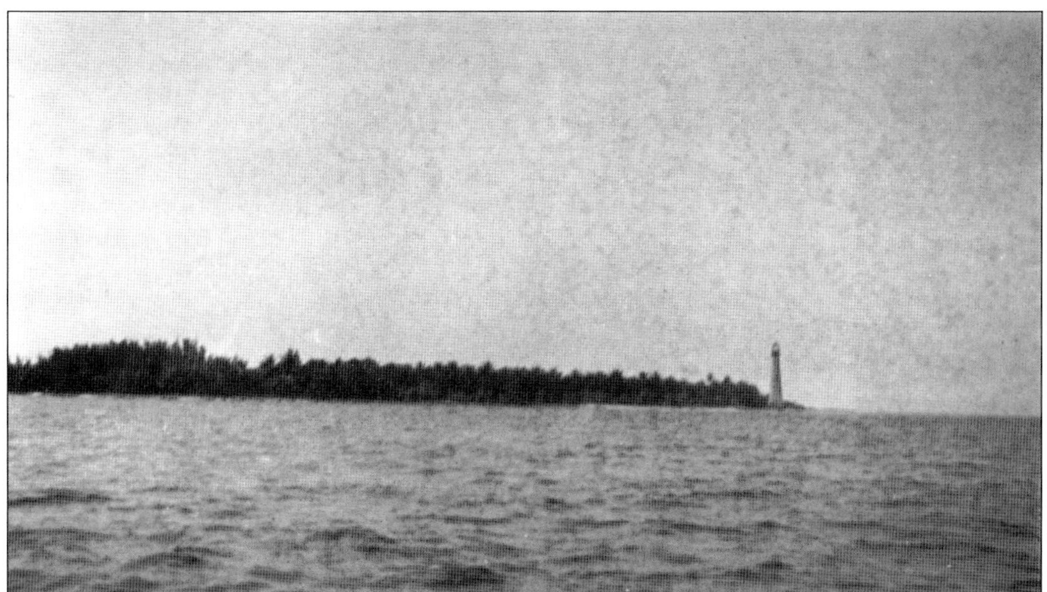

Due to ongoing hostilities between the US government and the Seminoles, Cape Florida remained without a replacement lighthouse until 1846. The new light rose 70 feet, and its 17 lamps had a range of 13 nautical miles. Although taller than the Key West light, it was similar in its construction, that is, a brick cone. (Photograph by Ralph Middleton Munroe, courtesy of the University of Miami Library.)

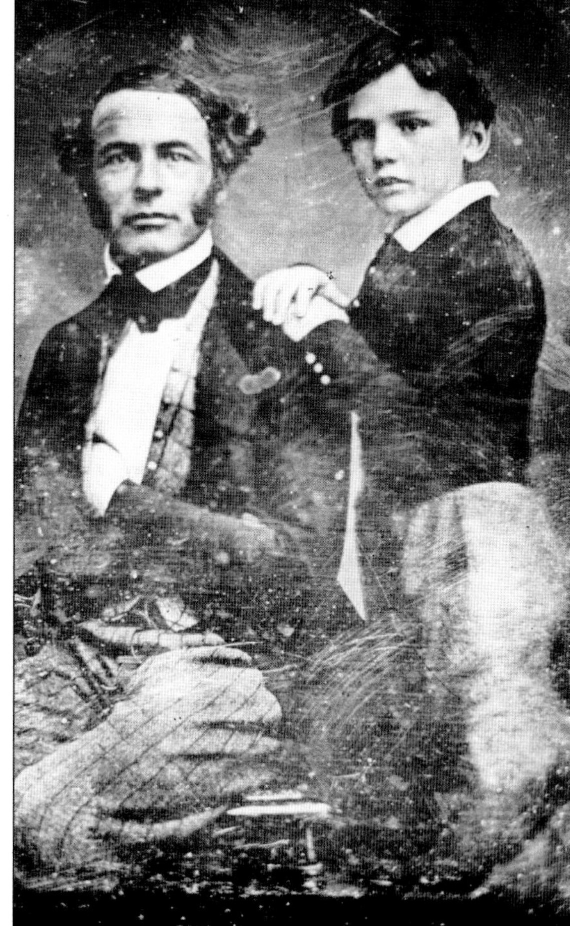

Army engineer Lt. Col. Robert E. Lee (left) journeyed to Key Biscayne in 1849 and saw the lighthouse as part of a team conducting a US Board of Engineers coastal survey. Lee also visited Key West and the Dry Tortugas. The coastal survey helped to shape the government's future plans for Florida Reef lighthouses. (Courtesy of Encyclopedia Virginia.)

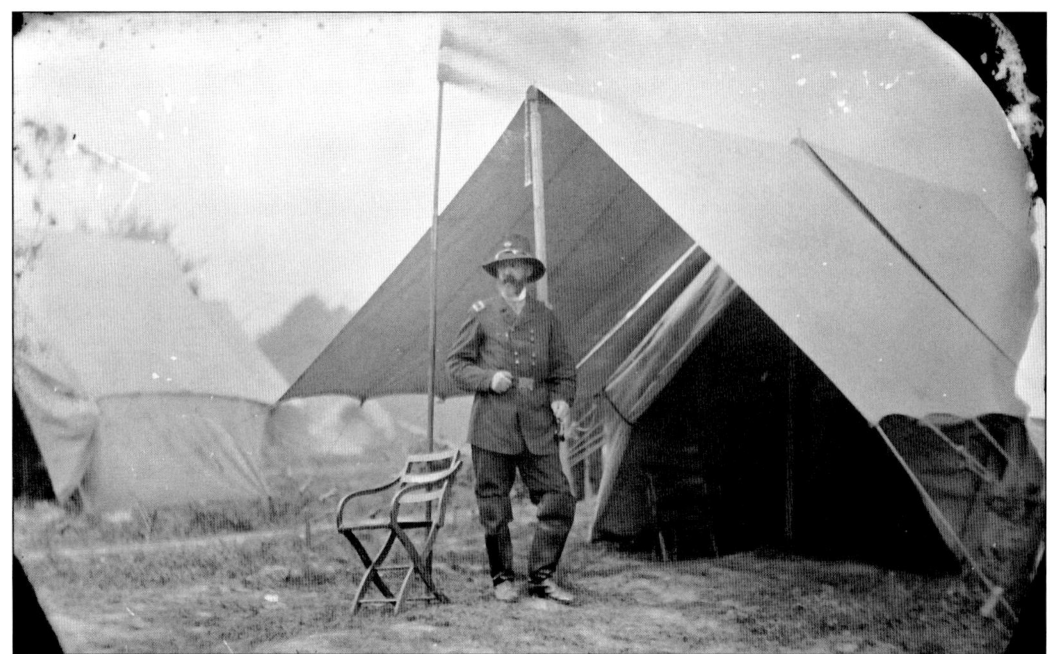

While supervising construction of Carysfort lighthouse, George Meade, Lee's future opponent at the Battle of Gettysburg, suggested changes to the Cape Florida light: installation of a Fresnel lens, raising of the brick tower, and the addition of an iron watch room. In 1854, the US Congress designated a budget for the work. (Courtesy of the National Archives.)

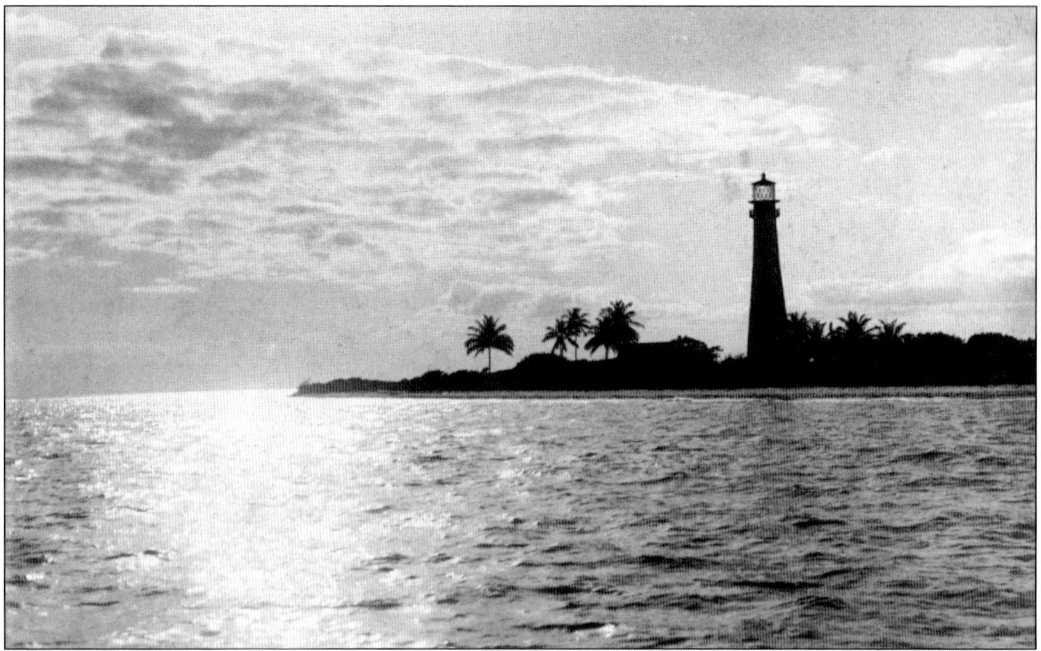

This photograph shows Cape Florida's additional 20 feet of brickwork. With a second-order Fresnel lens and a focal plane of 100 feet, the lighthouse had been improved for a budget of $15,000. Nevertheless, ships continued to founder off Cape Florida. (Photograph by Ralph Middleton Munroe, courtesy of the University of Miami Library.)

Three

INNOVATION

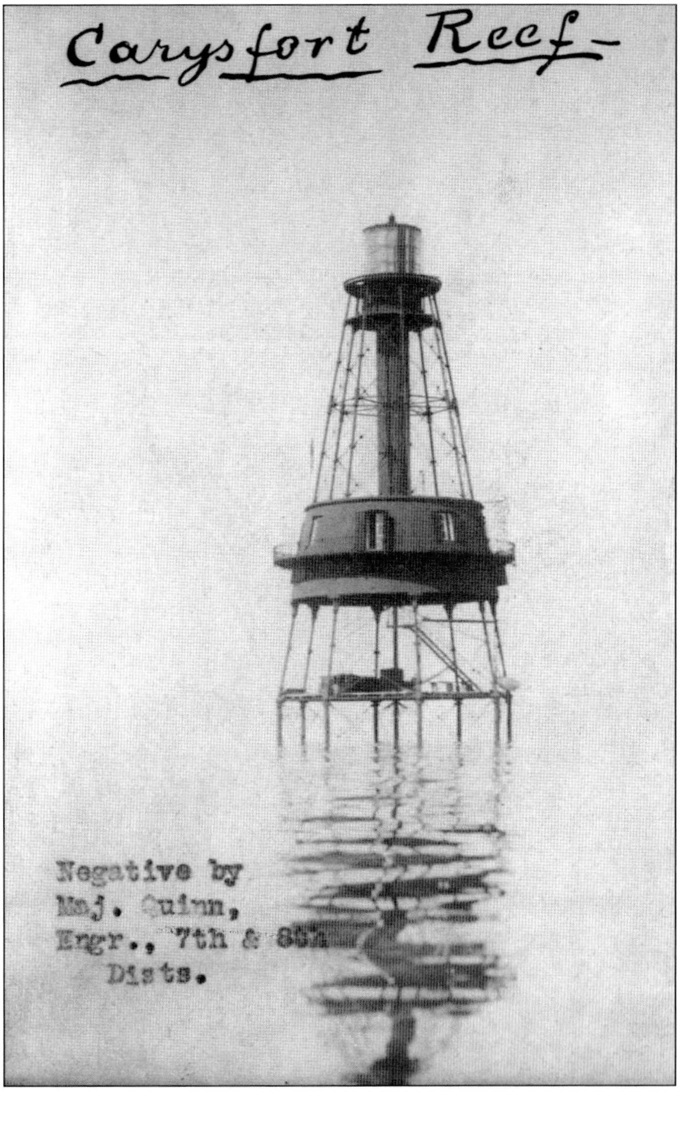

Up until the construction of the Carysfort lighthouse (pictured), the Florida Reef lights had been built of masonry; the government's lighthouse board relied on traditional plans. Innovation, however, arrived in the Keys with the next three lights. Their fabrication, even their lanterns, reflected the forward-thinking mentality of those who designed and supervised their construction. (Courtesy of the National Archives.)

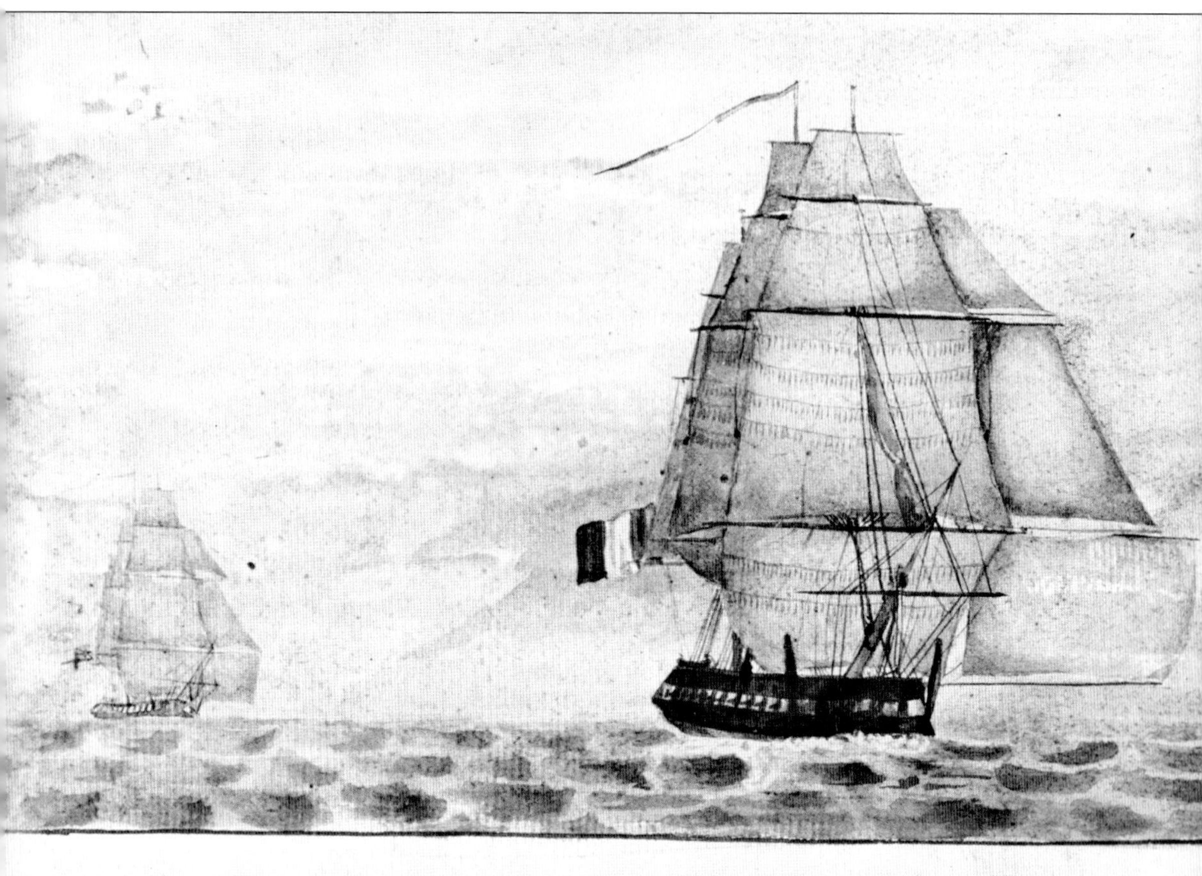

As the Key West and Cape Florida lights were replaced, the US government recognized the need for more lighthouses along the Florida Reef. One reef that had proven especially treacherous was Carysfort, off north Key Largo. It was named for the British frigate HMS *Carysfort*, which foundered there in 1770 (although fortunately, it did not sink). This reef had previously been marked only by a lightship. In 1826, Capt. John Whalton had taken command of the lightship *Caesar*; by 1828, the ship had rotted to such an extent that a new lightship, *Florida*, was built in 1830. Conditions were very difficult for captain and crew: they had to row 45 miles to access fresh water. In 1847, Captain Whalton and four sailors went ashore to see to their vegetable garden and were attacked by Seminoles. (Courtesy of the Naval History and Heritage Command.)

This 1853 survey illustrates the location of Carysfort Reef (box, bottom) vis-à-vis the closest lighthouse at the time, the Cape Florida light (box, top). Carysfort Reef lies six nautical miles off northern Key Largo. In some places, the corals rest 5 to 40 feet below the ocean's surface, while the Carysfort Trench descends 80 feet. (Courtesy of the Library of Congress.)

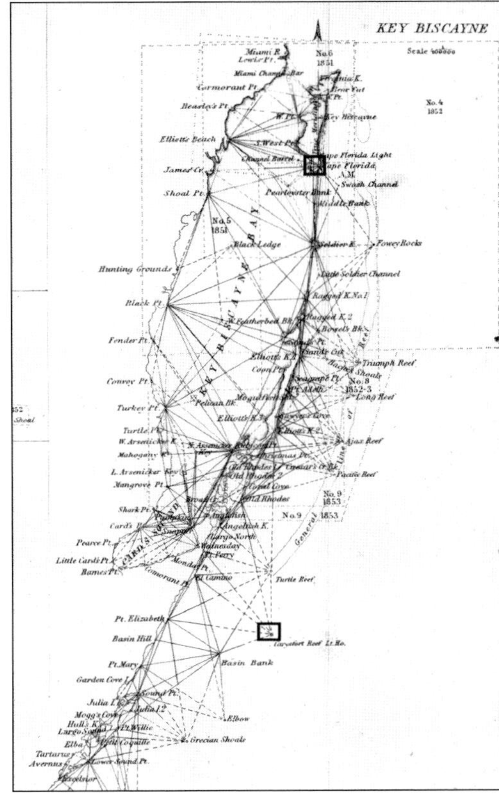

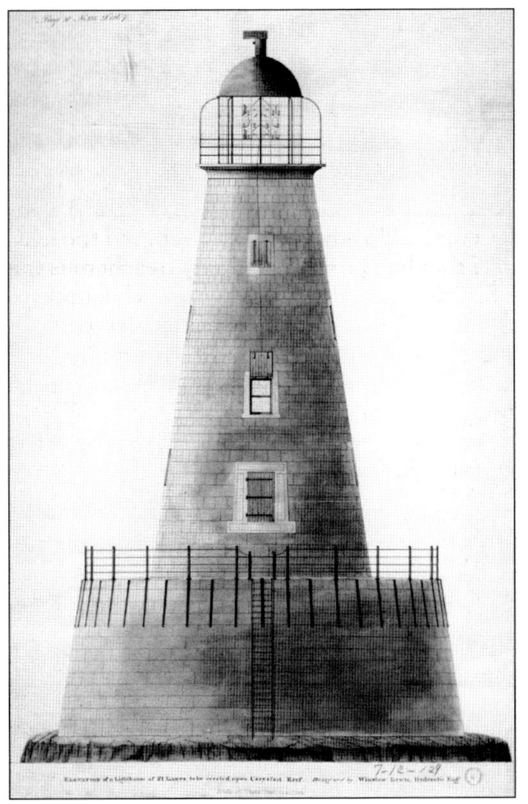

Superintendent of lights Stephen Pleasanton was a friend of Winslow Lewis, who submitted the first plan (pictured) for the Carysfort lighthouse. Lewis had also patented a reflective lighthouse lantern that Pleasanton installed in numerous American lighthouses. Both men had a vested interest in Lewis's design being chosen, and if it had been, the Carysfort light would have been constructed of masonry. (Courtesy of the National Archives.)

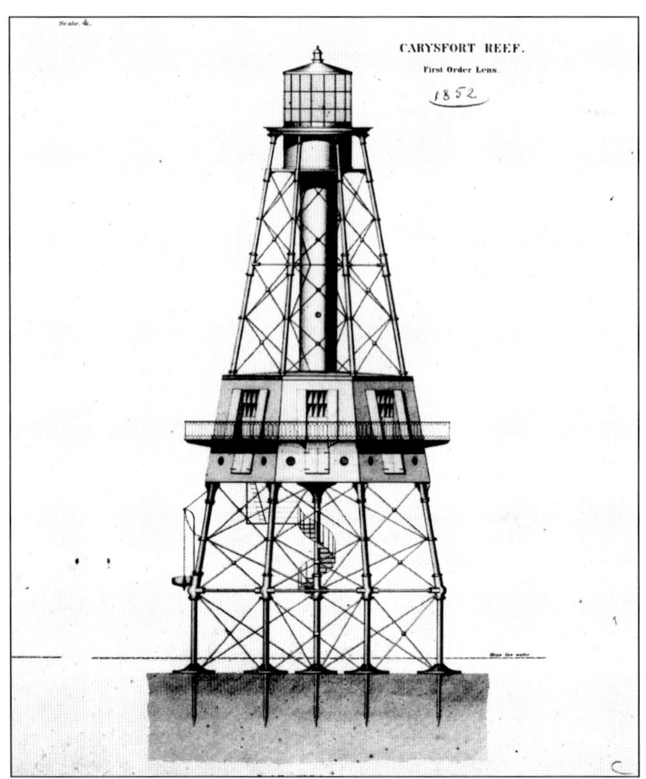

Winslow Lewis's nephew, Isaiah W.P. Lewis, was a civil engineer and understood the weaknesses of his uncle's design and patented lantern. He acquired the patent for the screwpile from its inventor, Alexander Mitchell; his innovative plan for a screwpile lighthouse was selected for the Carysfort Reef. According to Neil Hurley, Howard Standsbury also contributed to Carysfort's design. (Courtesy of Monroe County Library, Key West.)

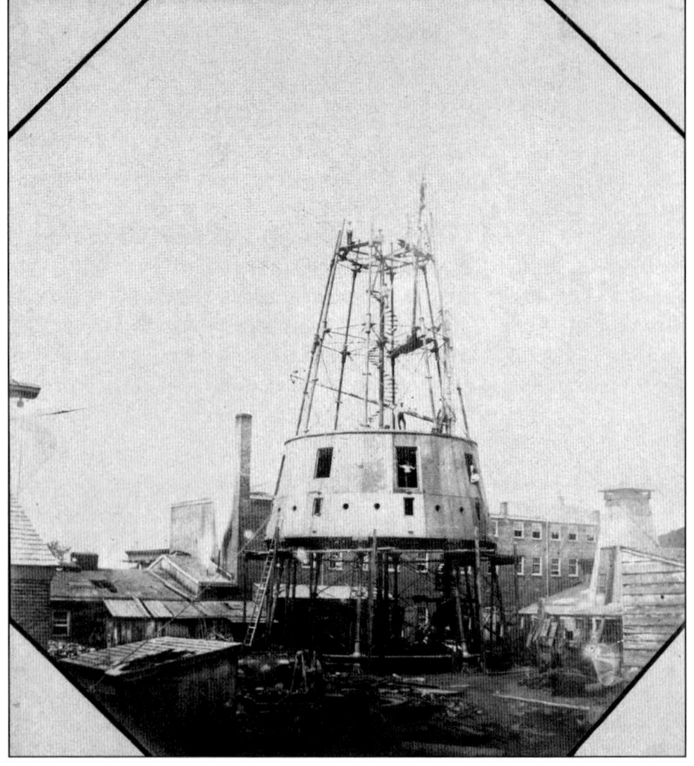

This photograph shows the 112-foot Carysfort lighthouse under construction in Pennsylvania. To ensure that the engineers and workers encountered no problems once on the reef, all the wrought iron segments of the light were produced at the northern factory, and the lighthouse was constructed on-site. Then, workers took the structure apart so it could be shipped to the Florida Keys. (Courtesy of Monroe County Library, Key West.)

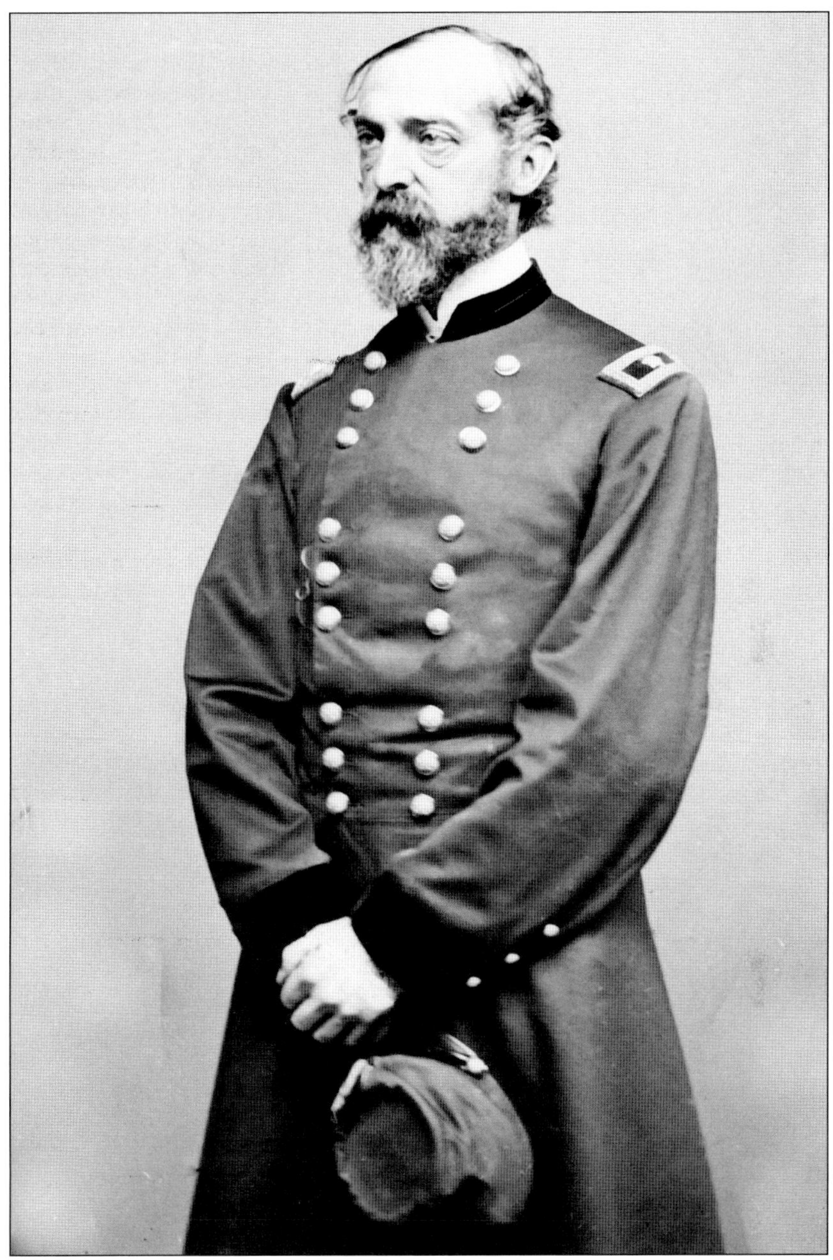

Capt. Howard Stansbury, of the US Army Corps of Topographical Engineers, immediately ran into problems with Carysfort's construction. Because he was drilling in sand, not coral, Stansbury used eight-foot-diameter cast-iron footplates or disks to allow the piles sufficient purchase. Unfortunately, the project ran out of money and came to a halt. Maj. Thomas Lippard later took over the project until he died in 1851; he was followed by Lt. George Meade (pictured). In the early 1850s, officer and engineer Meade served in the Florida Keys with the US Army Corps of Topographical Engineers. With his prior experience of lighthouse construction and coastal surveying, he had some appreciation for the daunting tasks before him. He played an important role in building three Keys lights, Carysfort, Sand Key, and Sombrero Key, and was a proponent of the innovative Fresnel lens. (Courtesy of the National Archives.)

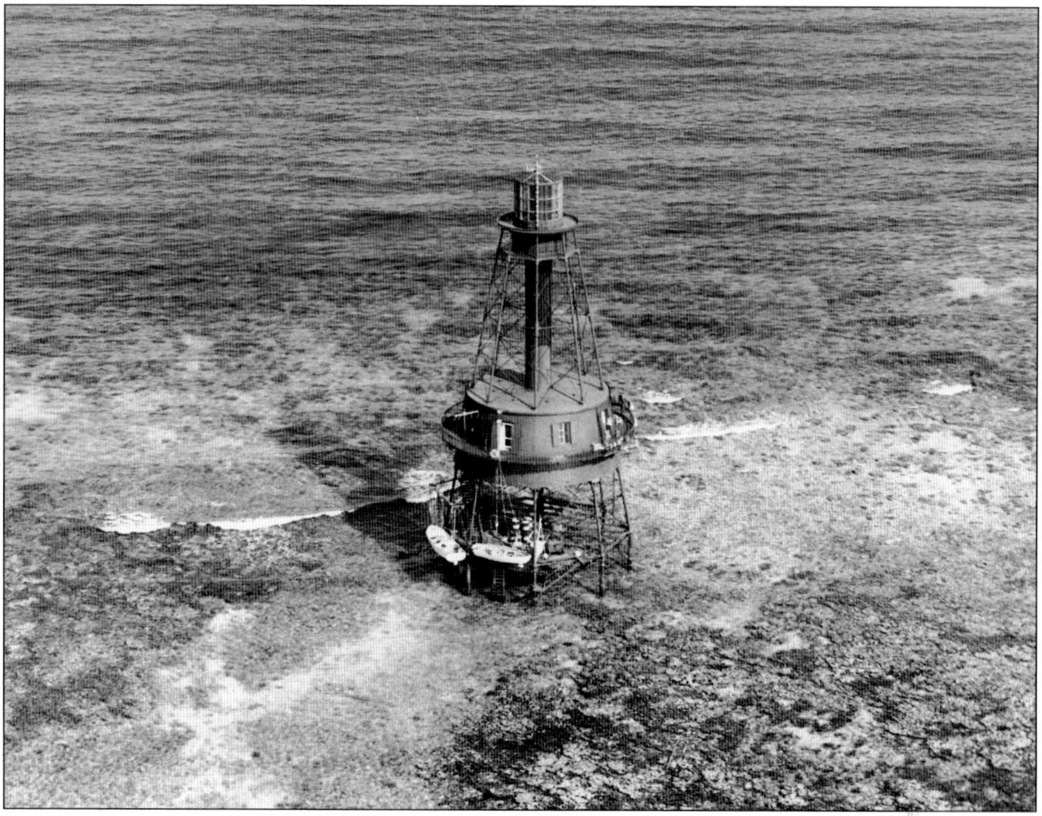

Carysfort's open ironwork constituted another design advance. Tropical storms, hurricane-force winds, and storm surge did not encounter the same resistance as they would with a solid brick lighthouse. Although initially meant to have a Fresnel lens, Carysfort light was first outfitted with 18 traditional Lewis lamps, to which Meade added reflectors. The lighthouse, completed in 1852, received its Fresnel lens in 1855. (Courtesy of the US Coast Guard Historian's Office.)

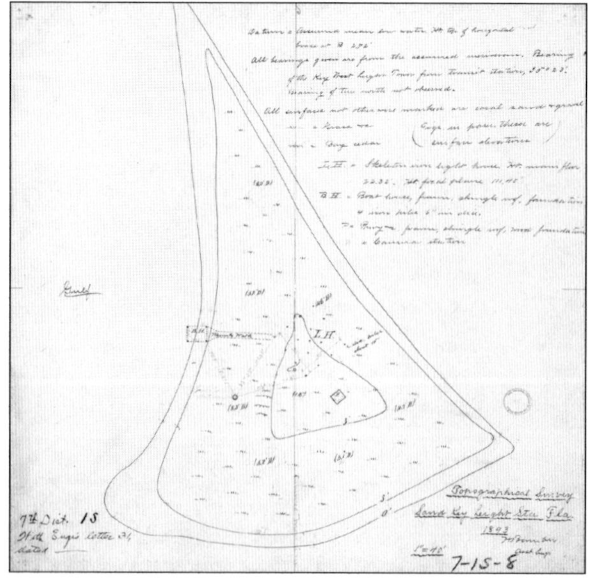

Lt. Comdr. Matthew Perry raised the question of whether Sand Key was stable enough for a lighthouse; the events of the 1846 hurricane and the utter destruction of that masonry light further underlined the challenges of the location. Sand Key is and was a shape shifter, growing and completely disappearing at times. This survey, conducted in the 1890s, shows that the key was not all that much larger than the lighthouse itself. (Courtesy of the National Archives.)

After his successful design for the Carysfort Light, Isaiah W.P. Lewis was the natural choice to design the next Florida Keys lighthouse. This drawing for the Sand Key light closely resembles that of Carysfort, with iron piles and a skeleton-type design that allowed wind and waves to pass through the structure fairly unimpeded. Yet this light, once erected, looked distinctive from Carysfort. (Courtesy of Monroe County Library, Key West.)

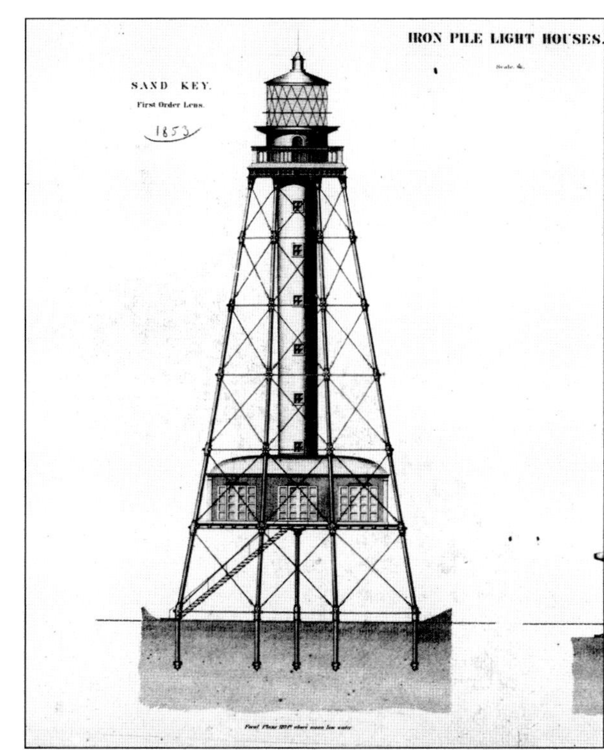

The 132-foot Sand Key lighthouse had a more pyramidal form than Carysfort. This 1853 article reported that "The focal plane is one hundred and ten feet above the sea, and the light can be seen from . . . the distance of eighteen miles." The focal plane is the distance from the surface of the water to the optical center of the lens. (Courtesy of Monroe County Library, Key West.)

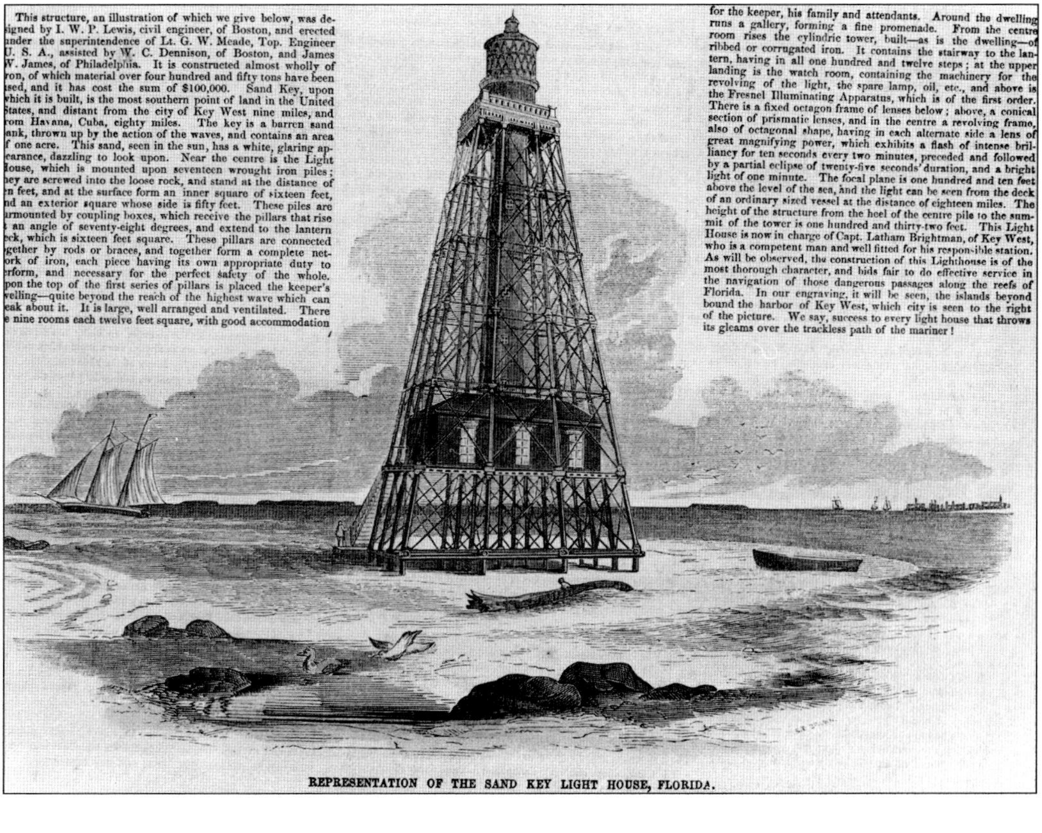

This structure, an illustration of which we give below, was designed by I. W. P. Lewis, civil engineer, of Boston, and erected
under the superintendence of Lt. G. W. Meade, Top. Engineer
U. S. A., assisted by W. C. Dennison, of Boston, and James
W. James, of Philadelphia. It is constructed almost wholly of
ron, of which material over four hundred and fifty tons have been
ised, and it has cost the sum of $100,000. Sand Key, upon
which it is built, is the most southern point of land in the United
States, and distant from the city of Key West nine miles, and
rom Havana, Cuba, eighty miles. The key is a barren sand
ank, thrown up by the action of the waves, and contains an area
f one acre. This sand, seen in the sun, has a white, glaring ap-
earance, dazzling to look upon. Near the centre is the Light
House, which is mounted upon seventeen wrought iron piles;
hey are screwed into the loose rock, and stand at the distance of
n feet, and at the surface form an inner square of sixteen feet,
nd an exterior square whose side is fifty feet. These piles are
urmounted by coupling boxes, which receive the pillars that rise
t an angle of seventy-eight degrees, and extend to the lantern
eck, which is sixteen feet square. These pillars are connected
gether by rods or braces, and together form a complete net-
ork of iron, each piece having its own appropriate duty to
erform, and necessary for the perfect safety of the whole.
pon the top of the first series of pillars is placed the keeper's
welling—quite beyond the reach of the highest wave which can
eak about it. It is large, well arranged and ventilated. There
e nine rooms each twelve feet square, with good accommodation
for the keeper, his family and attendants. Around the dwelling runs a gallery, forming a fine promenade. From the centre room rises the cylindric tower, built—as is the dwelling—of ribbed or corrugated iron. It contains the stairway to the lantern, having in all one hundred and twelve steps; at the upper landing is the watch room, containing the machinery for the revolving of the light, the spare lamp, oil, etc., and above is the Fresnel Illuminating Apparatus, which is of the first order. There is a fixed octagon frame of lenses below; above, a conical section of prismatic lenses, and in the centre a revolving frame, also of octagonal shape, having in each alternate side a lens of great magnifying power, which exhibits a flash of intense brilliancy for ten seconds every two minutes, preceded and followed by a partial eclipse of twenty-five seconds' duration, and a bright light of one minute. The focal plane is one hundred and ten feet above the level of the sea, and the light can be seen from the deck of an ordinary sized vessel at the distance of eighteen miles. The height of the structure from the heel of the centre pile to the summit of the tower is one hundred and thirty-two feet. This Light House is now in charge of Capt. Latham Brightman, of Key West, who is a competent man and well fitted for his responsible station. As will be observed, the construction of this Lighthouse is of the most thorough character, and bids fair to do effective service in the navigation of those dangerous passages along the reefs of Florida. In our engraving, it will be seen, the islands beyond bound the harbor of Key West, which city is seen to the right of the picture. We say, success to every light house that throws its gleams over the trackless path of the mariner!

REPRESENTATION OF THE SAND KEY LIGHT HOUSE, FLORIDA.

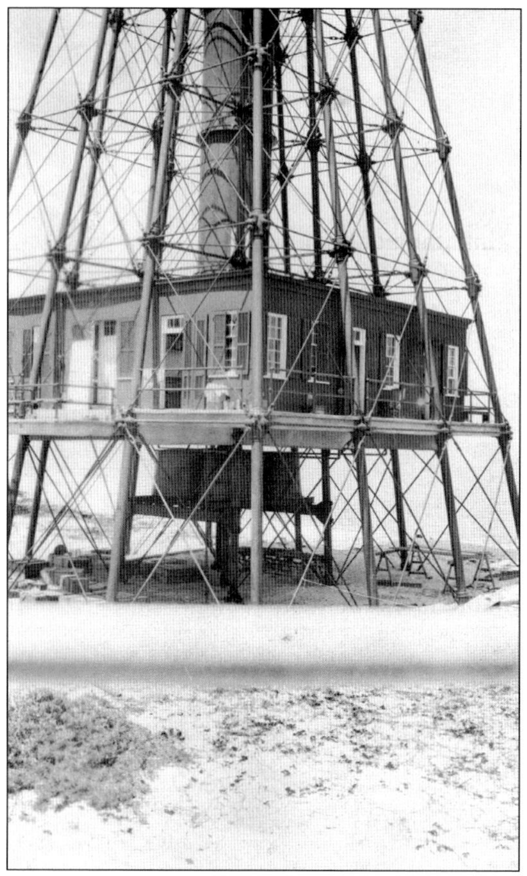

The Sand Key light's piles extend 10 feet below the surface. All the iron elements of the lighthouse were first fitted together at John F. Riley Ironworks in South Carolina. Designer Isaiah Lewis oversaw the installation of the state-of-the-art screwpiles into the coral. He might have completed the lighthouse had the project not run short of money. (Courtesy of the National Archives.)

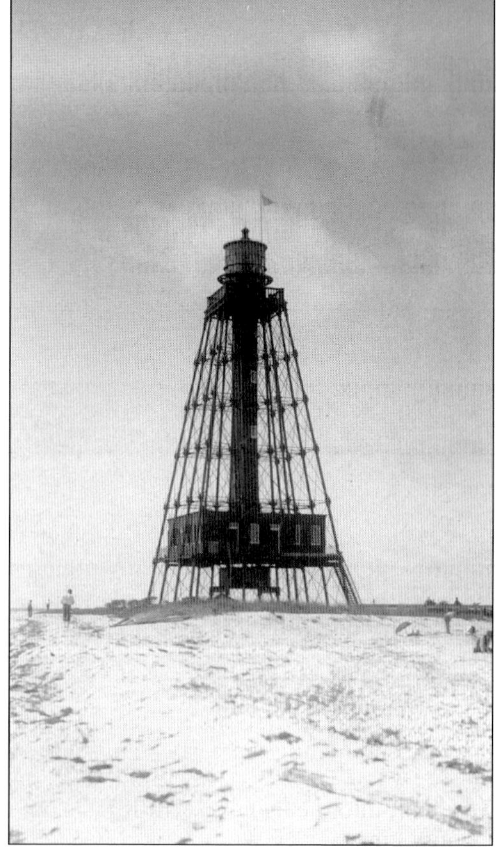

Work stopped at Sand Key and did not resume until 1853, when George Meade took over as the lead engineer and decided to make changes to Isaiah Lewis's design. This image shows the keeper's quarters, divided into nine rooms; the tube-shaped element in the center of the light contains the stairs, which are protected from the elements. (Courtesy of the National Archives.)

Installed in the Sand Key lighthouse was a Fresnel-type lens designed by George Meade and manufactured by Merrick & Towne in Pennsylvania. The lens consisted of "three rows of triangular glass panes," according to Josh Liller. Meade also made the keepers' lives easier by inventing the Meade Hydraulic Lamp, which delivered oil more efficiently from a reservoir in the dome of the lantern. (Courtesy of the US Lighthouse Society Archives.)

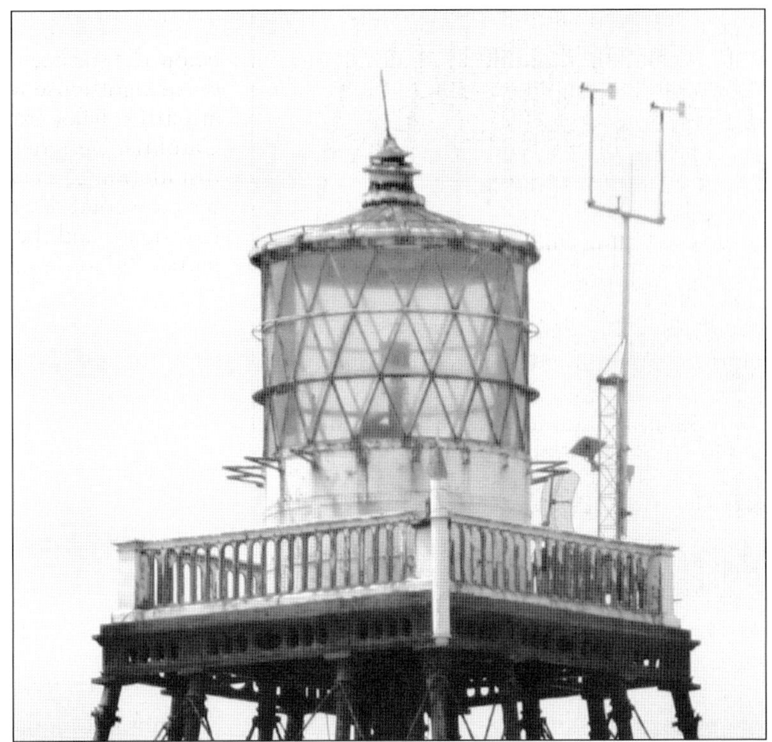

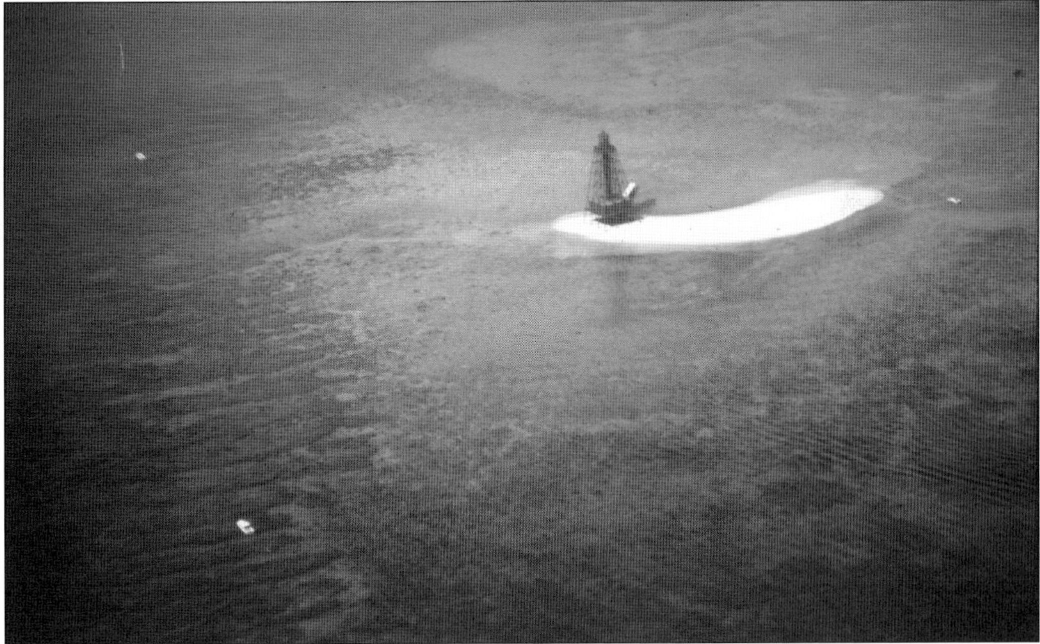

A hurricane struck the Sand Key lighthouse three years after its completion. Despite the destruction of every outbuilding there, the lighthouse survived that storm, as well as one in 1865, the twin hurricanes of 1870, and the 1875 hurricane. Due to hurricane damage, new keeper's quarters were built into the lighthouse in 1875. (Photograph by Raymond L. Blazevic, courtesy of Monroe County Library, Key West.)

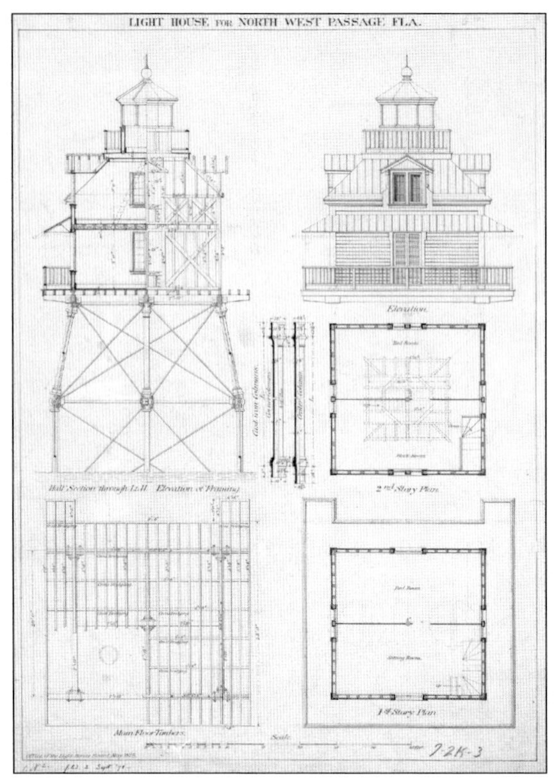

A lightship once marked the Northwest Passage or Northwest Channel, a channel to the northwest of Key West. The lightship had neither sufficient illumination nor satisfactory range, and lightships could be extremely unpleasant to handle when the weather grew rough. Historian Josh Liller points out that George Meade "designed a screwpile cottage lighthouse" for the Northwest Passage, although Meade did not oversee its construction. (Courtesy of the National Archives.)

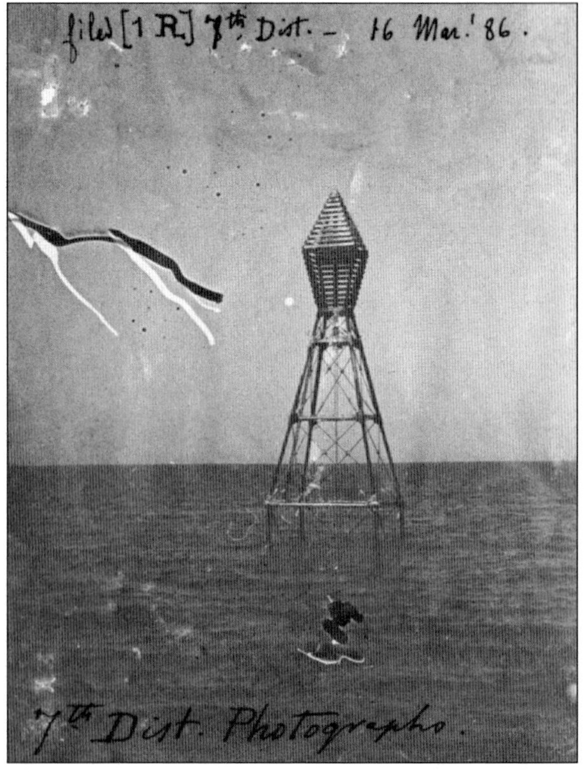

One of the most remote locations in need of a lighthouse was at Rebecca Shoal. Forty-three miles west of Key West, the shoal presented some of, if not the most, challenging construction conditions of any of the Keys lighthouses. Although George Meade designed a beacon to be erected here in 1854, storms and sea conditions delayed construction for over two decades. (Courtesy of the US Lighthouse Society Archives.)

As more and more American ships wrecked in the Middle Keys (or Vacas Keys), the need for a lighthouse became evident. George Meade examined potential sites at various reefs, including Coffins Patches, the Turtle Shoals, and Sombrero Key reef. This drawing illustrates the ventilator and chimney for a Coffins Patches light, although Sombrero Key was ultimately chosen. (Courtesy of the National Archives.)

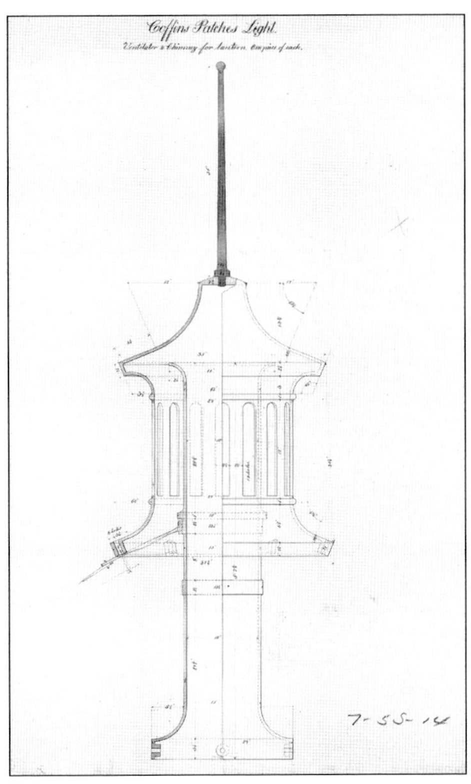

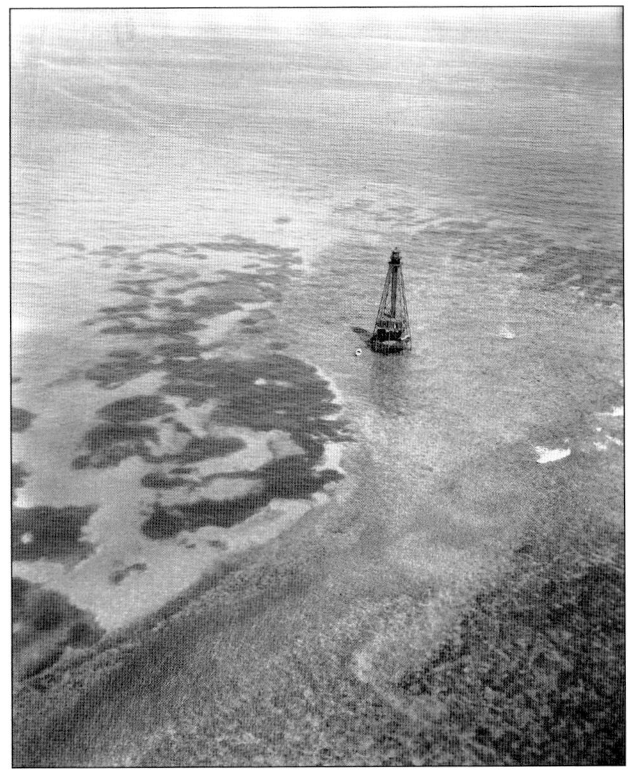

In 1743, Spanish missionary Fr. Joseph Alana drew a chart of the Keys and recorded the name Cayo Sombrero (or Hat Key). In 1765, one British surveyor described the key as "the shoal of Sombreros, with its barren sand-hills," while in 1775, George Gauld called it a "small sandy key on the reef." In the 19th century, the low-lying key disappeared and reappeared. (Courtesy of the State Archives of Florida.)

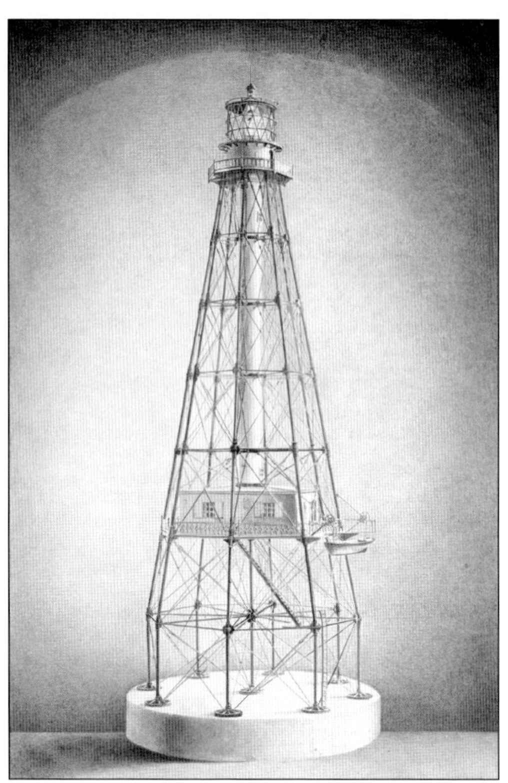

This drawing, meant to give a three-dimensional sense of the Sombrero lighthouse, shows how the piles form an octagon, as opposed to the squarish arrangement of piles at Sand Key. George Meade initially suggested using masonry construction but then changed his mind; he himself designed this wrought iron light, with galvanized iron for any elements below the waterline. (Courtesy of the National Archives.)

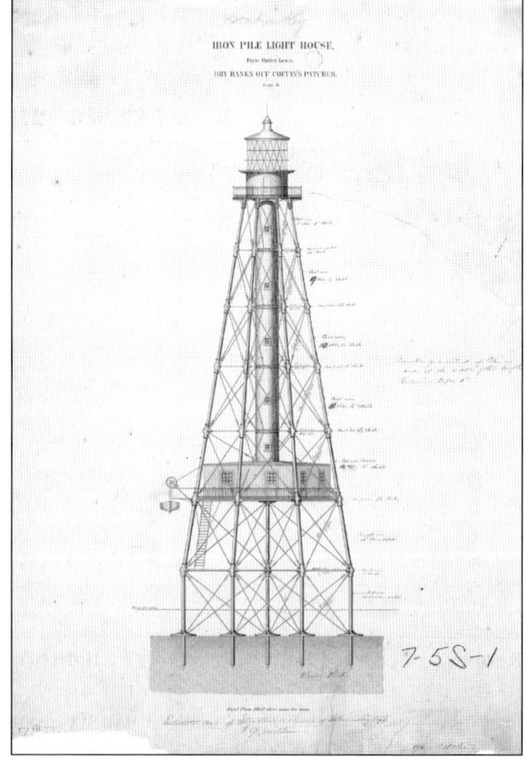

This Sombrero lighthouse drawing is annotated with notes and measurements. At top, the printed heading reads "Dry Banks off Coffin's Patches," but penciled above that is "Sombrero Key." Penciled at the bottom is "Estimated Cost of Structure Exclusive of Illuminating App. $98.641.46." Transportation of the light's parts, the lens, and workers' salaries were not included. (Courtesy of the National Archives.)

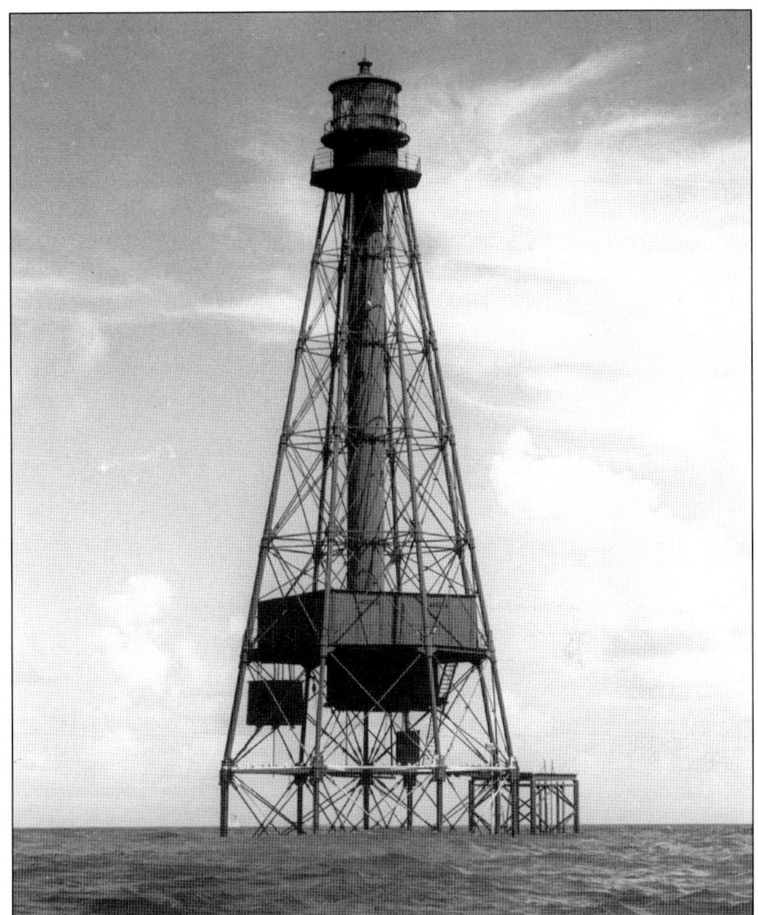

Although construction began in 1856, a hurricane destroyed what had been completed thus far. In 1857, Meade returned to Sombrero Key and this time succeeded in completing the lighthouse. As at Sand Key, nine piles descended 10 feet through eight-foot-wide footplates or disks. In this photograph, the cross-braces are visible. (Courtesy of Monroe County Library, Key West.)

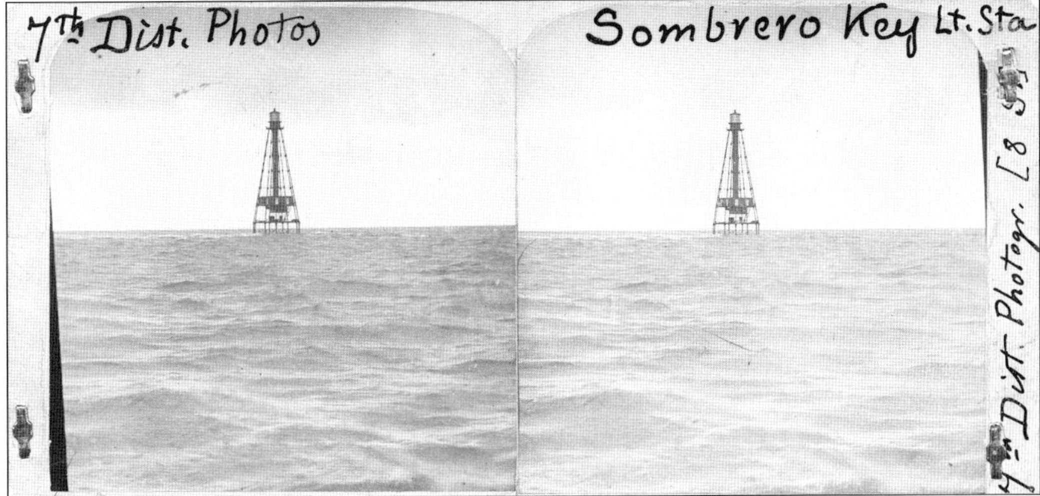

Keeper Joseph Bethel lit Sombrero Key lighthouse's fixed light in March 1858 and took residence in the 35-foot square quarters with the assistant keepers. The keeper had to climb 133 steps to reach the lantern. Although the lighthouse structure itself rose 156 feet, the focal plane (distance from the water to the lantern's optical center) was 142 feet. (Courtesy of the National Archives.)

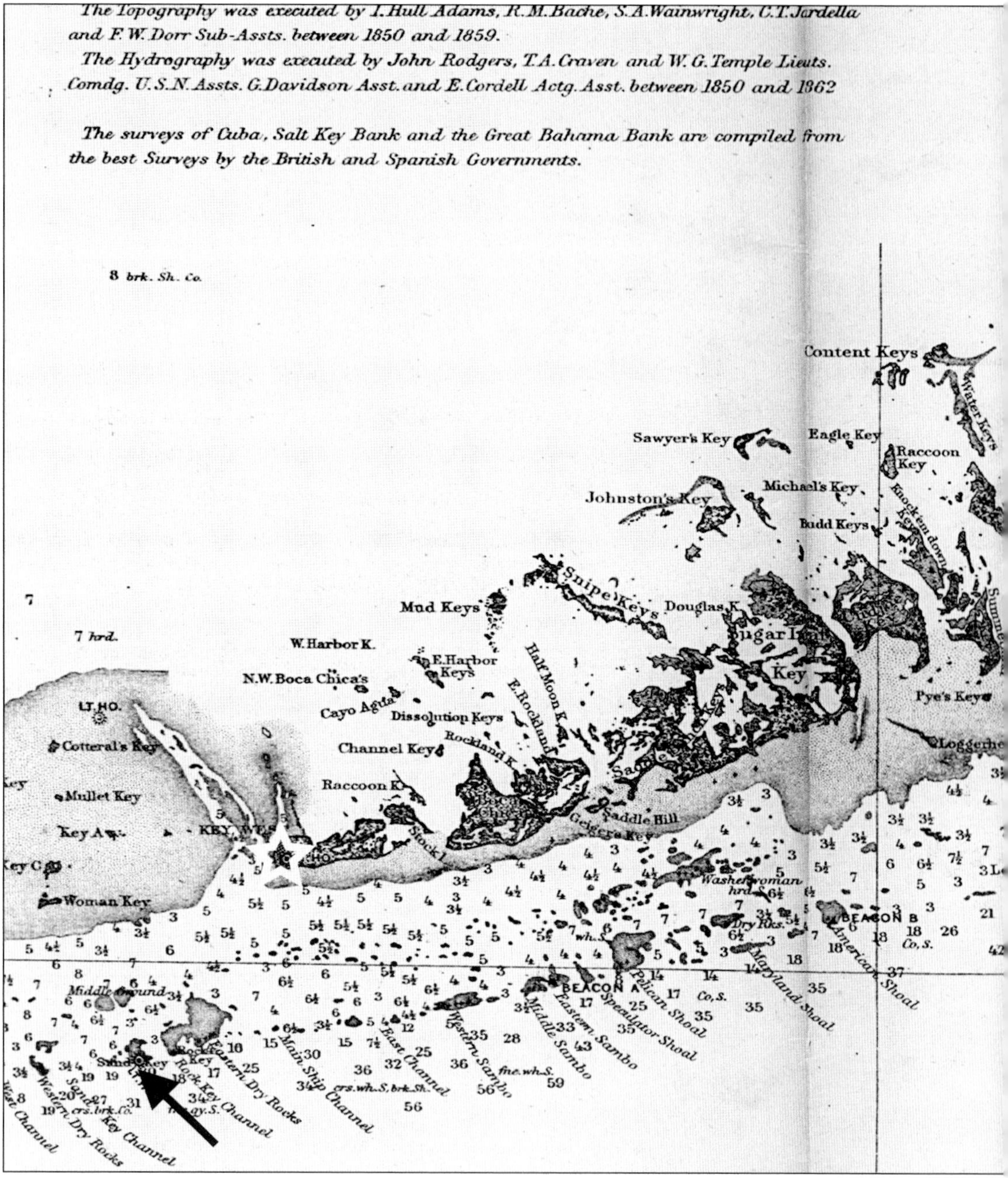

The Topography was executed by I. Hull Adams, R. M. Bache, S. A. Wainwright, C. T. Jardella and F. W. Dorr Sub-Assts. between 1850 and 1859.

The Hydrography was executed by John Rodgers, T. A. Craven and W. G. Temple Lieuts. Comdg. U.S.N. Assts. G. Davidson Asst. and E. Cordell Actg. Asst. between 1850 and 1862

The surveys of Cuba, Salt Key Bank and the Great Bahama Bank are compiled from the best Surveys by the British and Spanish Governments.

This hydrographic map starts on the right approximately at Duck Key and ends just west of Key West. The black arrow at left shows the location of the Sand Key lighthouse; for reference, a white star indicates the location of Key West. The black arrow to the far right shows Sombrero Key reef, south of the Middle Keys, including "Key Vaccas" and "Nights Key." At Sand Key,

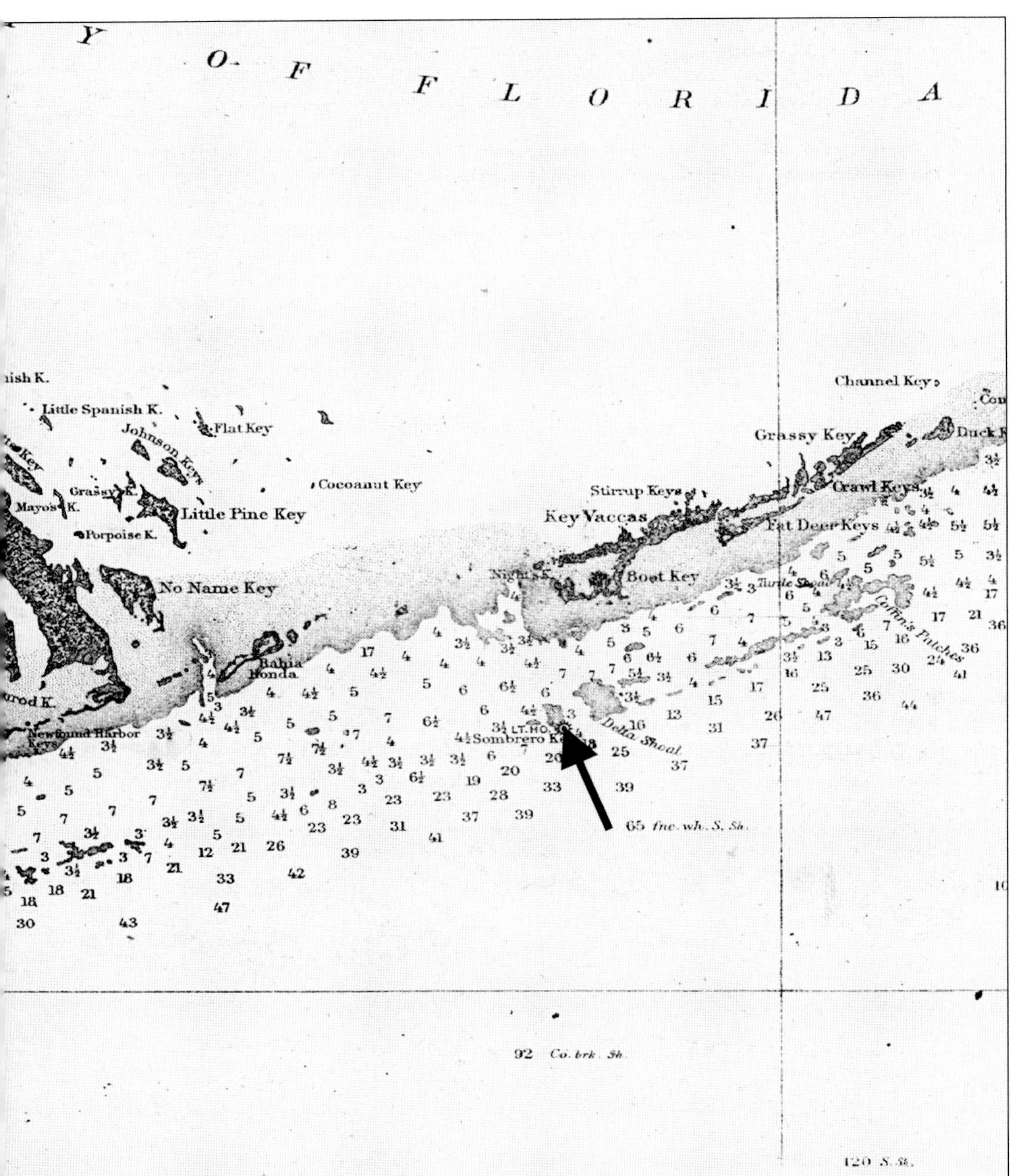

the lighthouse keepers had a relatively close "commute" to seek supplies or medical care at Key West. A few settlers pioneered the Vacas Keys, particularly the family of Temple and Mary Pent. Nonetheless, the Sombrero Key location was very remote both for the settlers and the keepers who tended the lighthouse. (Courtesy of the Library of Congress.)

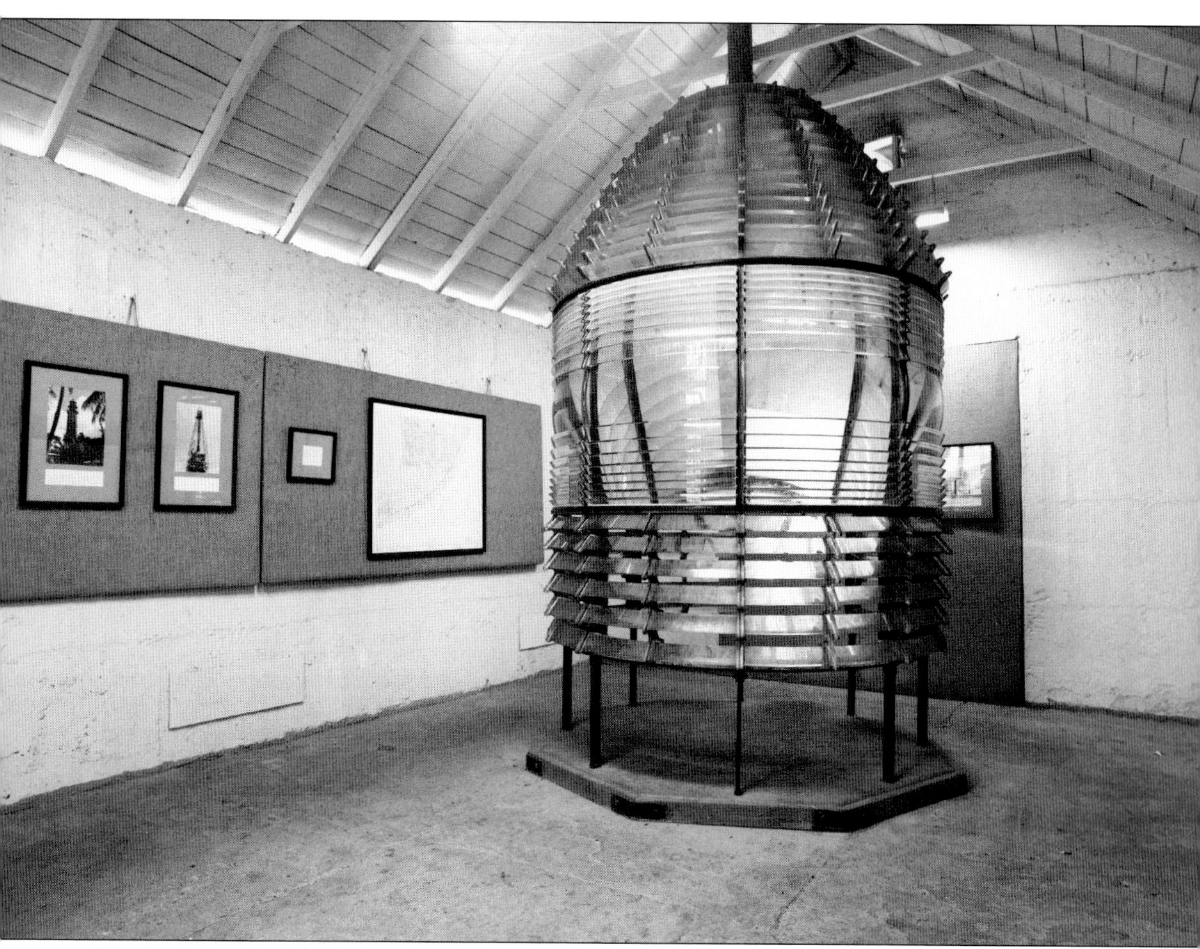

The Sombrero Key lighthouse once housed this stunning Fresnel lens, a first-order lens made by French firm L. Sautter and Company. First-order lenses are the largest, measuring approximately eight feet by six. Born in 1788, engineer and physicist Augustin-Jean Fresnel invented the catadioptric (reflective and refractive) lens. Before Fresnel, lighthouse lantern reflectors only reflected about half the light, and thus lost a great deal of potential illumination. With multiple, thin prisms arranged to both reflect and refract light, the lens required less glass and increased the visibility of the lighthouse beam. Sadly, Fresnel himself died before a full-sized version of his lens could be crafted, but his invention profoundly changed lighthouse technology. The Sombrero Key lighthouse's lens was eventually removed and taken to the lighthouse museum in Key West. (Courtesy of the State Archives of Florida.)

Four

Near the Site of Wrecks

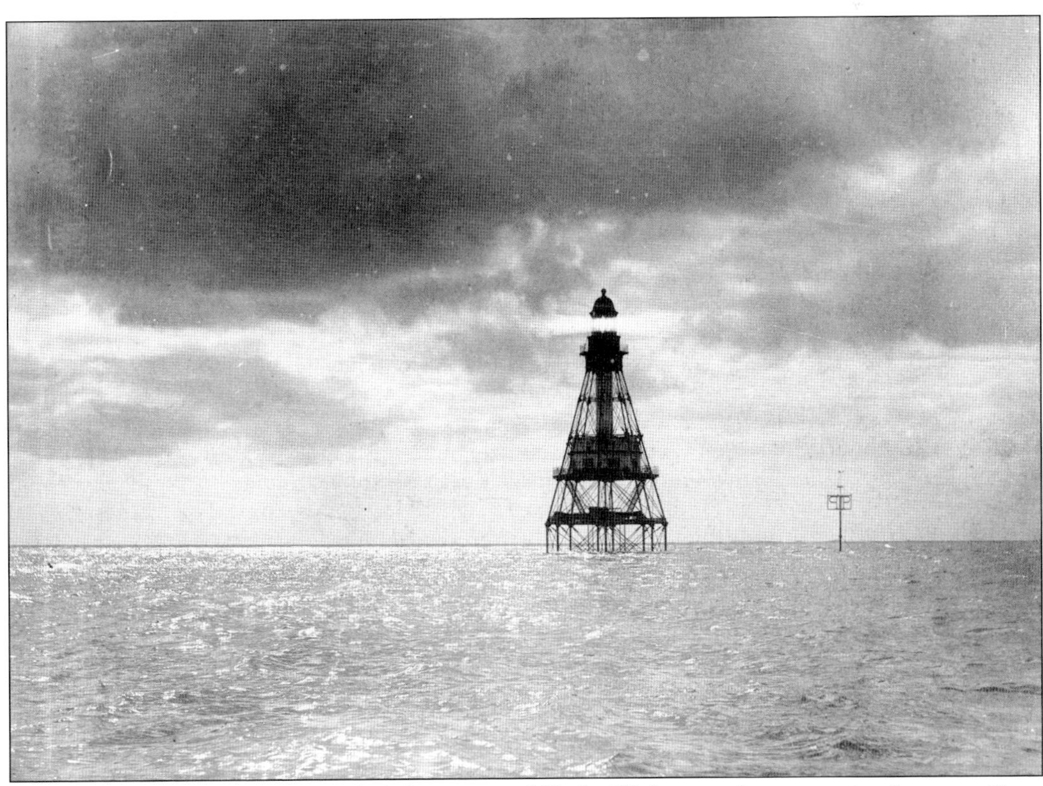

The construction of three more lighthouses would help fill the gaps for navigation between Cape Florida and Key West. In 1873, 1878, and 1880, one iron lighthouse after the other arose, each positioned near a section of the Florida Reef named for a famous wreck. (Photograph by Ralph Middleton Munroe, courtesy of the University of Miami Library.)

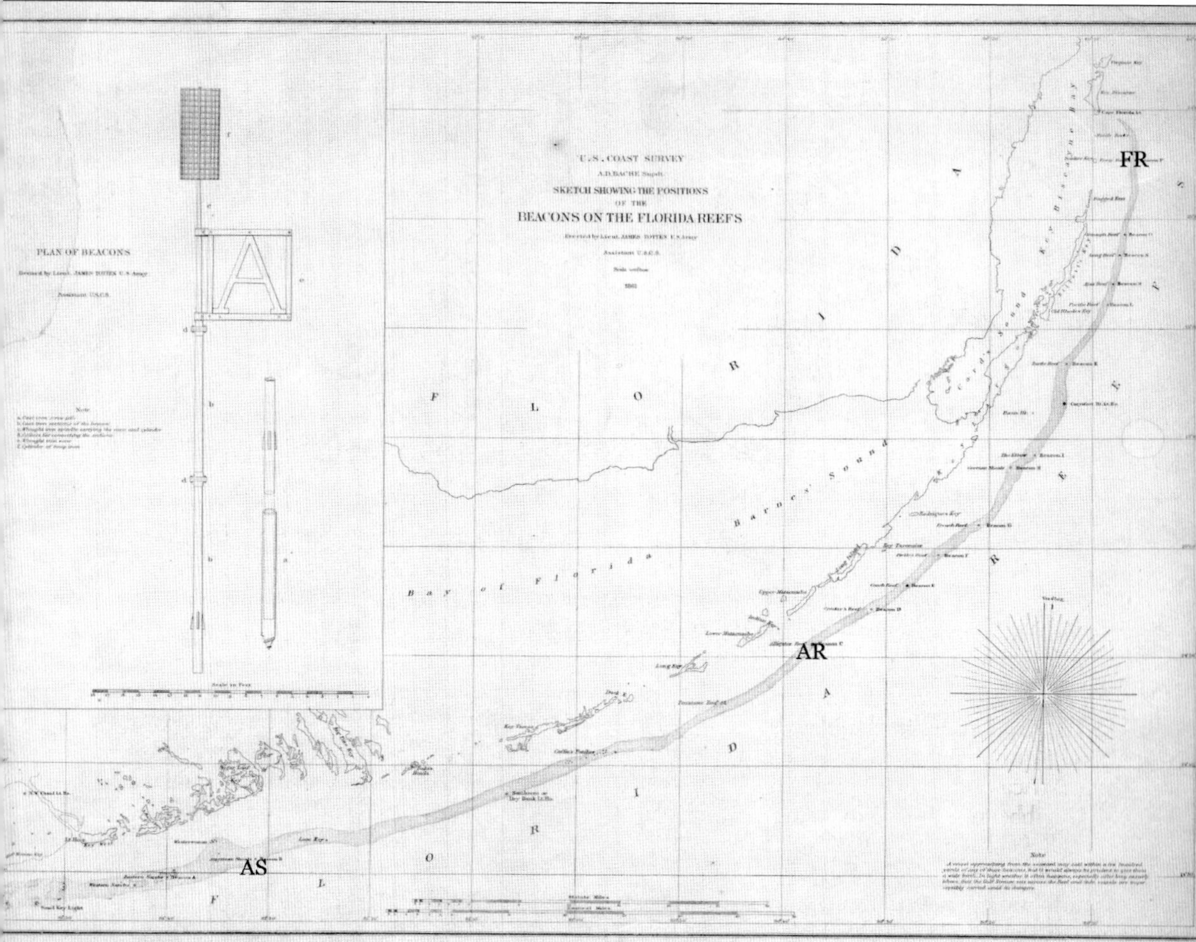

This 1861 coast survey was produced by the Office of the Chief of Engineers for the US War Department. It is titled "Sketch Showing the Positions of Beacons on the Florida Reef, Erected by Lieut. James Totten, U.S. Army." Also indicated are the lighthouses: Northwest Channel (also known as the Northwest Passage light), Key West, Sand Key, Sombrero, Carysfort, and Cape Florida. The 16 beacons are lettered from A to P. "AS" on the map indicates the American Shoals beacon (more typically used is the singular American Shoal). AR situates the Alligator Reef beacon off the islands of Islamorada, and FR shows Fowey Rocks, not far south of Cape Florida. These three beacons would be replaced by lighthouses after the Civil War. Lighthouses were strategically important to both the Union and the Confederacy. Confederate supporters attacked and disabled the Cape Florida light; it was not relit until 1866. Union troops held the island of Key West, and thus that light remained in Union hands. (Courtesy of the National Archives.)

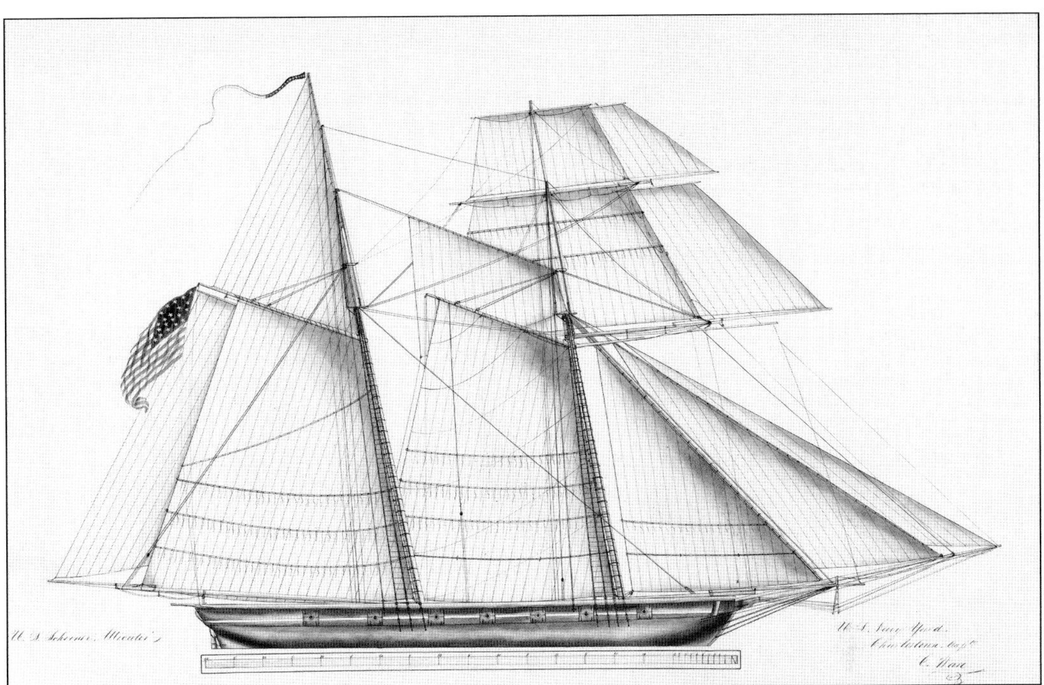

This handsome 1820 schooner was USS *Alligator*, used in the Navy's efforts to interrupt the slave trade from Africa and to quell piracy in the Caribbean. After foundering on the reef three and a half miles from Upper Matecumbe Key, the captain and crew were rescued by a wrecking vessel. Lt. John Dale burned the *Alligator* so that pirates would not seize it. This section of reef became known as Alligator Reef. (Courtesy of the National Oceanic and Atmospheric Administration.)

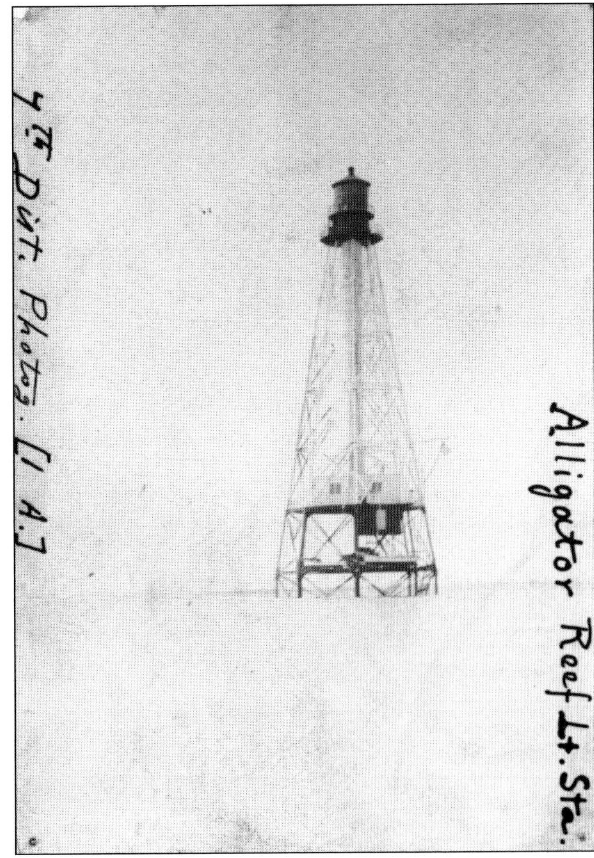

Seventh District inspector M. Carrington Watkins communicated to the Lighthouse Board that a light was urgently needed on Alligator Reef: "four vessels have been wrecked there . . . in the last four months." Although the decision had been made in 1857 to construct a lighthouse at Alligator Reef, the Civil War intervened. Florida joined its fellow slave states in the Confederacy. Work only started in 1872. (Courtesy of the National Archives.)

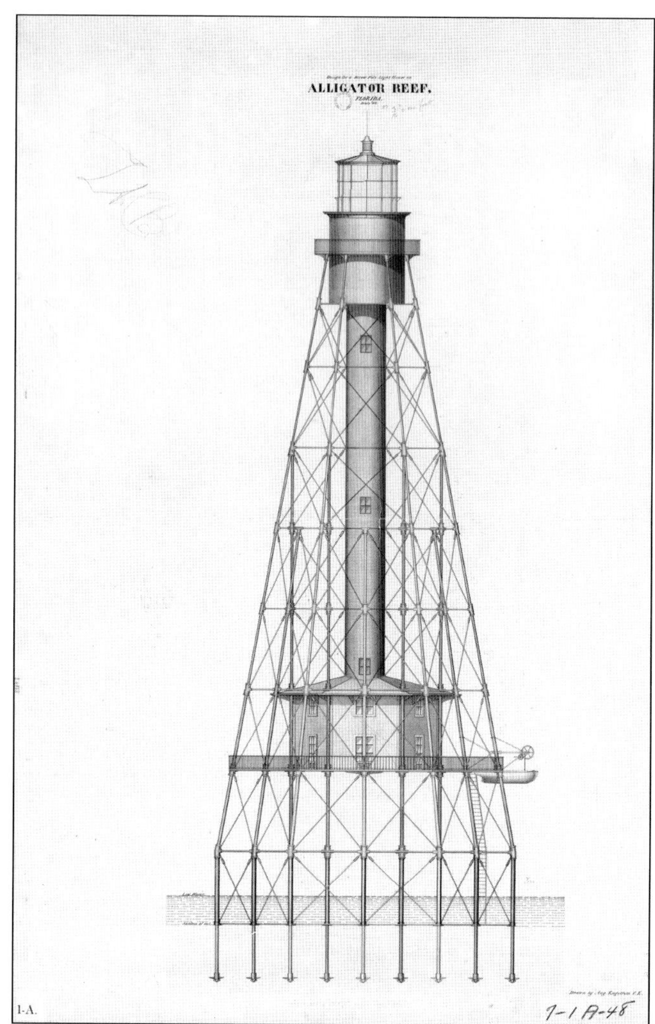

This illustration is headed "Design for a Screw Pile Light House on Alligator Reef Florida." Like the Sombrero lighthouse, the footprint of the Alligator Reef light formed an octagon. Unlike at Carysfort, the engineers were able to secure the piles in coral rock (rather than sand). And, as at the other wrought iron lighthouses, the piles were driven down 10 feet. (Courtesy of the National Archives.)

To enable the work on the reef, the workers and engineers used 11-acre Indian Key as a base. They also installed a platform next to the site itself. At times, the sea conditions made work on the project impossible, and the Alligator Reef lighthouse was not completed until November 1873. (Courtesy of the National Archives.)

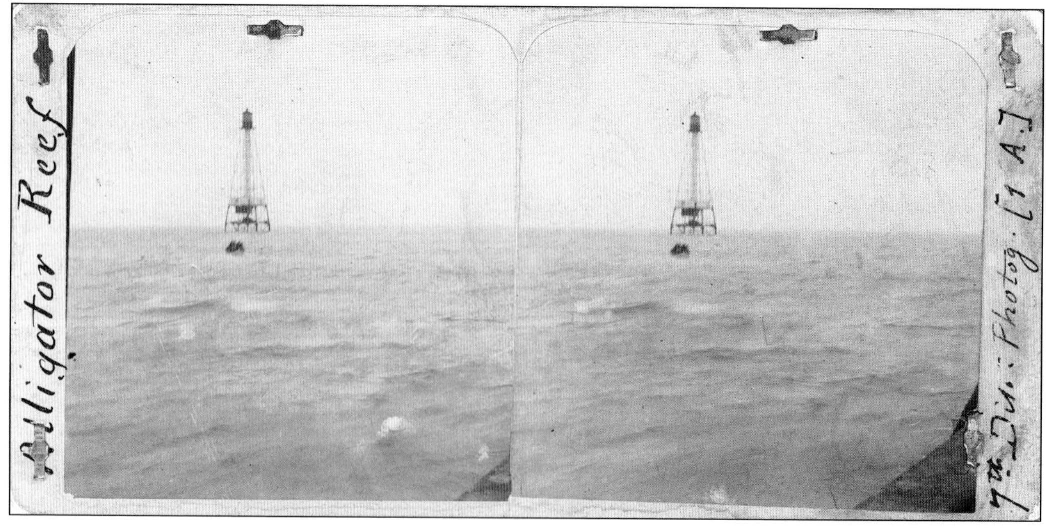

This design document shows one piece of machinery absolutely essential for the lighthouse keepers: the boat hoist. A reliable, functional hoist allowed the keepers some freedom of movement, at least when the weather remained manageable. Otherwise, they had to wait for a mail or supply vessel or a ship that happened to be passing. (Courtesy of the National Archives.)

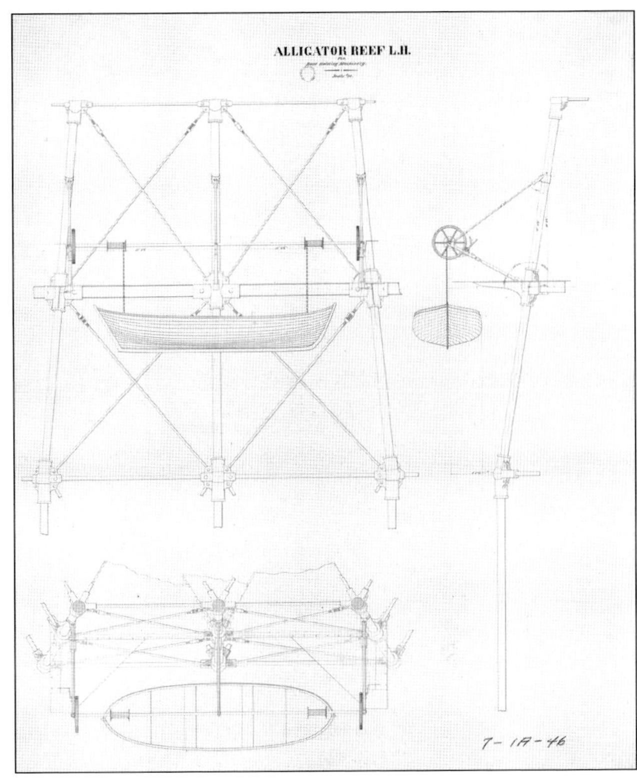

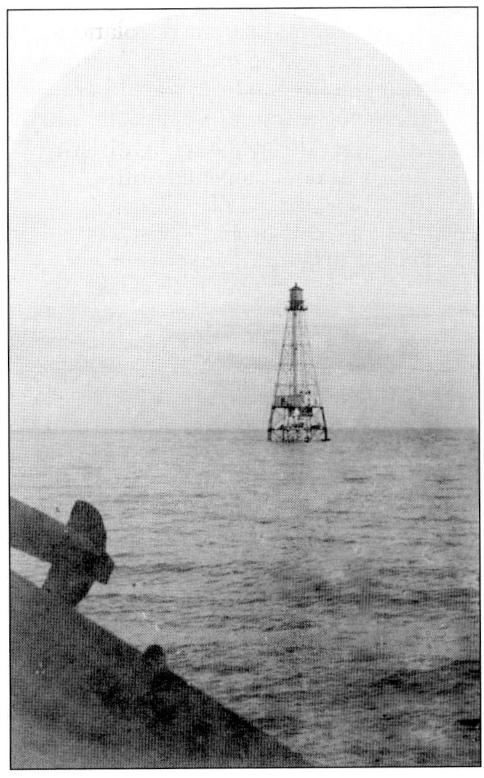

Alligator Reef's first keeper was George R. Billberry, who served from 1873 to 1885; Billberry had various assistant keepers, including Oscar Fish and Alexander Smith. The light's first-order Fresnel lens revolved and provided six flashes—five white and one red. (Courtesy of the National Archives.)

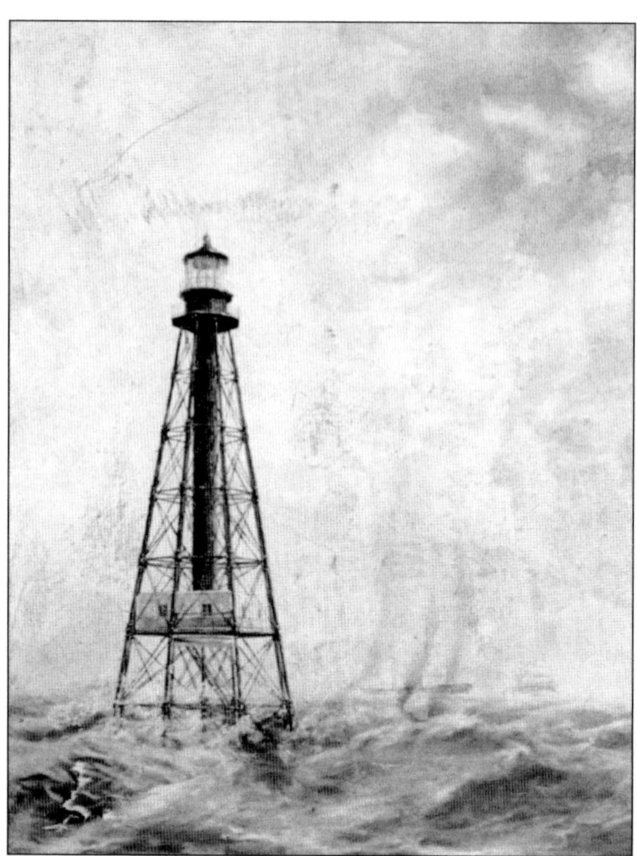

Mariners could spot the Alligator Reef light from up to 18 nautical miles; the completed 150-foot lighthouse could boast a focal plane of 136 feet, just 6 feet less than that of Sombrero Key. When the World's Columbian Exposition was held in 1893 to celebrate the anniversary of Columbus's voyage of 1492, a painting of Alligator Reef lighthouse was among the objects displayed. (Courtesy of the National Archives.)

The brick lighthouse on Cape Florida had survived for decades, but both its position and its technology left something to be desired. The Lighthouse Board instead designated Fowey Rocks as the site for a new iron lighthouse approximately seven miles southeast of Cape Florida. In 1748, the British warship HMS *Fowey* ran aground on the reef and subsequently sank here. (Courtesy of the National Archives.)

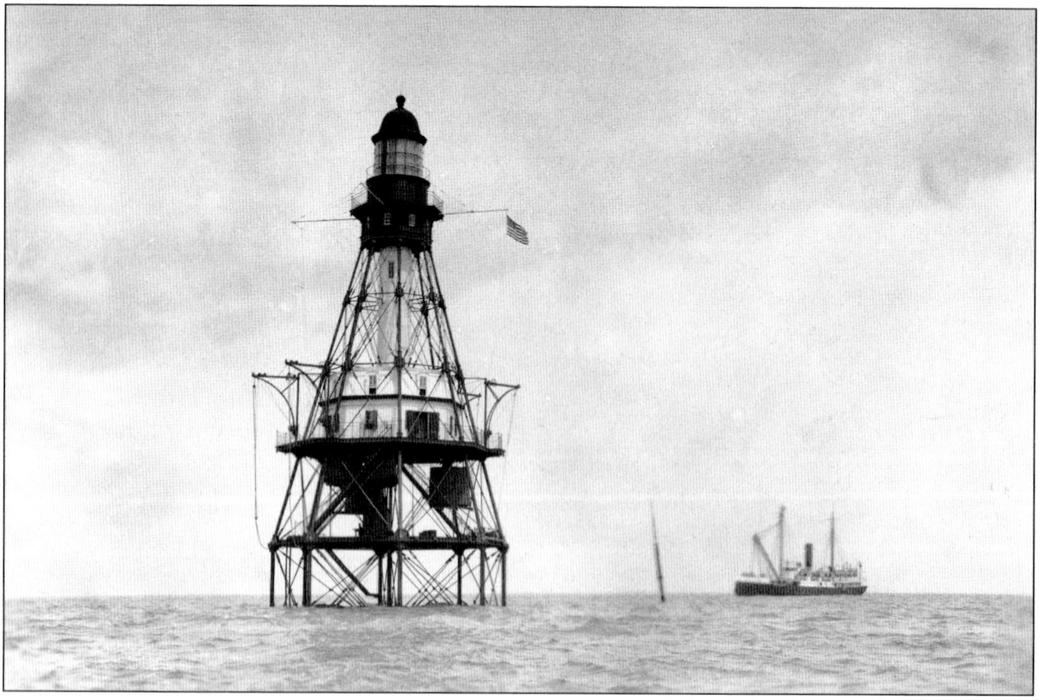

Fowey Rocks lighthouse's namesake, HMS *Fowey*, was a 127-foot warship launched by the Royal Navy in 1744. In 1748, *Fowey* was captained in the Americas by Francis William Drake, a descendant of Sir Francis Drake. As it sailed through Biscayne Bay, *Fowey* wrecked upon a reef and sank. Fortunately, sailors could seek refuge on British merchant ships they had been escorting. (Courtesy of the National Archives.)

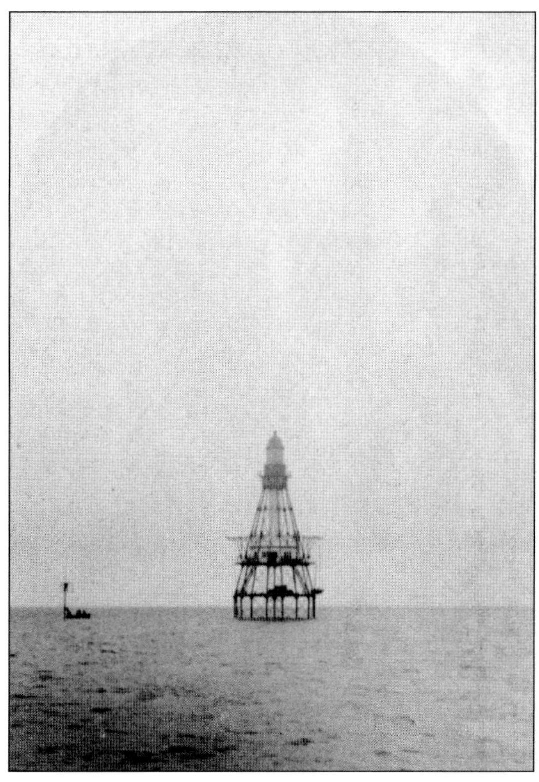

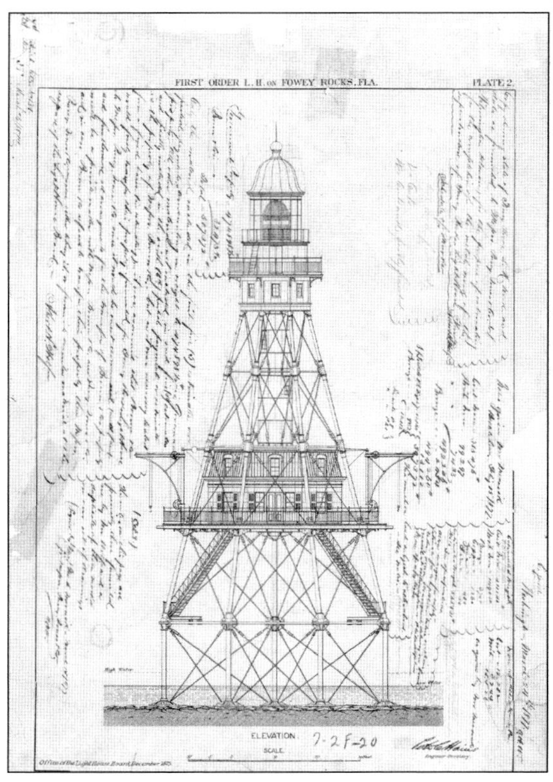

This extensively annotated drawing of Fowey Rocks lighthouse is titled "First Order L.H. on Fowey Rocks, Fla." One note reads "Copy showing state of Fowey Rocks L.H. work and data as furnished to [Messieurs] Pusy, Jones & Co of Wilmington, Delaware, for the purpose of estimating for the completion of the metal-work of the superstructure of Fowey Rocks Lighthouse, Florida." (Courtesy of the National Archives.)

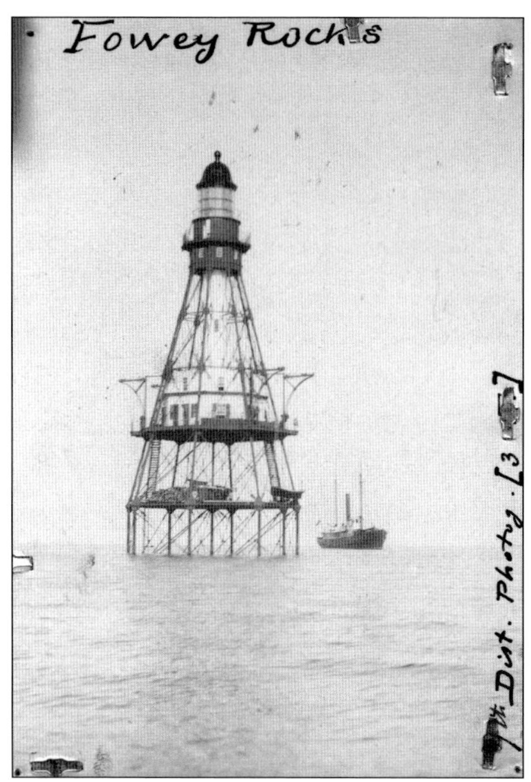

In this photograph, one can make out the distinctive dome that tops the Fowey Rocks lighthouse. Unlike the Alligator Reef or Sombrero lighthouses, this dome has only rounded edges and curves, like a child's hat in a storybook. According to lighthouse expert Tom Taylor, this "'bell-shaped' dome . . . had originally been designed in 1856." The same dome design was used for the Ponce Inlet lighthouse. (Courtesy of the National Archives.)

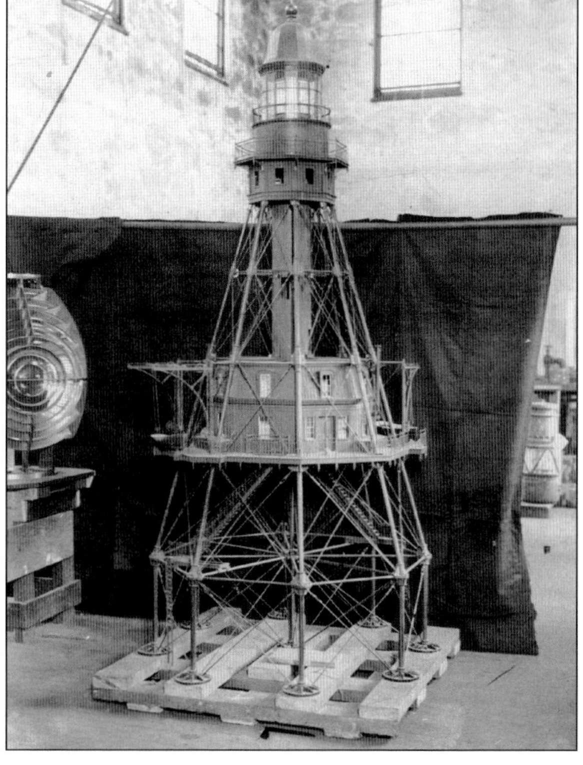

The beauty of this model is that is allows one to appreciate even the sections of lighthouse under the waterline. Fowey Rocks has an octagonal footprint and many cross-braces. One can make out the two stories of the keeper's quarters, the enclosed stairs, and the safety railing outside the lantern. This piece of government property has mysteriously gone missing. (Courtesy of the National Archives.)

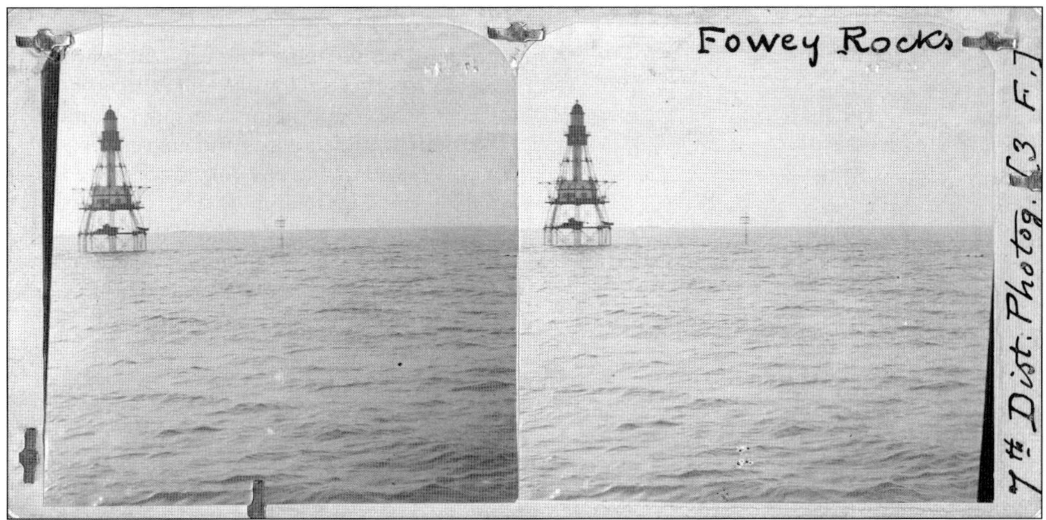

The Fowey Rocks lighthouse stands 125 feet and has a focal plane of 110 feet. Fowey Rocks light received a Fresnel lens from the Henry Lapaute Company in France, which had also crafted the Sombrero Key lighthouse lens. Sombrero's was first lit in 1858, Fowey Rocks' in 1878. Today, Fowey Rocks' lens is at the US Coast Guard's Aid to Navigation School in Virginia. (Courtesy of the National Archives.)

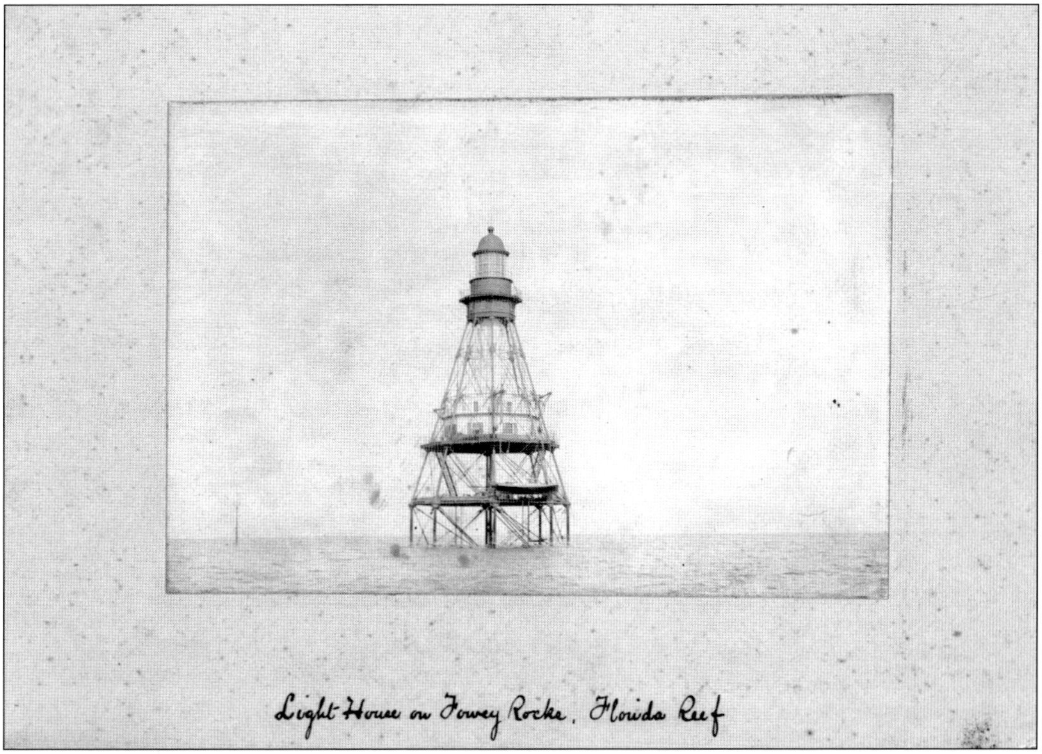

Light House on Fowey Rocks, Florida Reef

As the northernmost light of the Florida Keys, Fowey Rocks became a well-known outpost to visit for the nascent Coconut Grove community, south of the Miami River. A Coconut Grove pioneer, John Frow, had been keeper of the Cape Florida light and next served as keeper of Fowey Rocks. (Photograph by Ralph Middleton Munroe, courtesy of the University of Miami Library.)

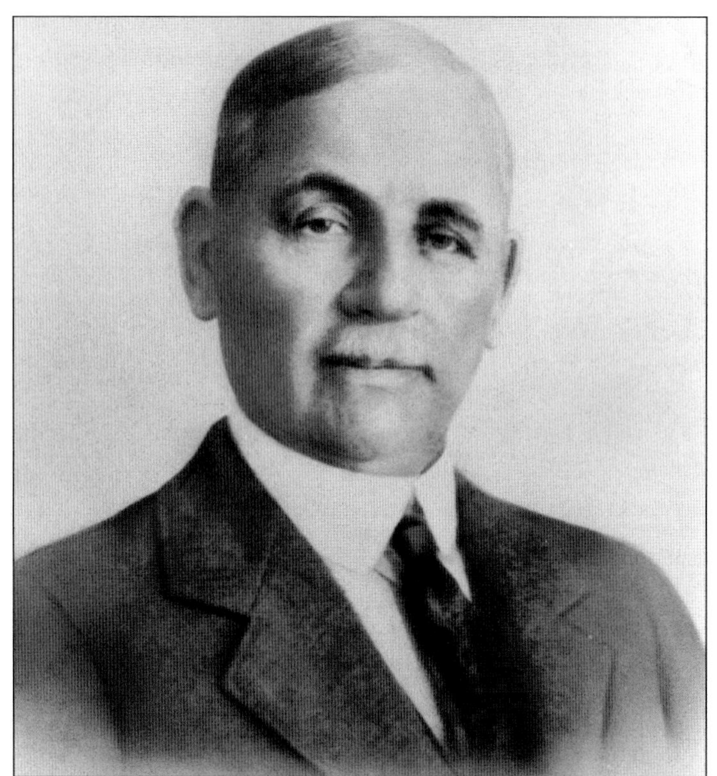

Florida Supreme Court chief justice Jefferson Browne worked as an assistant keeper at Fowey Rocks when he was a young man. He also wrote the history *Key West: The Old and the New*. In his book, he quotes author and Coconut Grove resident Kirk Munroe's poem, "Lights on the Florida Reef," which begins, "The fixed white light of Fowey Rocks, / And Carysfort's white flash." (Courtesy of Monroe County Library, Key West.)

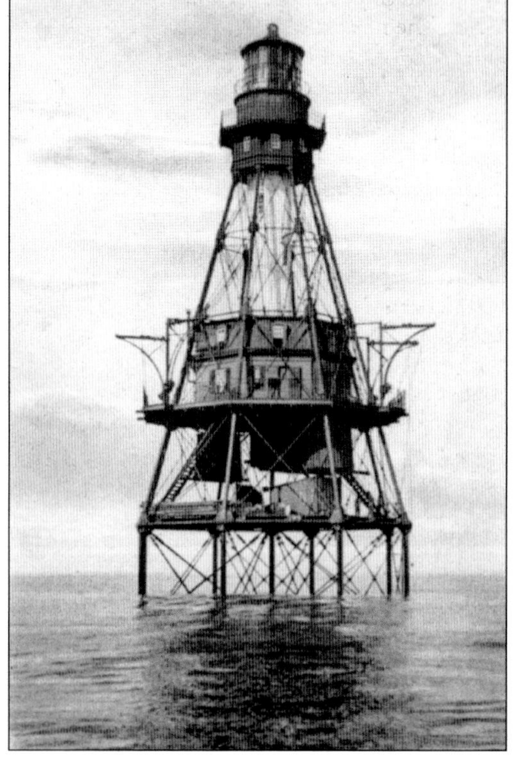

In his book, Jefferson Browne cites an 1835 recommendation from the governor of the Bahamas: "A light is necessary at each of the following places: Key Tavernier, Indian Key, Loo Key, and one in the intermediate space between the two last named places." The US government did not follow his advice exactly, but in 1880, the lighthouse pictured was indeed built near Looe Key. (Courtesy of Monroe County Library, Key West.)

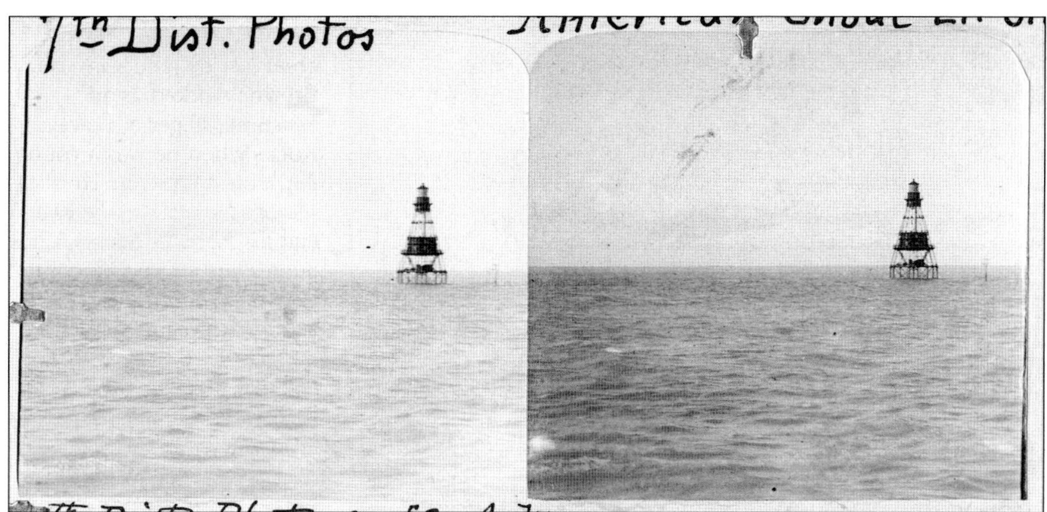

A number of ships wrecked on Looe Key and American Shoal; Looe Key was named for British frigate HMS *Loo*, which wrecked on that section of reef in 1744. However, the Lighthouse Board eventually chose nearby American Shoal as the site for the next iron light to be constructed on the Florida Reef. (Courtesy of the National Archives.)

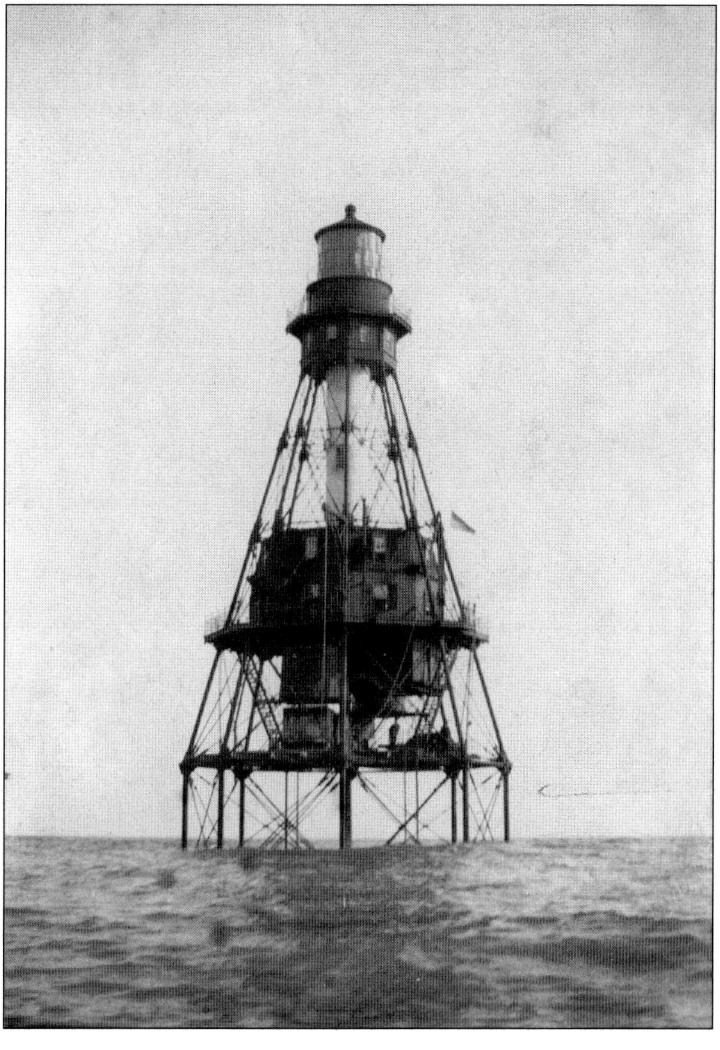

In this photograph, one can see the resemblance between American Shoal's keeper's quarters and those at Fowey Rocks. Although the plans for both lights look almost indistinguishable, American Shoal does not have Fowey's more ornate, bell-shaped dome or Victorian flourishes. With an iron structure manufactured in New Jersey and a first-order Fresnel lens from Henry Lapaute of Paris, the lighthouse first was lit in 1880. (Courtesy of the National Archives.)

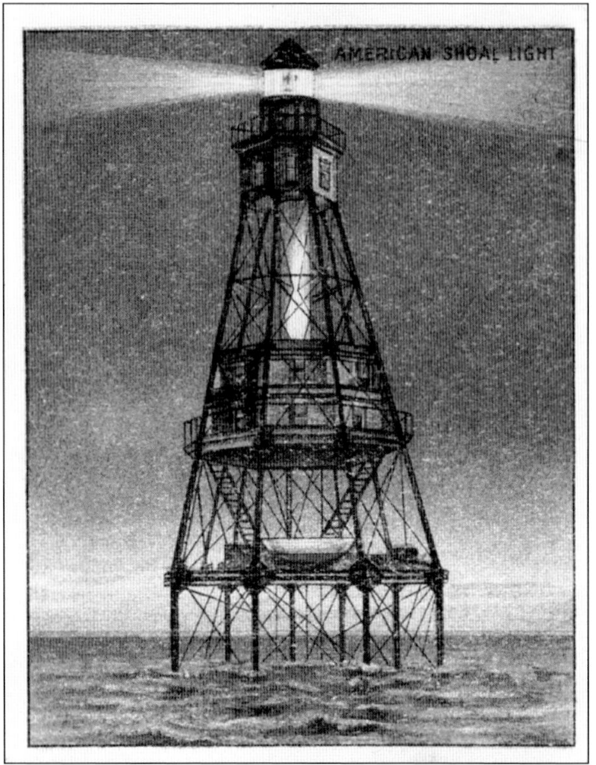

The Hassan cigarette company chose American Shoal lighthouse to be featured on one of its collectible tobacco card inserts. There were 50 lighthouse cards in all. The colored card depicts the light at night and contains a fair amount of detail, including the two staircases leading to the lower platform, the cross braces, the keeper's boat, and the two-story keeper's quarters, although the proportion of the watch room vis-à-vis the lantern height appears to be somewhat off. Approximately 124 feet high, the lighthouse stands in shallow water; the reef here lies 5 to 15 feet before the ocean's surface. Directly to the north of the reef is Sugarloaf Key, and to the northwest are the Saddlebunch Keys. (Both, courtesy of Laura Albritton.)

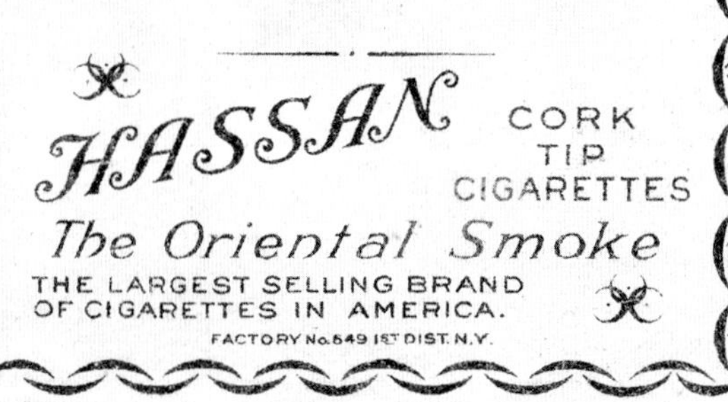

LIGHT HOUSE SERIES 1 TO 50

AMERICAN SHOAL LIGHT.

In five feet of water on American Shoal, off the coast of Florida. Has a flashing white and flashing red oil light, alternating at intervals of 5 seconds. Height above mean high water 109 feet. Visible 18¾ miles. Established 1880.

HASSAN CORK TIP CIGARETTES

The Oriental Smoke

THE LARGEST SELLING BRAND OF CIGARETTES IN AMERICA.

FACTORY No. 649 1ST DIST. N.Y.

Five

IN THE DRY TORTUGAS

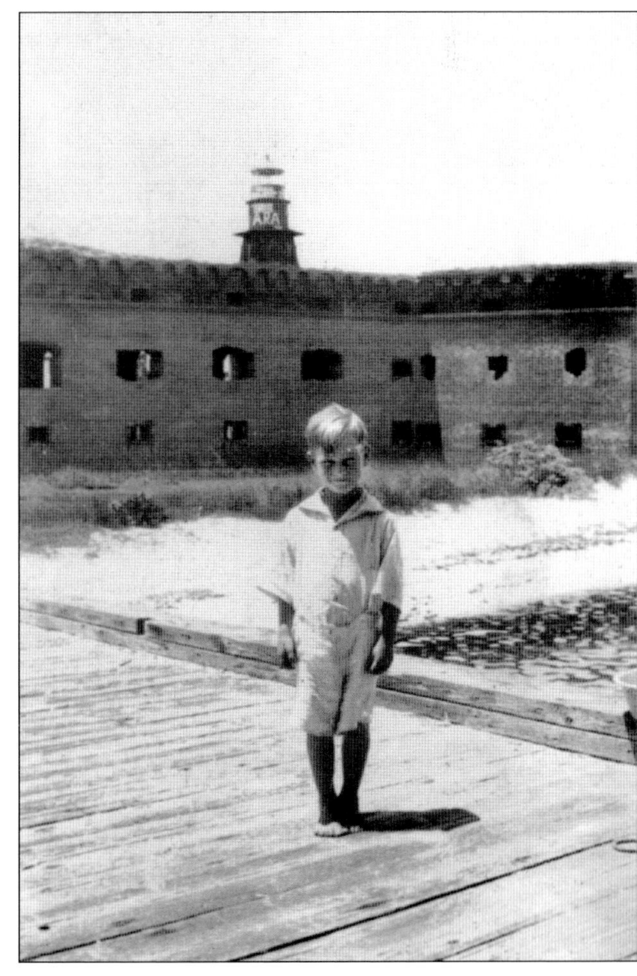

One of the earliest Florida Keys lights was built in the Dry Tortugas. The government eventually decided to construct a new light at Loggerhead Key and replace the 1826 lighthouse on Garden Key with a smaller structure. Before the fort pictured here (Fort Jefferson) was constructed, keepers faced an unusually solitary life in the Dry Tortugas. (Courtesy of Monroe County Library, Key West.)

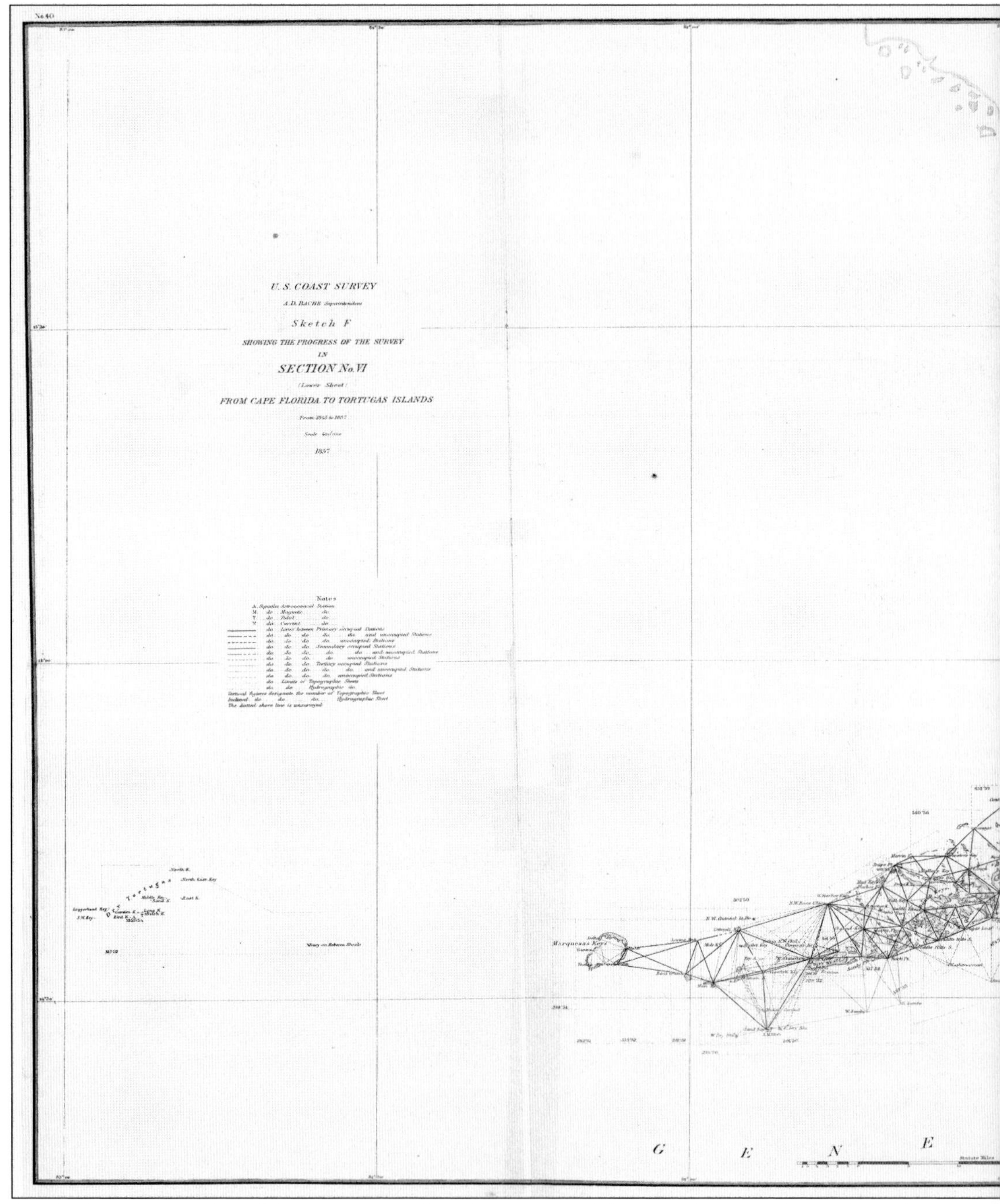

At the far western edge of the Florida Reef lie the islands of the Dry Tortugas. Spanish explorer Juan Ponce de León sailed along the Florida Keys in 1513; after seeing particularly large numbers of sea turtles in the area, he gave the islets the name "Tortugas." English-speaking sailors later called them "Dry Tortugas," since they could not find fresh water. These tiny isles appear as specks

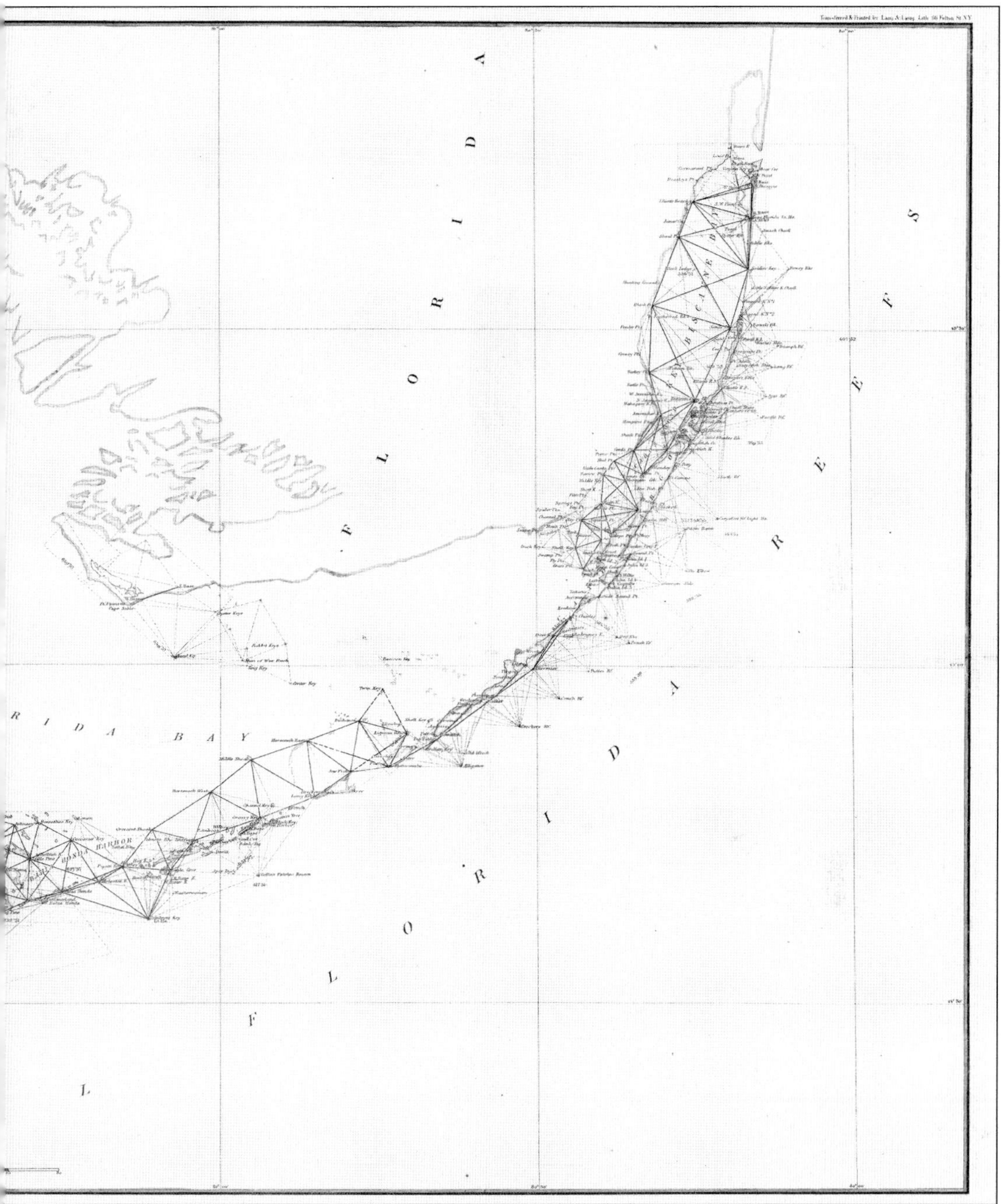

on the far left side of this 1857 coastal survey. Roughly 68 to 70 miles west of Key West, they have long been inhospitable to human inhabitation and the seas here problematic to navigate. (Courtesy of the State Archives of Florida.)

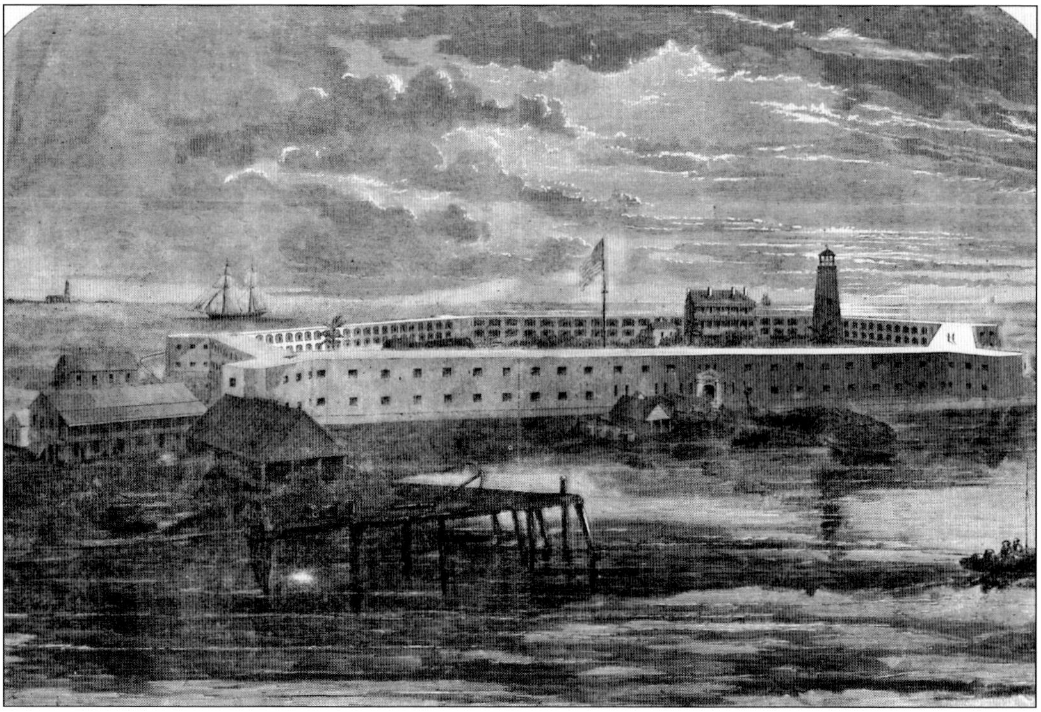

Before the construction of Garden Key's lighthouse, the island had remained untouched by human beings, save for sailors who might have gone onshore to hunt birds. The lighthouse project got its start in 1824 but was not completed until 1826, when the Garden Key light was lit by keeper John Flaherty. (Courtesy of Monroe County Library, Key West.)

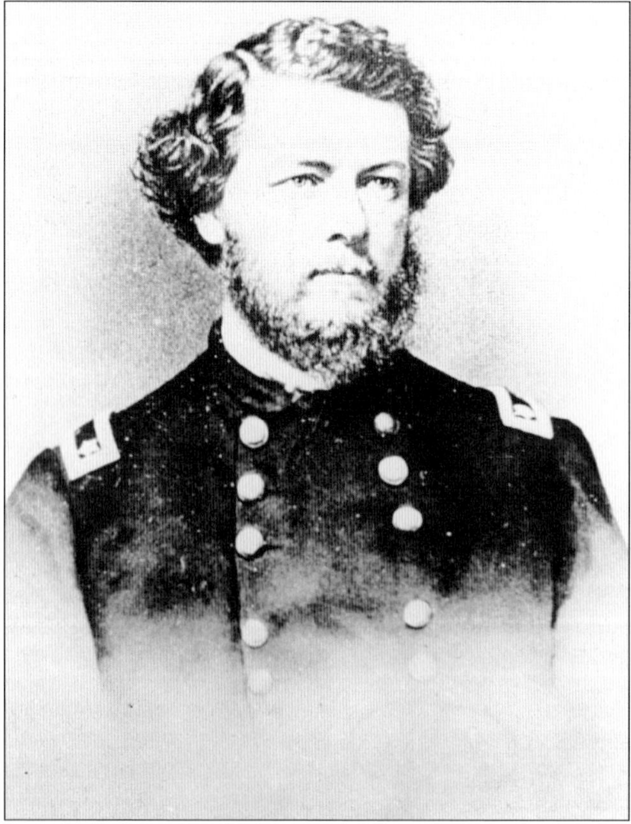

Beginning in 1846, 2nd Lt. (later captain) Horatio Wright of the US Army Corps of Engineers directed the construction of Fort Jefferson on Garden Key, much of it with enslaved labor. Although Wright designed a new lighthouse for Garden Key, the federal Lighthouse Board chose Loggerhead Key as the location instead. (Courtesy of Monroe County Library, Key West.)

Capt. Daniel R. Woodbury took over the development of a new Dry Tortugas lighthouse from Captain Wright in 1856. Although Woodbury made significant changes to Wright's design, the Loggerhead light would still be constructed in brick as originally planned. Woodbury created this illustration, which shows the stairways to the watch room and the lantern. (Courtesy of the National Archives.)

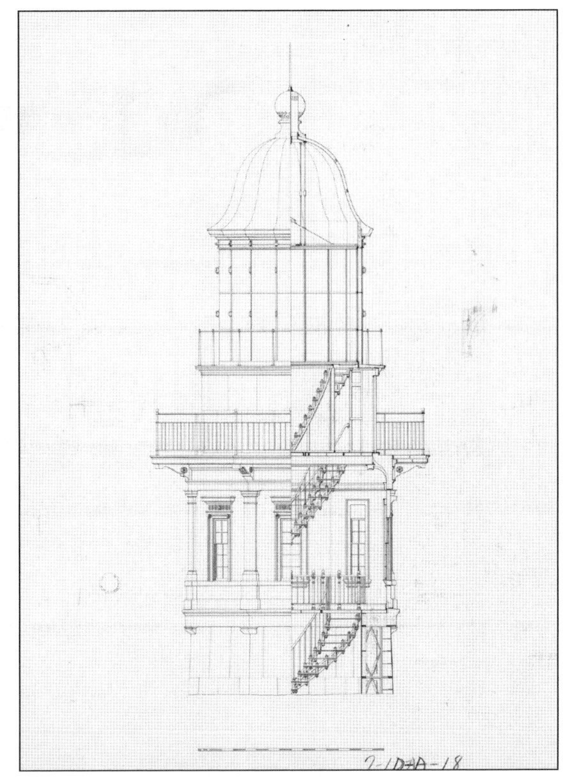

This photograph gives some sense of the isolation of the 49-acre Loggerhead Key. Of the seven islands in the Dry Tortugas, Loggerhead is the largest. Before they were cut down, buttonwood trees flourished here. Since then, coconut trees, Geiger trees, cacti, and mangroves have grown, while offshore lies the Little Africa Reef. (Courtesy of the State Archives of Florida.)

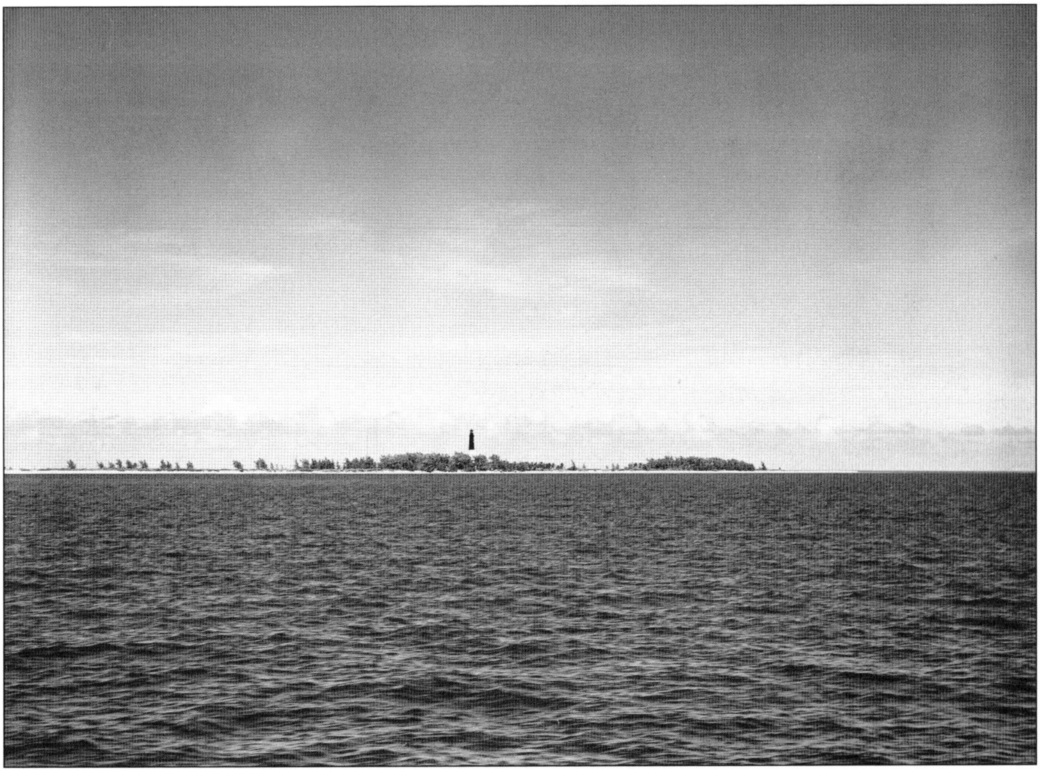

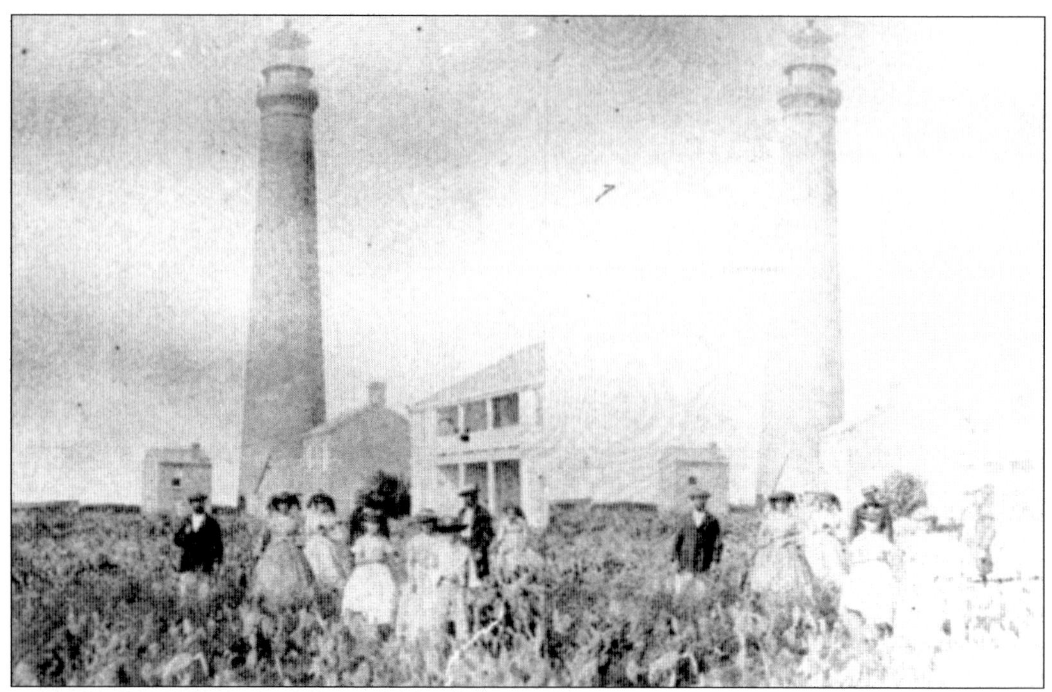

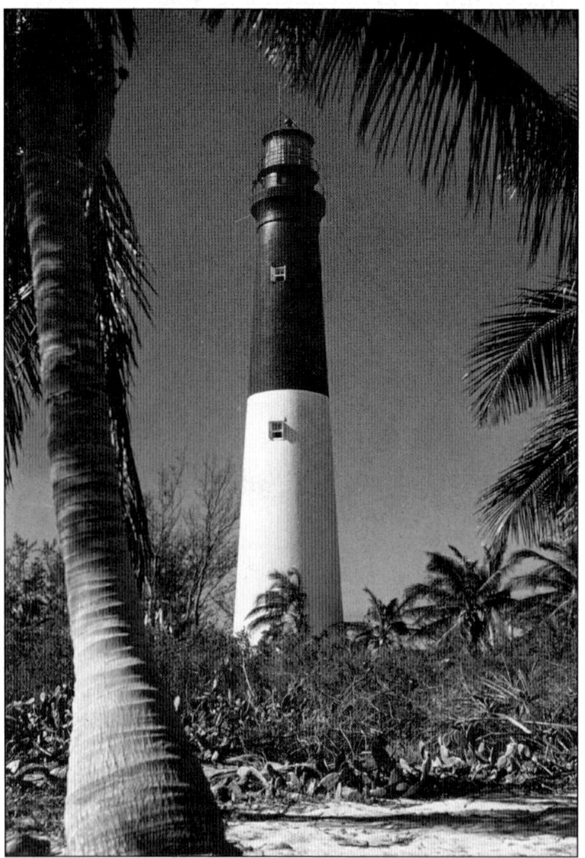

This ghostly 1860 image by Joseph B. Holder shows the completed Loggerhead Key light in the Dry Tortugas. Only a few years before the Civil War, slave-owning Key Westers rented out people held in bondage to work on both the fort at Garden Key and this lighthouse. The lighthouse, along with brick cisterns for water, an oil house, keeper's quarters, and a kitchen/guesthouse, was finished in 1858, the same year the Sombrero Key lighthouse was completed. Here five white women, three men, and one boy pose in a field of cacti. They may possibly be the principal keeper Benjamin Kerr, his wife, Henriette Kerr, their children, and assistant keepers. Interestingly, in 1860, Henriette Kerr, one of their daughters, and the assistant keepers attempted to murder Benjamin Kerr. Why they did so is not clear, but Kerr escaped. Note that in the more recent image, Loggerhead Key lighthouse has acquired its distinctive half-white, half-black paint. (Above, courtesy of the University of Miami Library; left, courtesy of the National Archives.)

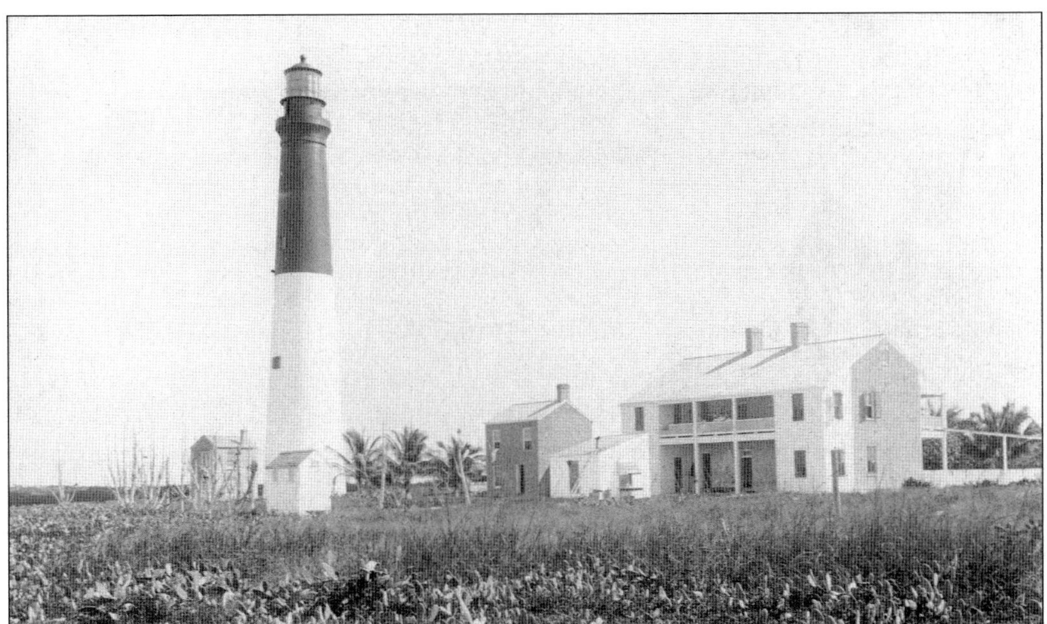

Palm trees surround Loggerhead lighthouse's various outbuildings. Just in front of the lighthouse is small white building that may be an outhouse. The two-story house has shutters, some of which are closed in this picture. One can also see the house's two chimneys and the two porches on the other side of the home. On the second-floor porch, people pose for the distant photographer. (Courtesy of the National Archives.)

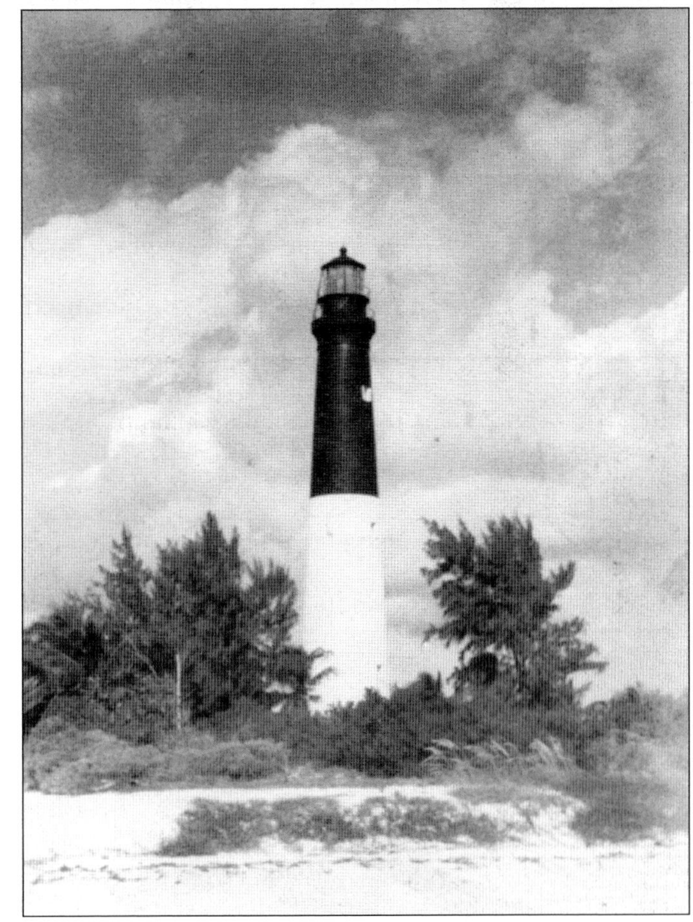

The Dry Tortugas Light on Loggerhead Key was constructed of brick with a stone foundation. The brick tower itself rose 150 feet, apparently 157 feet including the lantern. A Fresnel lens, this one manufactured by L. Sautter, was imported from France for use at the light. The internal stairway is constructed not of iron but of granite. (Courtesy of Monroe County Library, Key West.)

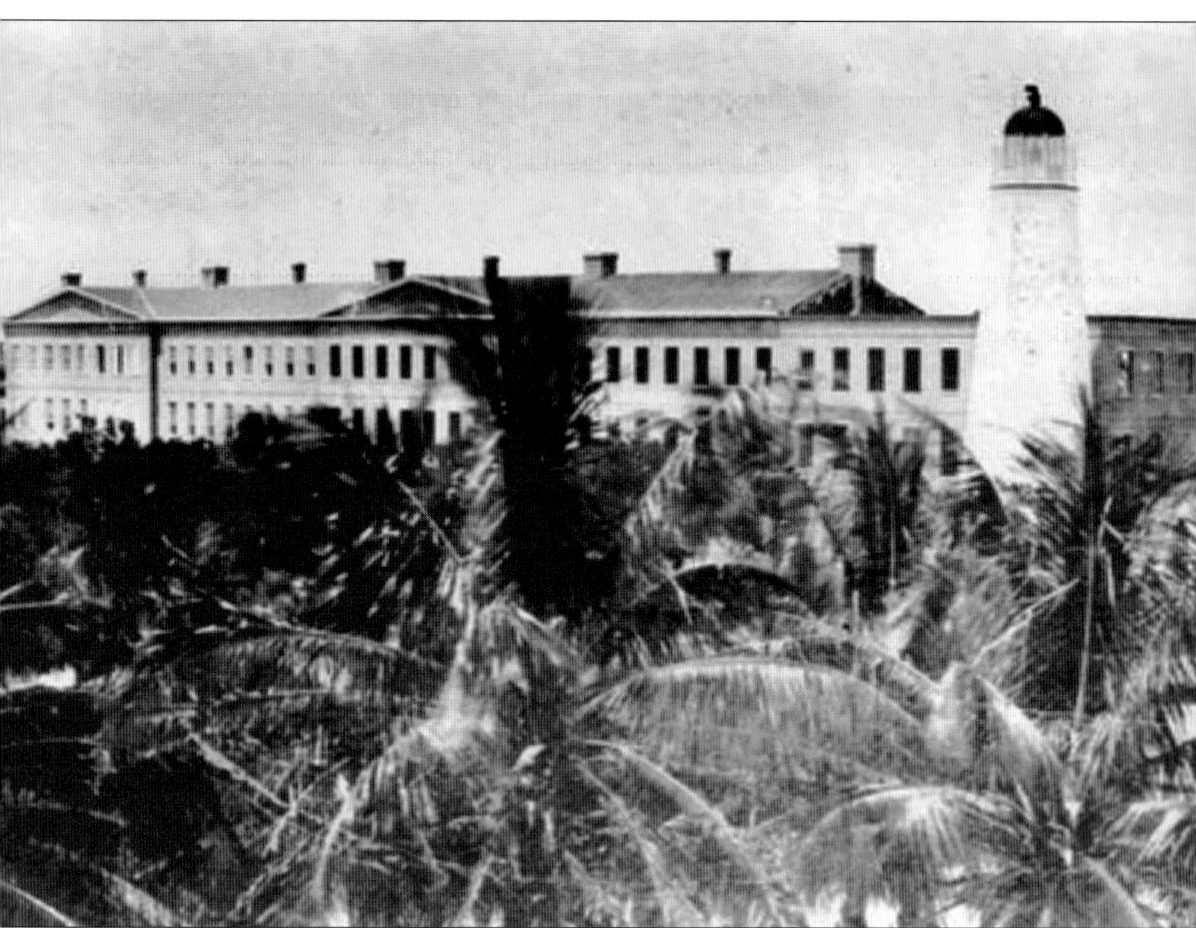

Construction on Fort Jefferson took over 30 years, starting in 1846; the fort, built with 16 million bricks, grew up around the lighthouse. Although the lighthouses at Key West, Sand Key, and Cape Florida had not survived, this 65-foot tower (with a 70-foot focal plane) dating from the 1820s endured. After Florida seceded from the Union in January 1861, the Union continued to hold several Florida Keys lighthouses, including those on Loggerhead Key, Garden Key, and Key West. Fort Jefferson had enough military personnel to make it probably impregnable; on Key West, Union troops seized Fort Taylor, still under construction, and secured it for the United States. The Union also held lighthouses at Carysfort, Sand Key, the Northwest Passage, and Sombrero Key. Thus the only Confederates to live under the watchful eye of the Garden Key light were prisoners, up to 900 at a time. (Courtesy of the US Lighthouse Society Archives.)

The most notorious prisoner to inhabit the fort is allegedly pictured here: Dr. Samuel Mudd. He and three other men, Edman Spangler, Michael O'Laughlen, and Samuel Arnold, had been convicted of giving aid to or conspiring with John Wilkes Booth. Dr. Mudd had treated Booth for his injuries after his assassination of Pres. Abraham Lincoln at the Ford Theater in Washington, DC, in 1865. (Courtesy of the Open Parks Network.)

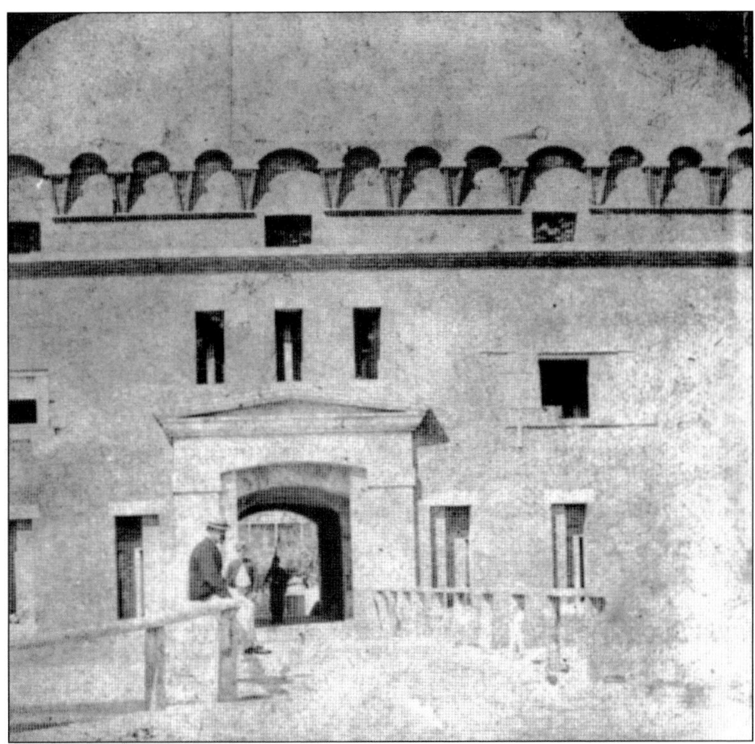

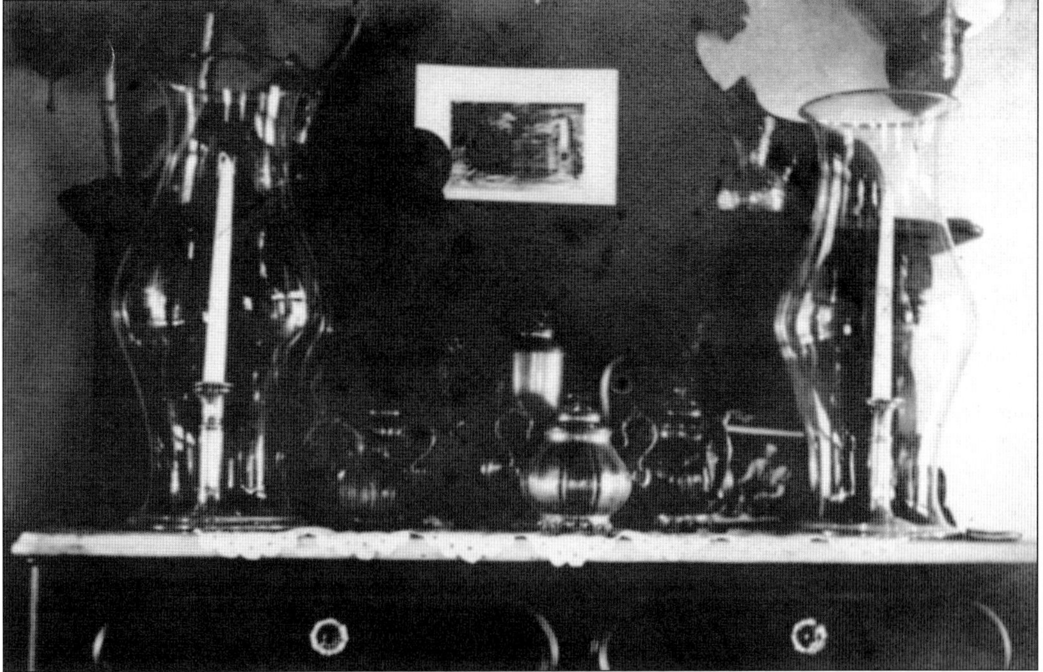

Fort Jefferson's lighthouse keeper and his wife, Mr. and Mrs. Henry Beuners, knew Dr. Mudd. In fact, they both helped the doctor survive yellow fever after he became stricken with the often-fatal disease. After he was freed, Dr. Mudd gave the Beuners this tea set in gratitude for saving his life. (Courtesy of Monroe County Library, Key West.)

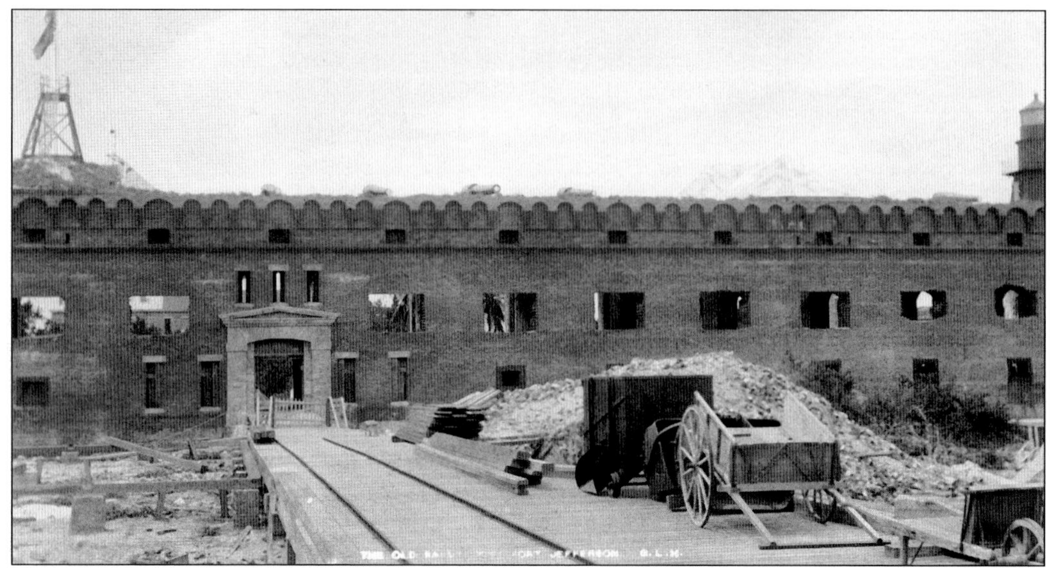

Once the Loggerhead Key lighthouse went into operation, it became the lighthouse for the Dry Tortugas. The Lighthouse Board no longer thought there was a need for the 1826 masonry Garden Key lighthouse and tore it down in 1876. The new harbor light, pictured here, was intended to aid vessels approaching Fort Jefferson. (Courtesy of Monroe County Library, Key West.)

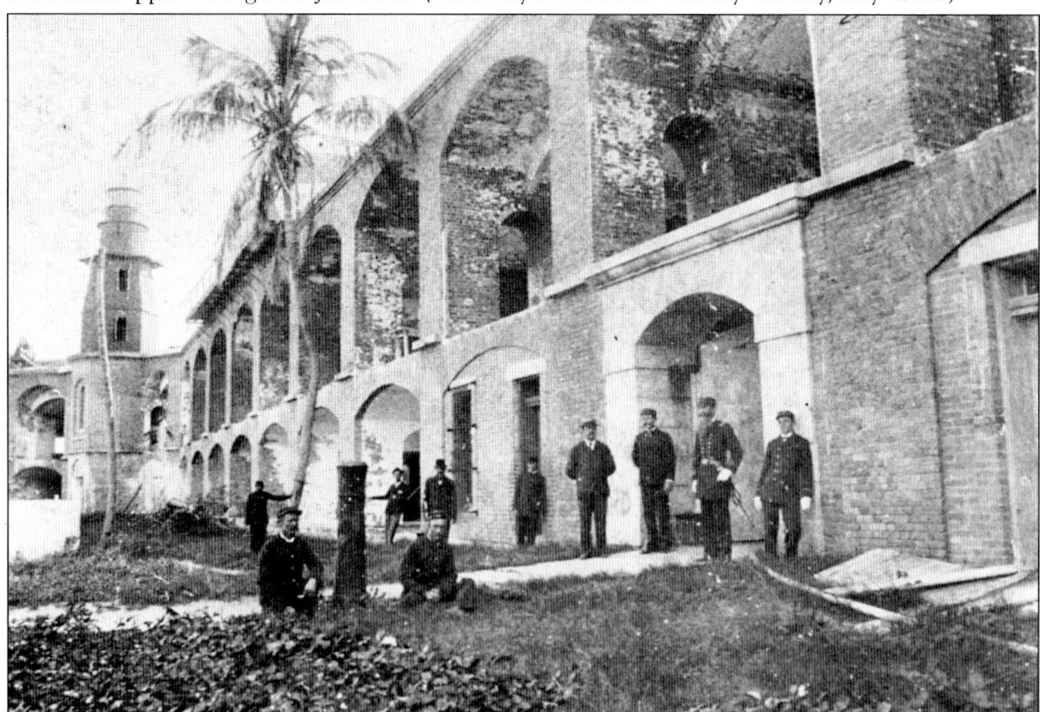

Soldiers stand inside Fort Jefferson, a new light in the background. In the 19th century, Emily Holder journeyed with her husband to live here on Garden Key. Although the fort's exterior looked "bare and repulsive" to Holder, she found "the interior offering a decided contrast," with "trees of the deep green belonging to tropical vegetation, so restful to the eye in the glaring sun." (Courtesy of Monroe County Library, Key West.)

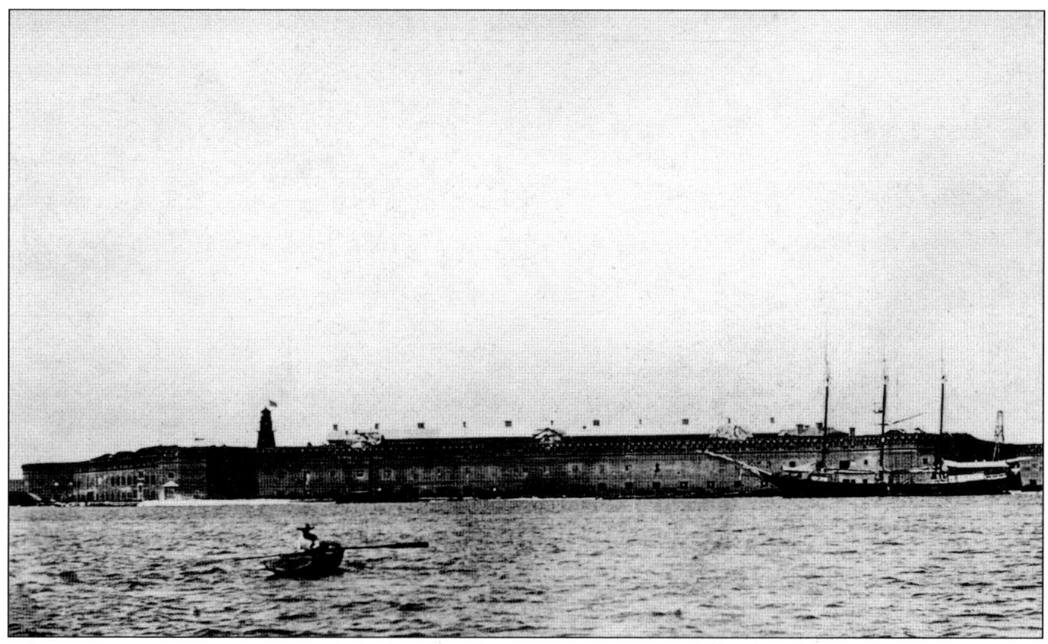

The 37-foot Tortugas Harbor lighthouse, also known as the Fort Jefferson harbor light, was lit on April 5, 1876. John Messina, the same keeper who tended the previous lighthouse, tended to the new light until 1889. Keepers worked here until 1912, when the lighthouse was automated. (Courtesy of Monroe County Library, Key West.)

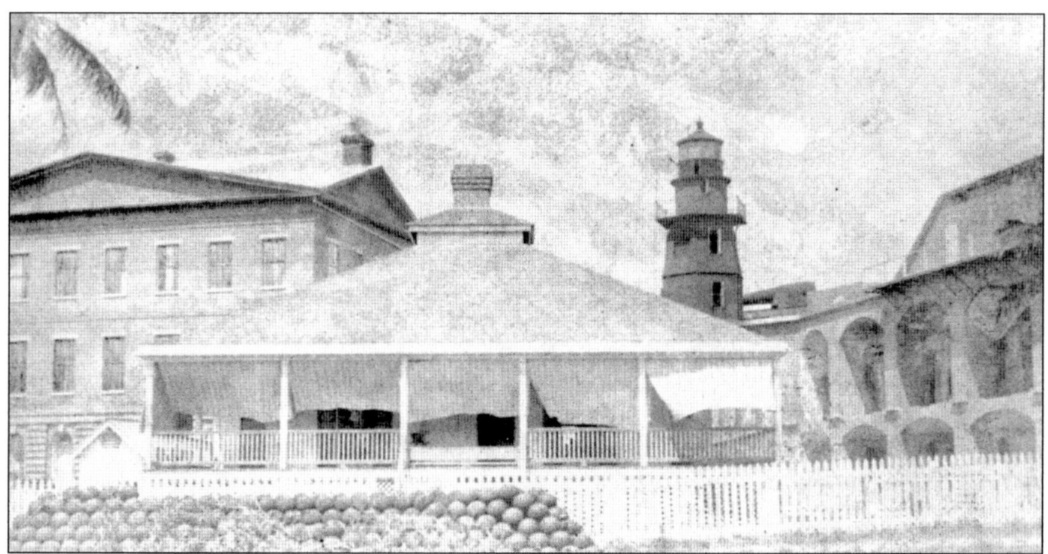

Garden Key's new light was built inside the walls at Bastion C rather than on the interior parade grounds. The construction and appearance of the harbor light at Fort Jefferson is singular in the Florida Keys: a three-story hexagonal structure of boiler-plate iron (thick plate iron used for boilers). (Courtesy of Monroe County Library, Key West.)

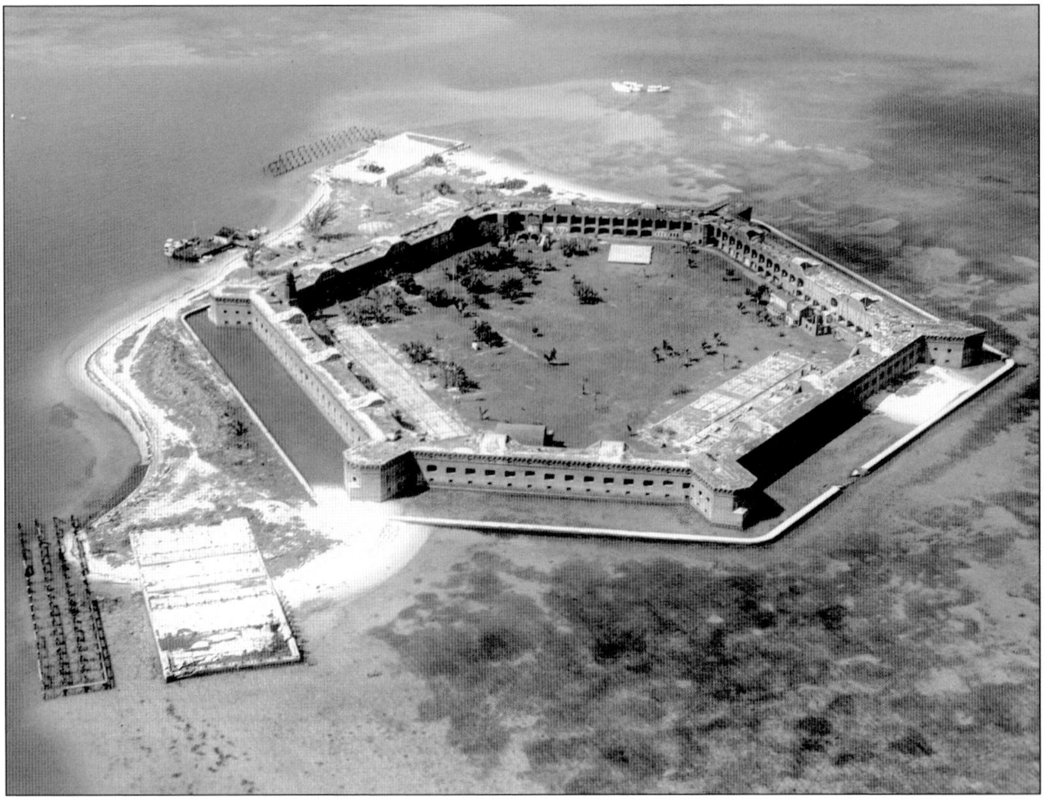

This aerial photograph shows the hexagonal shape of Fort Jefferson; the dark form of the harbor light is visible on the left, where Bastion C juts out from the walls. This picture also illustrates how shallow waters and reef surround the small island of Garden Key. (Courtesy of Monroe County Library, Key West.)

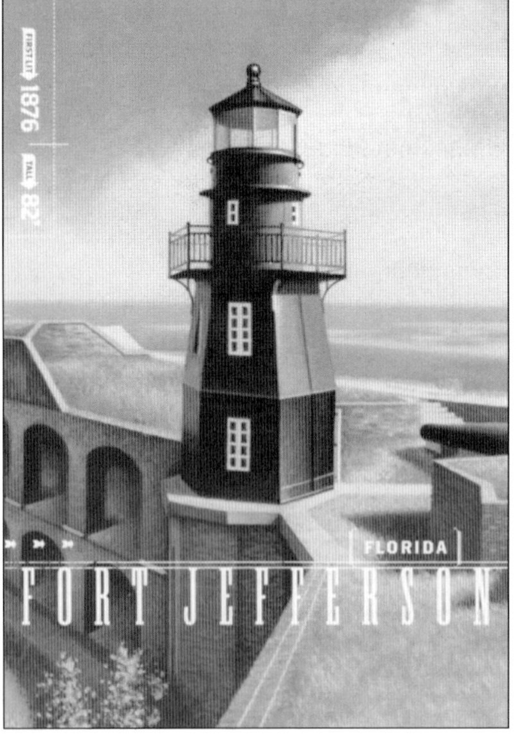

The harbor light on Garden Key (shown here on a US Postal Service postcard) rises 82 feet if measured from the base of the bastion, although the structure itself was only 37 feet tall. Its lens was accordingly smaller, a fourth-order Fresnel lens, as it did not need to have the long range of Loggerhead Key's lighthouse, for example. (Courtesy of Monroe County Library, Key West.)

Six

LESSER-KNOWN LIGHTHOUSES

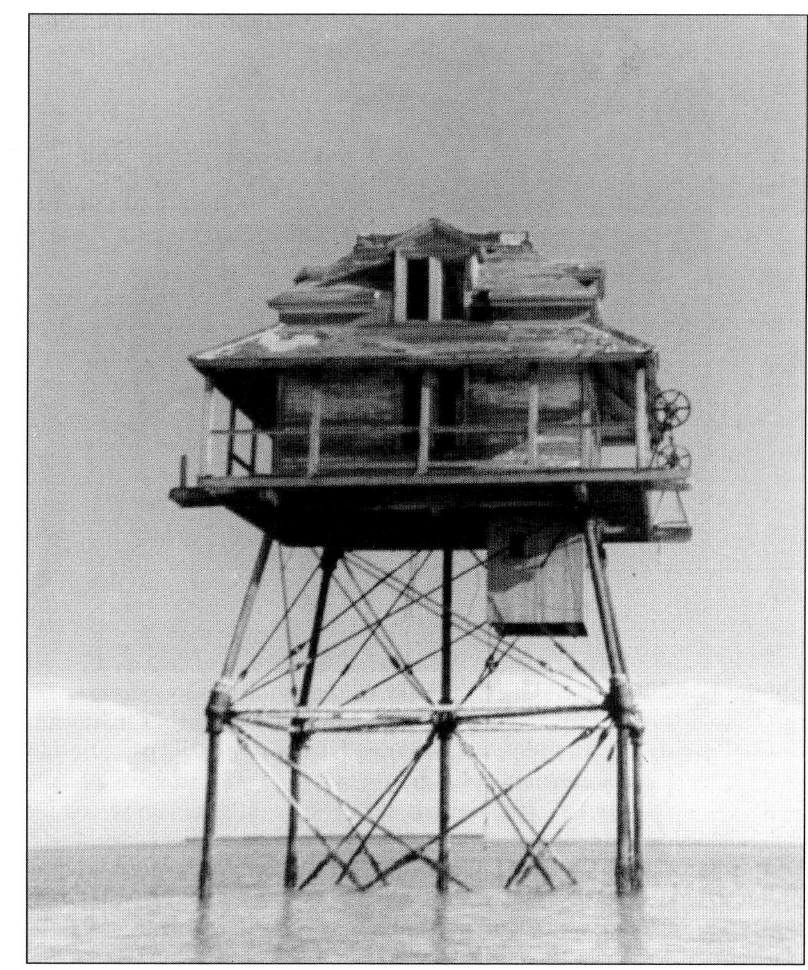

While some Florida Keys lighthouses have become regional icons, others have faded into obscurity; perhaps there remain only a few remnants to prove that once a light shone there. The lighthouses at the Northwest Passage and Rebecca Shoal resembled one another physically, although they were located in quite dissimilar oceanic conditions. (Courtesy of Monroe County Library, Key West.)

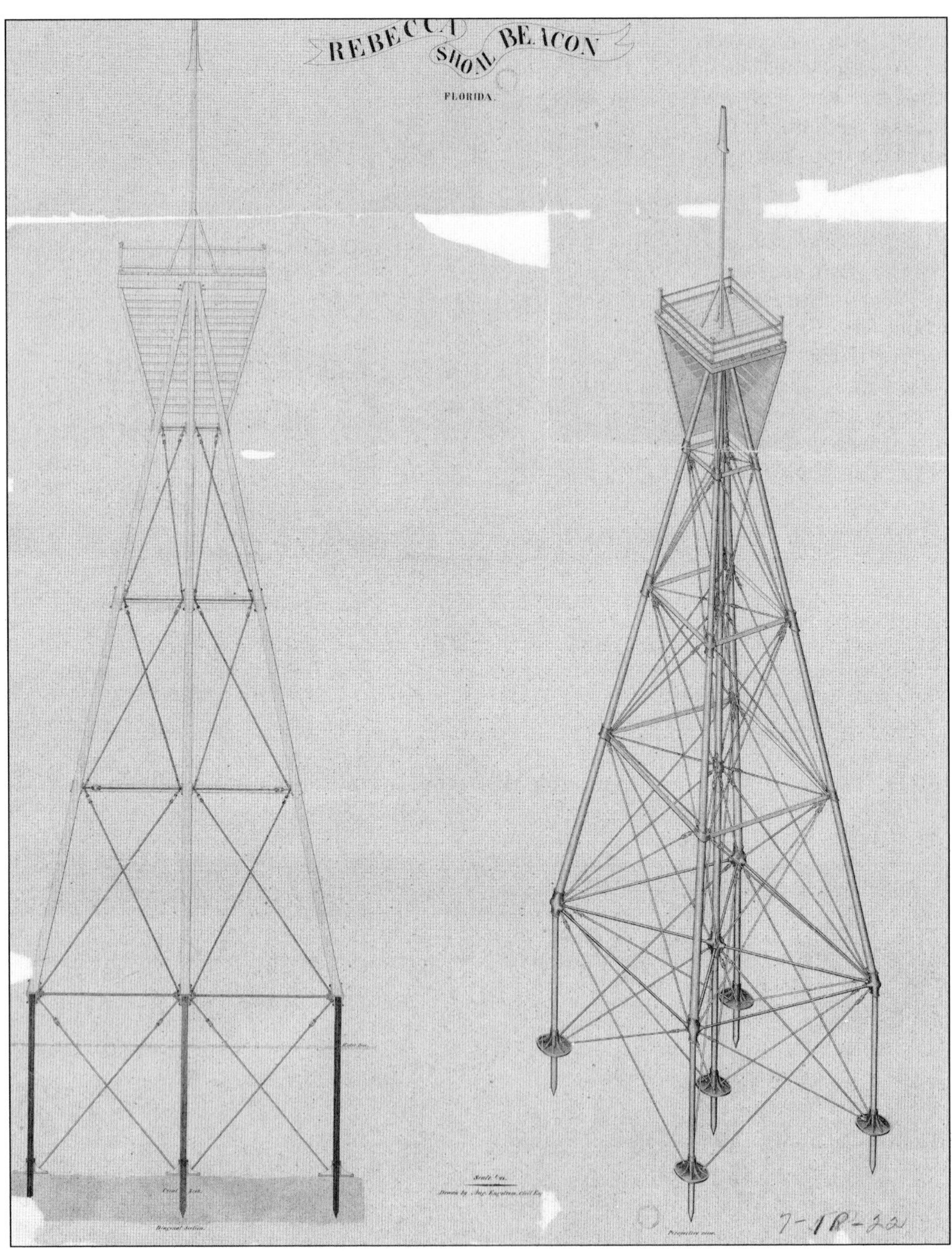

This 19th-century drawing depicts the design for the Rebecca Shoal day beacon. Engineer and officer George Gordon Meade succeeded in overseeing the construction of Florida Reef lighthouses, but at Rebecca Shoal, conditions thwarted the government's attempt to erect a beacon here on multiple occasions. This particularly tumultuous location, where gulf and ocean converge, created a host of problems. Twice, a work platform was swept away by storms, and on a third try, the weather proved so bad that laborers quit the job. Meade tried to get a beacon built here in 1857 and 1858, which constituted the fourth and fifth attempts. The officer who went onto defeat Robert E. Lee at Gettysburg was, in this case, vanquished by Rebecca Shoal. When a day beacon was finally built in 1873, it lasted only months, and it was replaced around 1879. (Courtesy of the National Archives.)

The Northwest Passage or Northwest Channel lies northwest of Key West and provides a medium-draft channel for ships to travel from Key West's harbor to the Gulf of Mexico. Reefs and shoals on either side of the passage created hazardous conditions. The lightboat *Key West*, with a range of 12 miles, was stationed there, but in 1854, work began on a lighthouse. (Courtesy of Monroe County Library, Key West.)

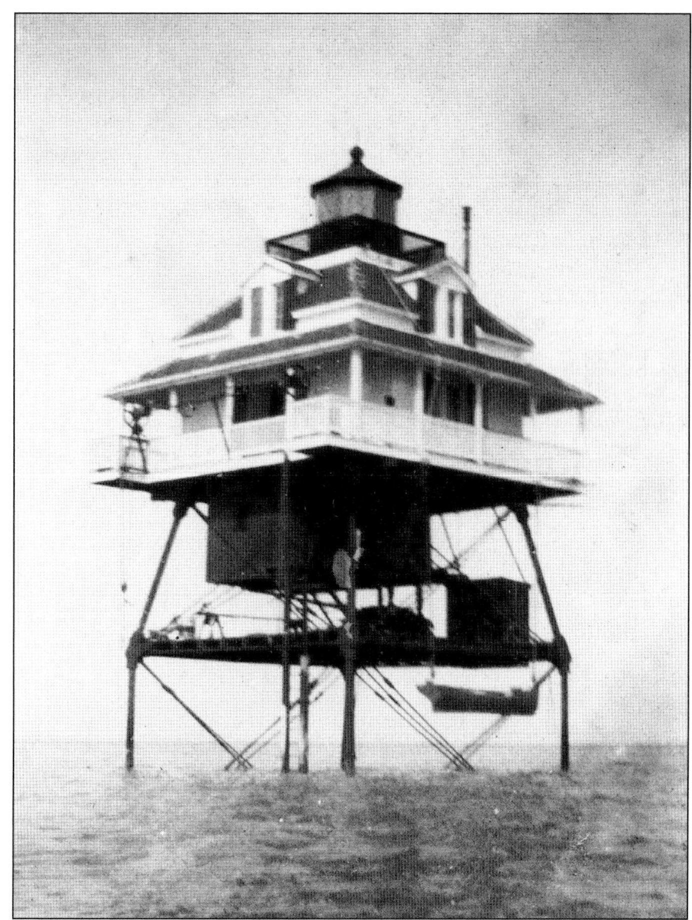

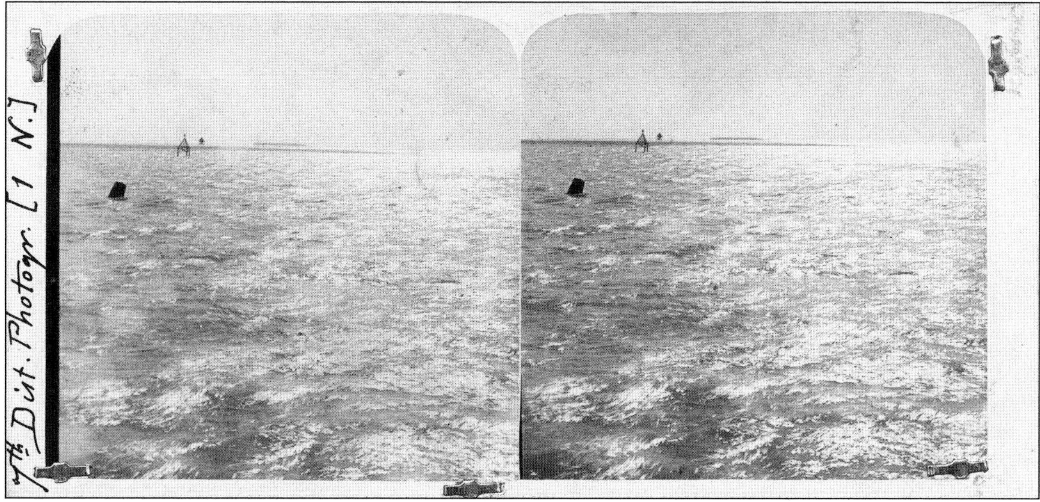

Superintendent Samuel Douglass advocated for a lighthouse and selected its ultimate location. The Northwest Channel light was constructed with iron piles, but its cottage-style design was unusual for the Keys. The wooden keeper's quarters obscured much of the lighthouse except for its lantern. (Courtesy of the National Archives.)

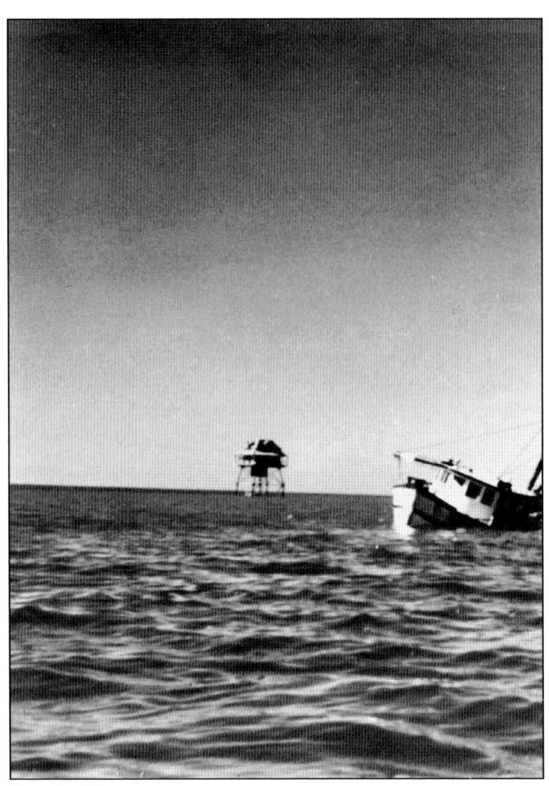

With a $12,000 budget, the Northwest Channel lighthouse was erected in six months and lit in 1855 by keeper William Richardson. After the quarters deteriorated severely, a new structure was designed and completed in 1879. Its original fifth-order Fresnel lens was changed to a larger, fourth-order lens. The lighthouse stood approximately 47 feet high, about one third the height of Sombrero Key. (Courtesy of Monroe County Library, Key West.)

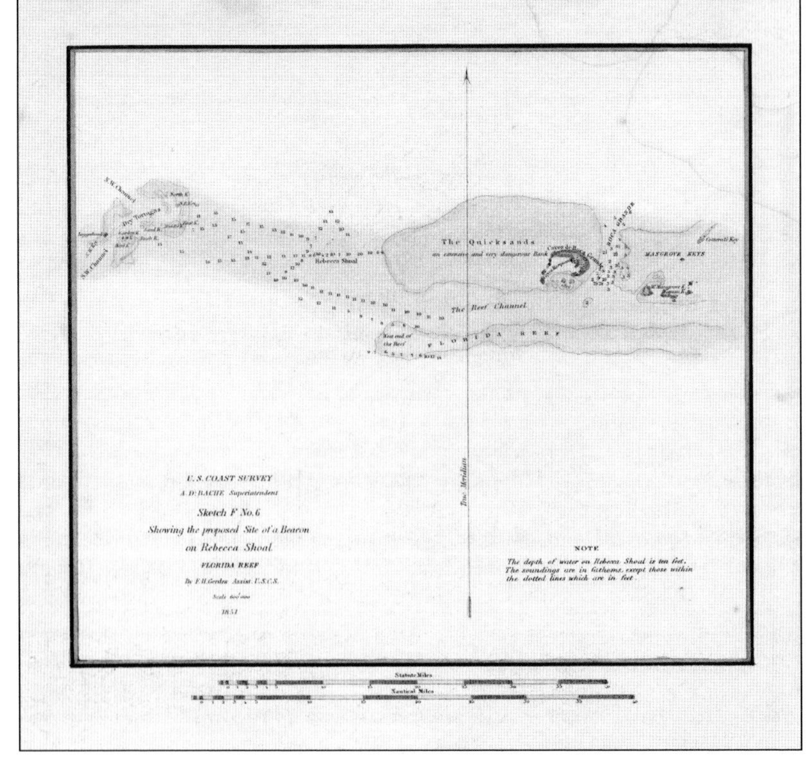

This 1851 illustration by F.H. Gerdes shows the location of Rebecca Shoal, and to the far west (left side) are the Dry Tortugas. A note says, "The depth of water on Rebecca Shoal is ten feet." To the east of the shoal are the Quicksands, "an extensive and very dangerous bank," while to the southeast lies the Florida Reef. (Courtesy of the State Archives of Florida.)

Here is one of the plans for the Rebecca Shoal Light Station, specifically its metal work. Tension rods, waste pipes, and rain pipes have been accounted for in this design, issued by the Office of the Lighthouse Board in 1885. The angular legs of the light can be made out, above which were situated the keeper's quarters, an internal staircase, and the lantern itself. (Courtesy of the National Archives.)

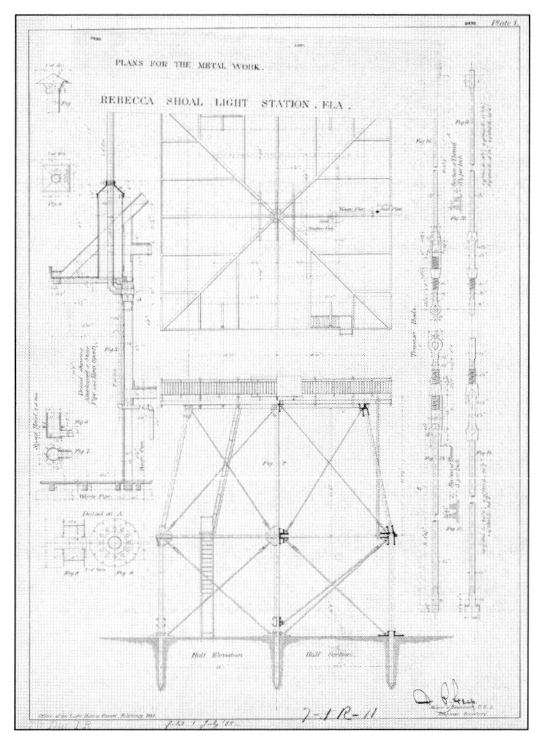

Completed in 1886, the Rebecca Shoal lighthouse had an utterly different appearance from the austere lines of Alligator Reef or Sand Key. The three-story house stood atop a deck of iron plates. In this picture, the keeper's boat is just above the landing deck and a lower ladder, perhaps 10 feet above sea level. (Courtesy of the National Archives.)

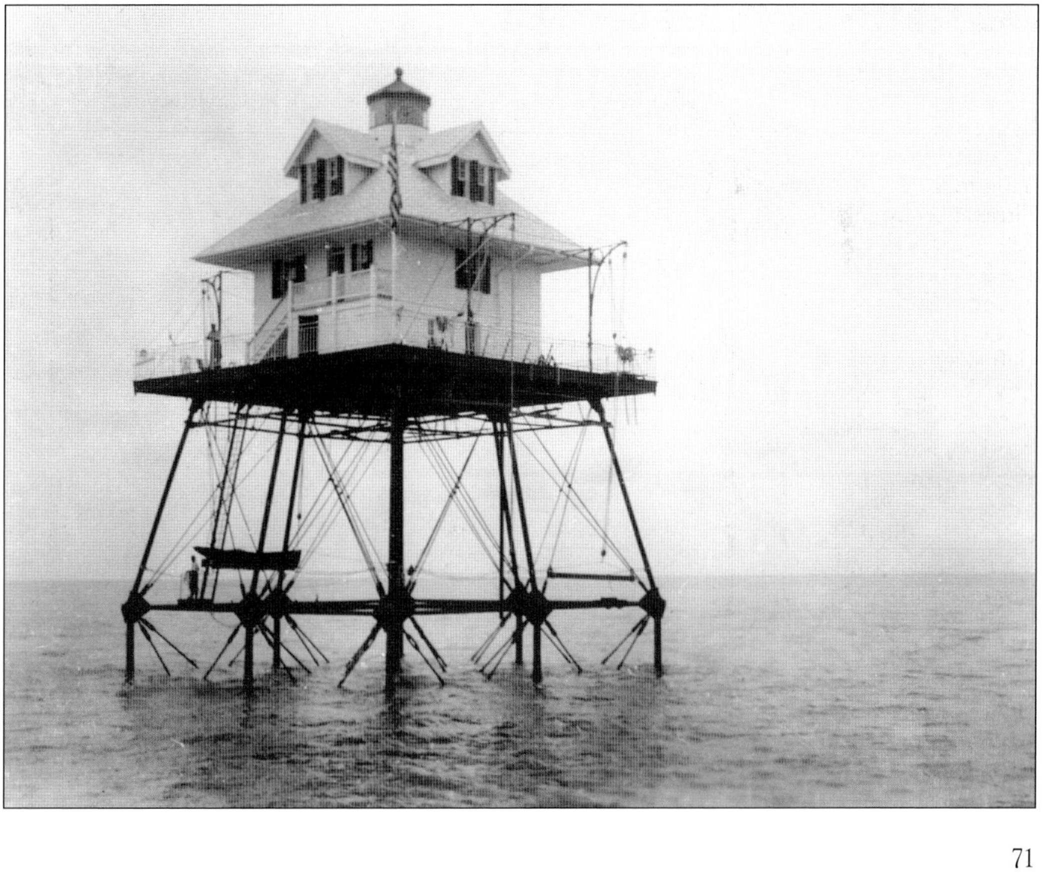

Rebecca Shoal Light Station
July 28th 1892

Comd Wm B. Newman U.S.N. L.H. Inspector

Sir

I herewith inform you of the First Keeper Henry Brown. I Think That He is capable of Filling My Place during My absence I have Questioned him and I Think He can Take charge in case any Thing Should Happen and Comd if you are Bothered in getting a man I Will Recommend Capt. Thomas W. Roberts for a good Man. Nothing More Every Thing is in good condition

Yours Obedient

Robert J. Fine

In this 1892 letter, principal keeper of Rebecca Shoal Robert Fine writes to lighthouse inspector Comdr. William B. Newman about his assistant: "I think he is capable of filling my place during my absence." One can only imagine how keepers looked forward to leave, considering that the shoal lies 43 miles west of any amenities or town. (Courtesy of the US Lighthouse Society Archives.)

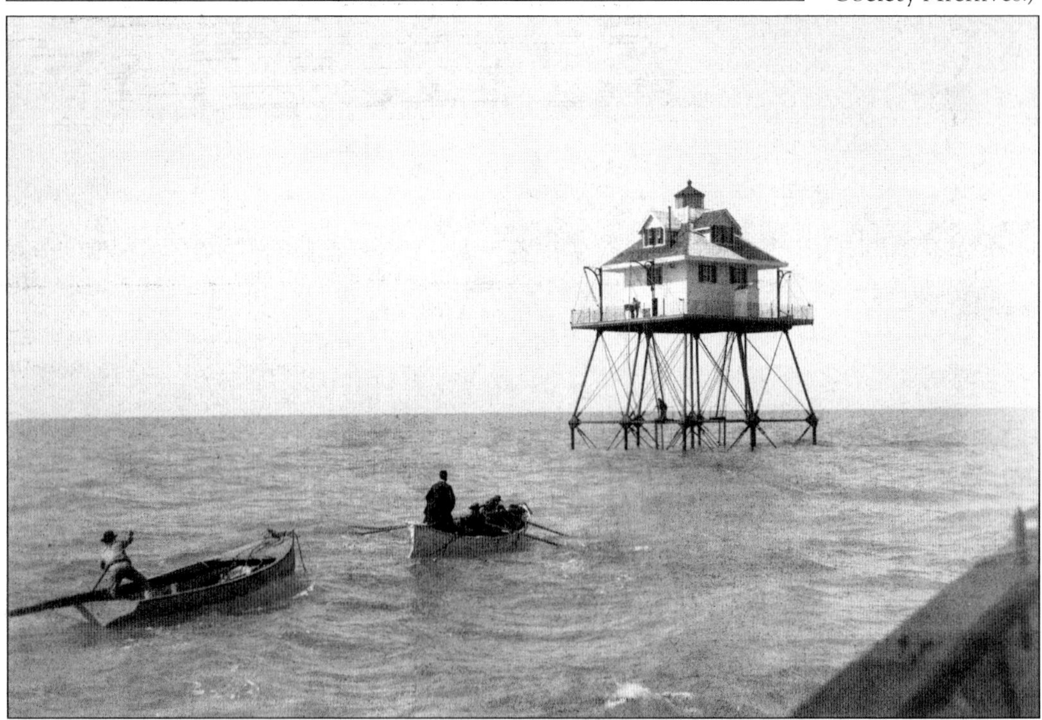

Despite the cozy appearance of the house, with its dormers and shutters, the intense weather conditions that arose and the perpetual isolation proved very challenging. In this photograph, taken from a larger vessel, two rowboats approach the light. Company, news, supplies, and mail were looked forward to by the keepers. (Courtesy of the National Archives.)

Seven

Women Who Kept the Lights

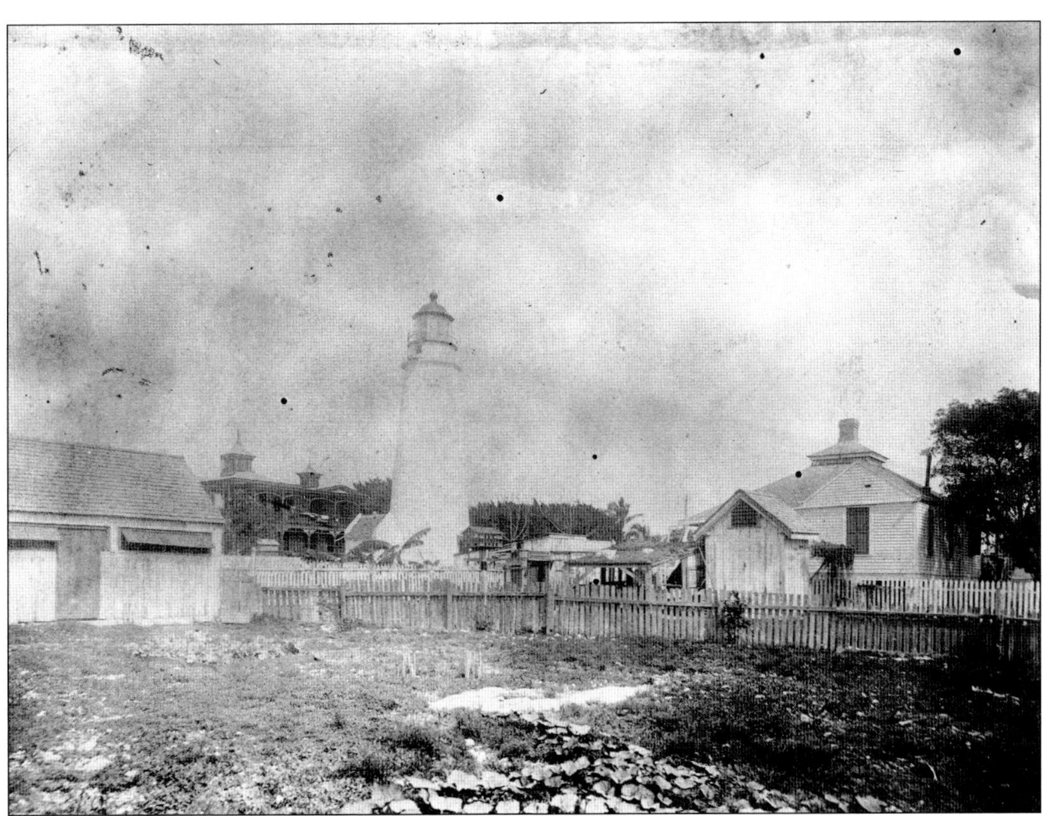

At least four women served as lighthouse keepers in the Florida Keys, at Sand Key and Key West. Although the profession of keeper was generally the domain of men, approximately 25 women worked as keepers in the state of Florida. In the Keys, Rebecca Flaherty, Barbara Mabrity, Mary Armanda Carroll, and Mary Elizabeth Bethel kept the lighthouse lanterns that illuminated the Florida Reef. (Courtesy of Monroe County Library, Key West.)

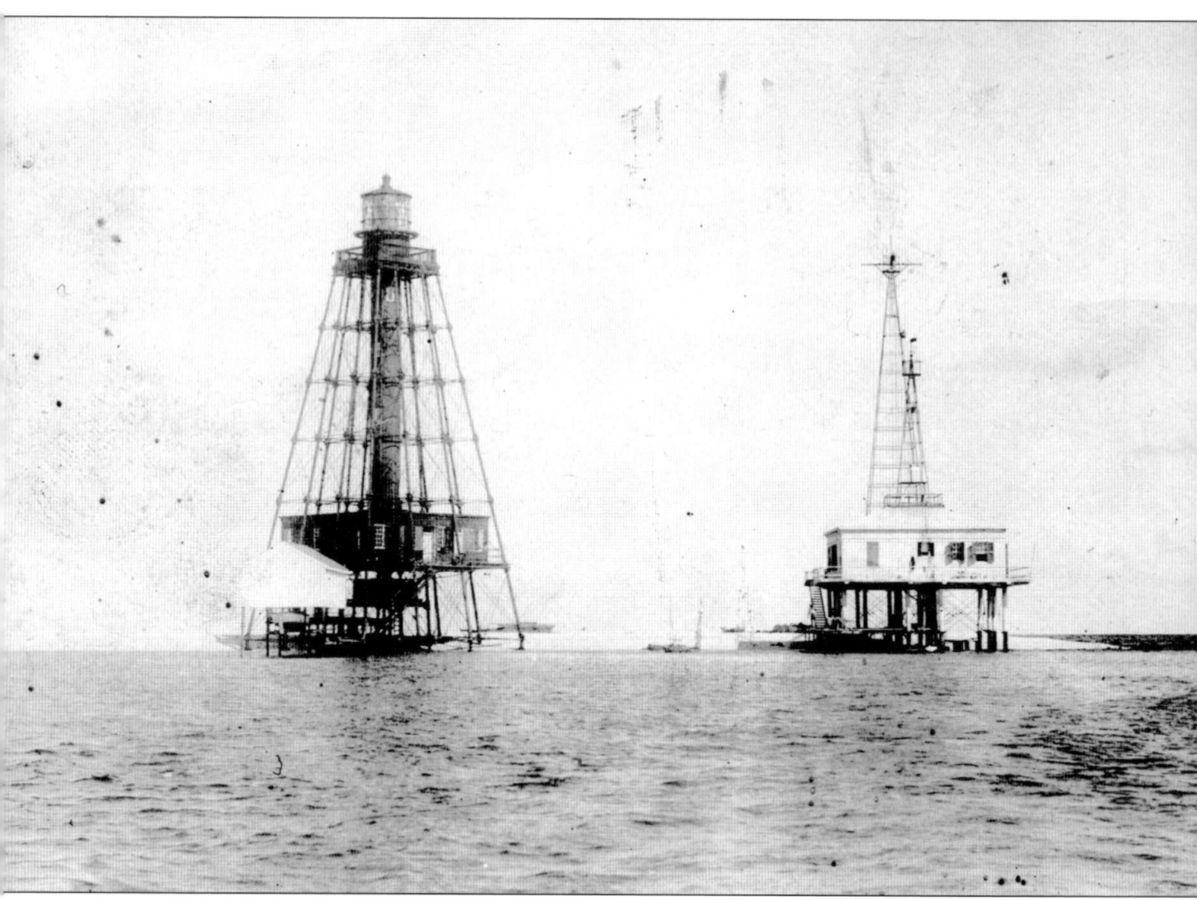

Rebecca Flaherty first moved to the Dry Tortugas with her husband, John, for his job tending the lighthouse on Garden Key. The couple gratefully relocated to Sand Key, much closer to Key West, not long after that lighthouse was completed in 1827. Although Sand Key is pictured here, the couple did not tend this light but the earlier brick version (destroyed in the 1846 hurricane). In 1828, John Flaherty fell ill and left Rebecca to keep the Sand Key lighthouse. After his death, she officially became the keeper and lived on the sliver of an island with her sister. In 1834, she married a captain named Fredrick Neill; some accounts then name Captain Neill as the keeper of record, but surely his wife, experienced as she was, fulfilled duties alongside him. Rebecca and Fredrick Neill left Sand Key sometime in 1836. (Courtesy of Monroe County Library, Key West.)

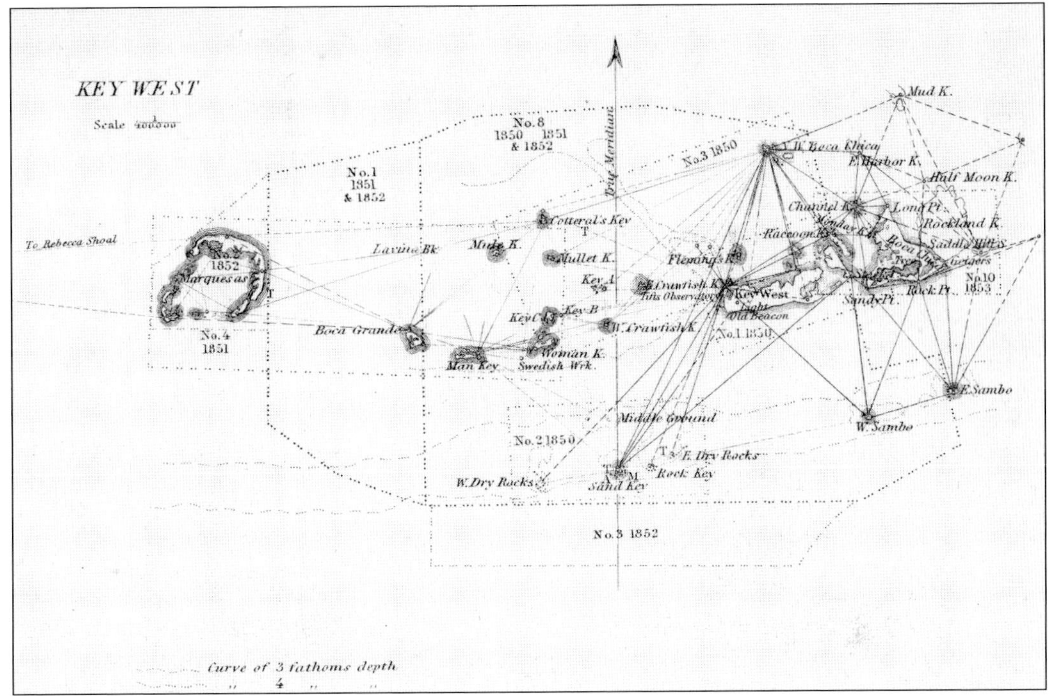

This 1853 Coast Guard survey shows the location of the Sand Key lighthouse (in the center, above "No. 3 1852"). Southwest of Key West, Sand Key was visited regularly by Key Westers, including attorney William Hackley in 1831. He reported that Rebecca Flaherty "with her sister and a hired man, are the only inhabitants of the key and sometimes there are none but the two females." (Courtesy of the State Archives of Florida.)

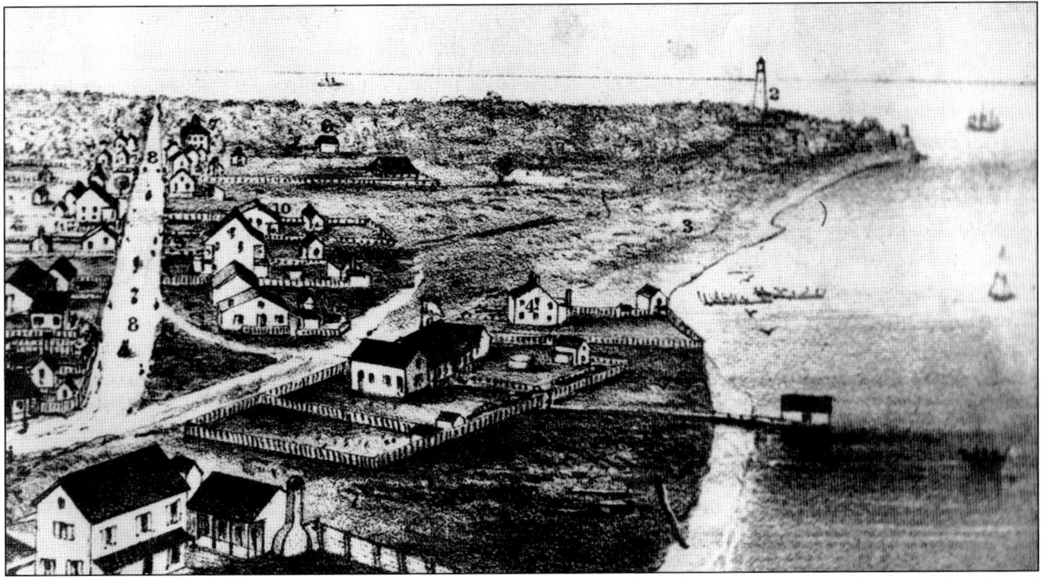

This is a detail of a sketch by Key West settler, surveyor, and one-time mayor William Whitehead that shows the original location of the Key West lighthouse on the southwest shore. After the first keeper, Michael Mabrity, died in 1832, his wife, Barbara, took over the position. (Courtesy of Monroe County Library, Key West.)

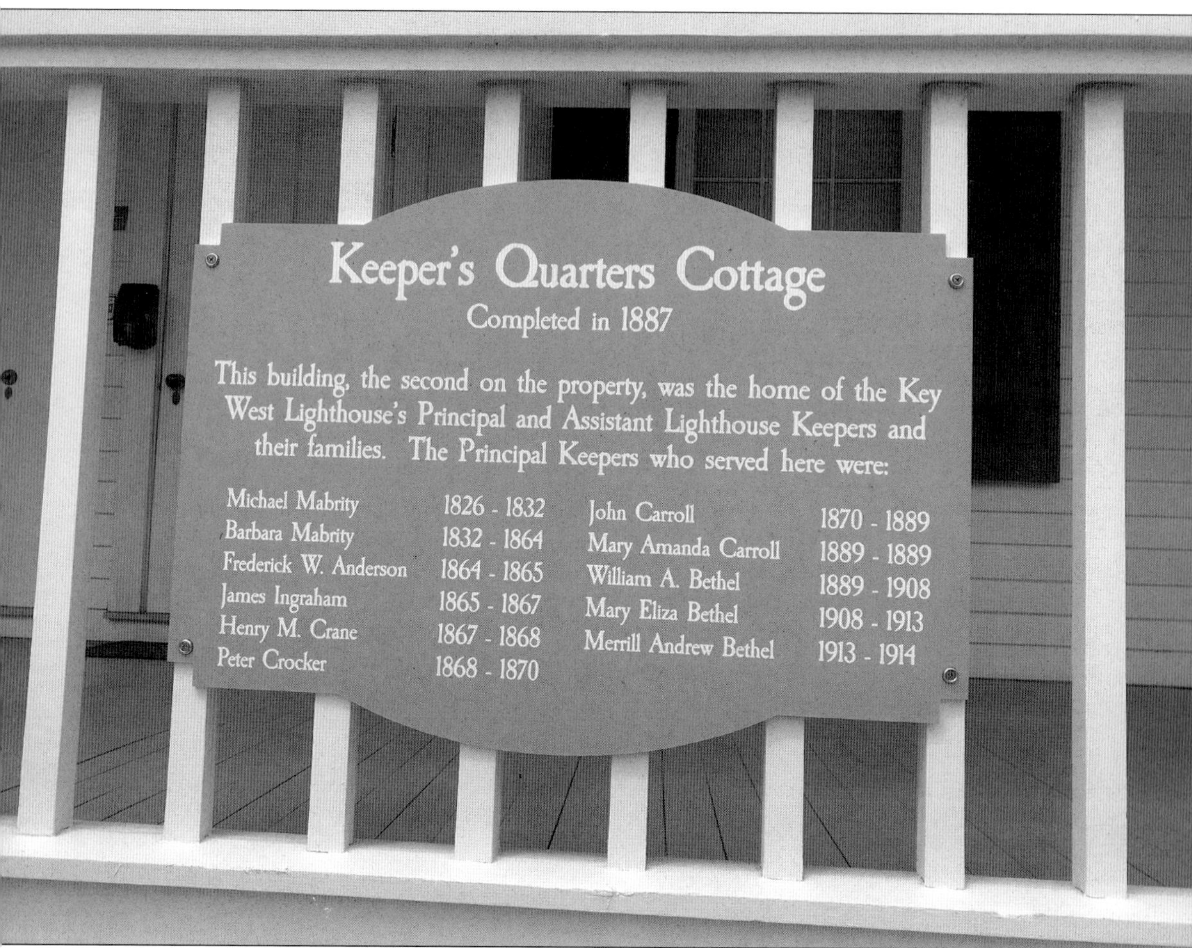

The Key West lighthouse museum displays this sign listing all the keepers. It was not unheard of for widows to take over their husbands' lighthouse duties, but in most cases, the widow was eventually replaced by a man. However, Barbara Mabrity continued to keep the Key West light for decades. She survived the terrible hurricane of 1846, which obliterated the lighthouse, and saw it replaced by a new structure in 1848. During the Civil War, Mabrity became embroiled in something of a scandal over her purported allegiance to the Confederacy (Key West was held by Union troops for the duration of the war despite being in Confederate Florida). Since lighthouse keeper was a government position, loyalty was of supreme importance during wartime. According to historian William H. Thiesen, Barbara Mabrity voluntarily retired at age 82. (Courtesy of Laura Albritton.)

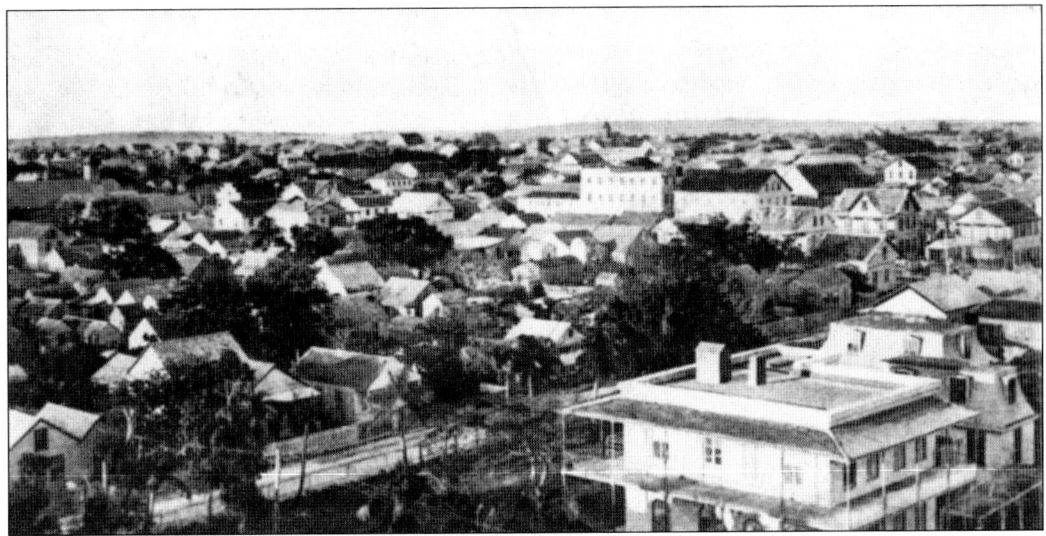

Barbara Mabrity and a subsequent female keeper, Mary Armanda Fletcher Carroll, saw this view from the Key West lighthouse. (At bottom right stands Asa Tift's home, now the Hemingway house.) Mary was Barbara Mabrity's granddaughter. Not only had her father been an assistant lighthouse keeper at Key West but Mary also married a keeper, John Carroll, who initially worked as Key West's assistant keeper. (Courtesy of Monroe County Library, Key West.)

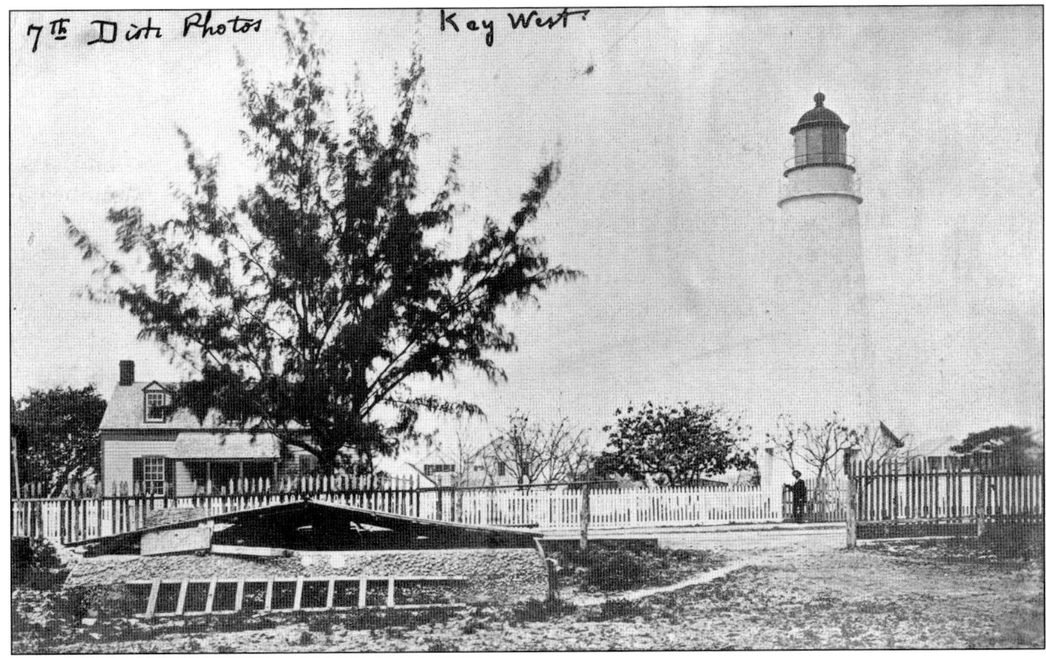

John Carroll became Key West's principal keeper in 1870 and Mary his assistant keeper in 1876. After her husband died in 1889, Mary Carroll took over the position. Mary Carroll died in 1889, not long after her advancement as principal keeper, of the same disease that killed her husband, John: typhoid fever. (Courtesy of the National Archives.)

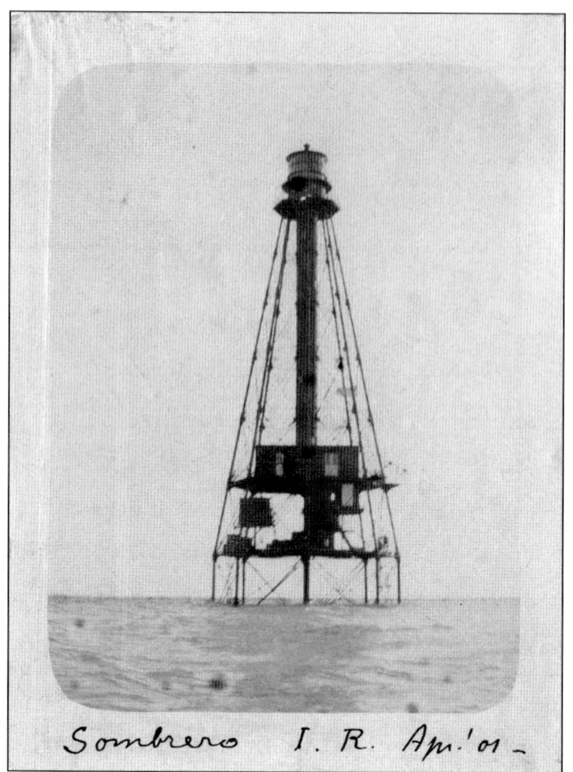

Barbara and Michael Mabrity's daughter Nicolosa also married a lighthouse keeper: Capt. Joseph Bethel. Bethel kept the Garden Key lighthouse in the Dry Tortugas from approximately 1839 to 1842; in 1858, he became keeper of the Sombrero Key lighthouse (pictured here). Nicolosa Mabrity Bethel may have assisted her husband in his duties, although she and their children had a home on Key West. (Courtesy of the State Archives of Florida.)

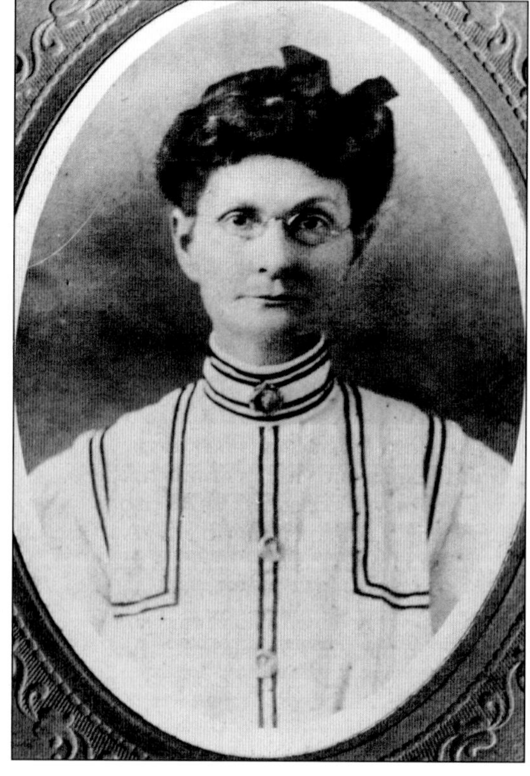

A native of Eleuthera in the Bahamas, Mary Elizabeth Sands married William A. Bethel, the son of Nicolosa Mabrity Bethel and Capt. Joseph Bethel, in 1874. William Bethel became the principal keeper of the Key West lighthouse in 1889. Mary Elizabeth (nicknamed Eliza) worked as his assistant keeper starting in 1891. (Courtesy of Monroe County Library, Key West.)

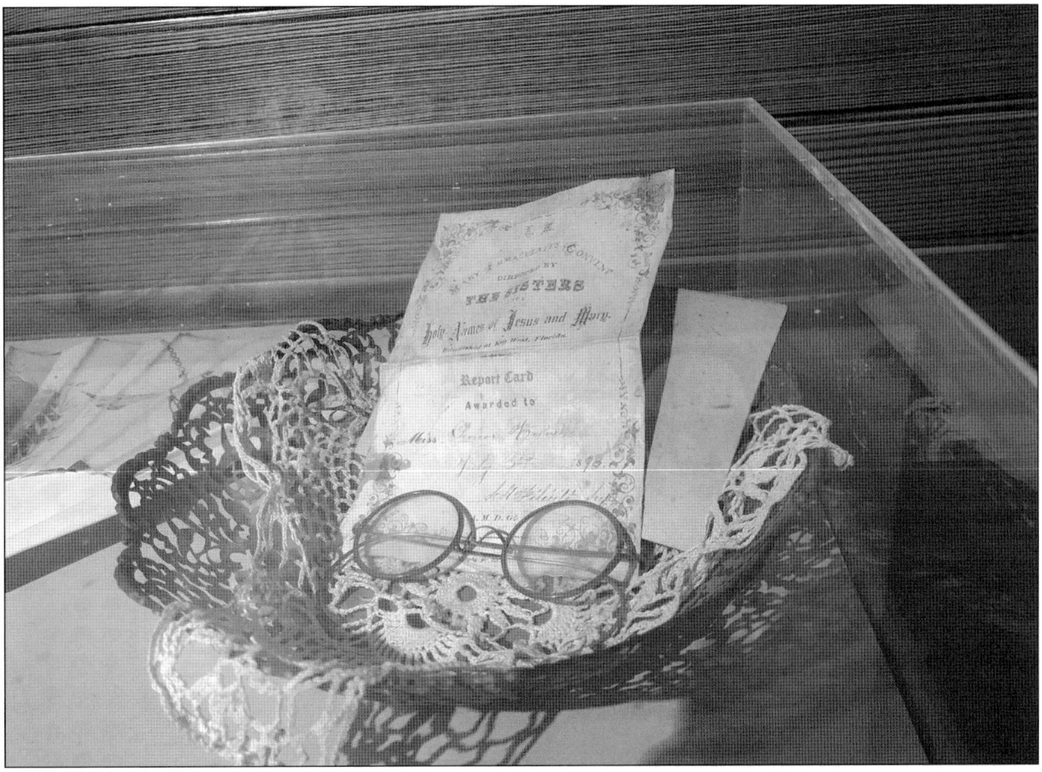

Pictured here are Mary "Eliza" Bethel's glasses, on display at the Key West lighthouse museum in the restored keeper's quarters. The same year Mary was appointed as assistant keeper, the lighthouse's lantern was updated to use kerosene; the next year, in 1892, the house's wood shingle roof was replaced by slate, according to Steve Mirsky. (Courtesy of Laura Albritton.)

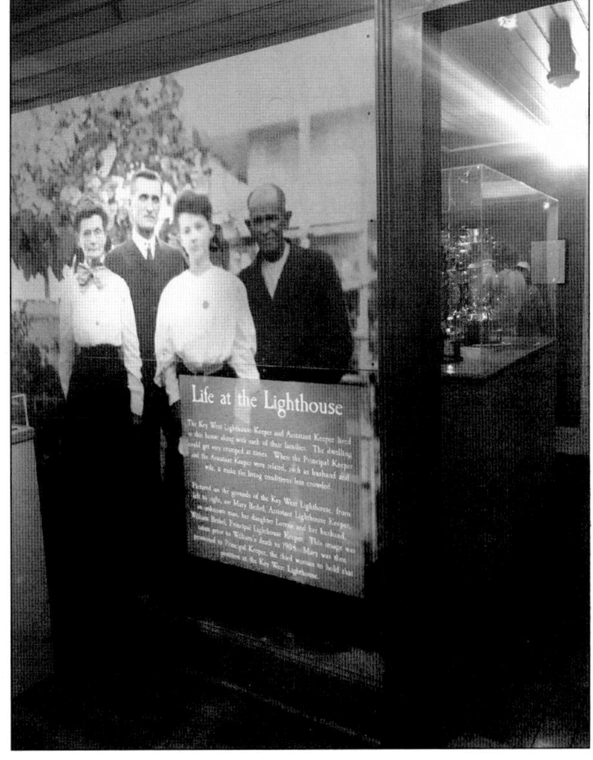

The Key West lighthouse museum exhibits a number of Mary Bethel and the Bethel family's belongings, including furniture and clothing. This part of the exhibit includes a photograph of Mary Bethel (left), their daughter Lorena, and William Bethel (far right). Their clothing and William's age place the photograph in 1907 or 1908. (Courtesy of Laura Albritton.)

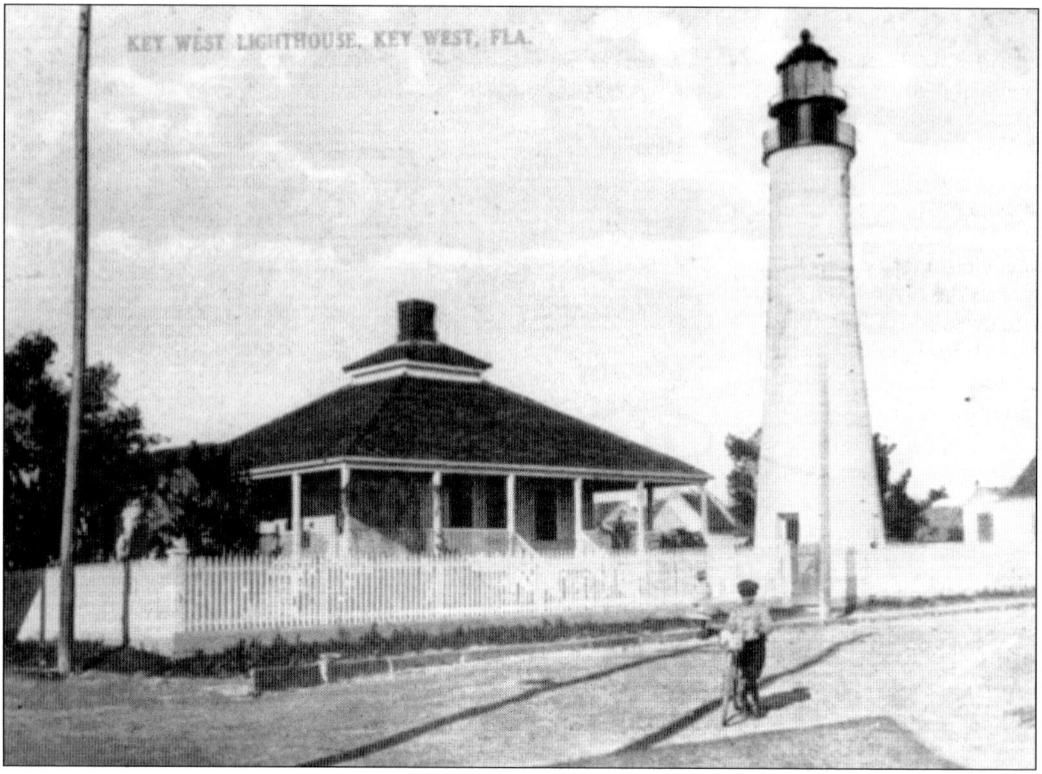

Mary Bethel lived with her family in these keeper's quarters from 1889 until at least 1913. Her husband, William, had two accidents while tending to the lighthouse, the second of which led to his death in 1908. Mary was made principal keeper, and her son Merrill was employed as the Key West light's assistant keeper. (Courtesy of Monroe County Library, Key West.)

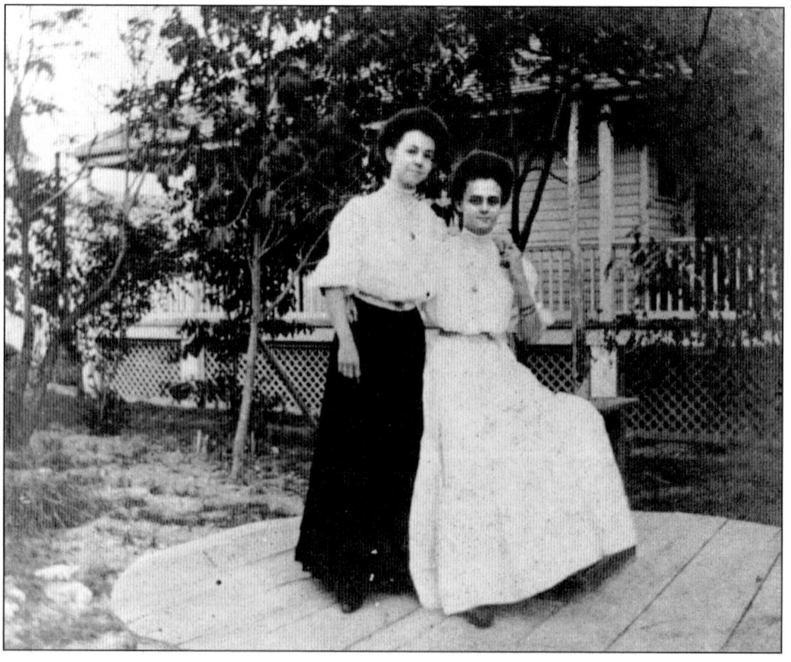

In this photograph, two of the Bethel daughters pose before the keeper's quarters, most likely Lorena on the left and Jennie on the right. The two young women were great-granddaughters of Michael and Barbara Mabrity, the original Key West keepers. Neither would serve as keeper, as the lighthouse was automated in 1915. (Courtesy of Monroe County Library, Key West.)

Jennie Bethel wore this delicate white lace dress when she got married in December 1911 at the keeper's quarters, where her family had lived since 1889. A photograph of Jennie with her new husband, Henry Johan de Boer, is exhibited with the dress in the Key West Lighthouse and Keeper's Quarters Museum. (Courtesy of Laura Albritton.)

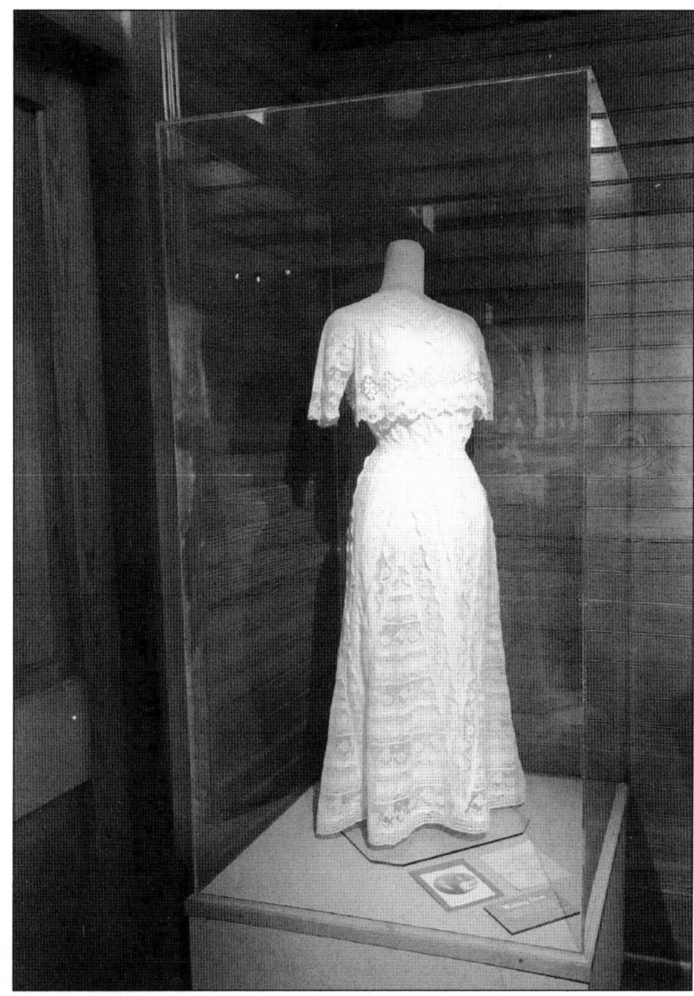

Key West lighthouse keeper Mary Elizabeth Bethel ordered this invitation made for her daughter Jennie's wedding. The wedding invitation reads "Mrs. Mary Elizabeth Bethel requests the honor of your presence at the marriage of her daughter Jennie Louise to Mr. Henry Johan de Boer on Tuesday evening, December the twenty-sixth at eight o'clock, 928 Whitehead Street, Key West, Fla." (Courtesy of Laura Albritton.)

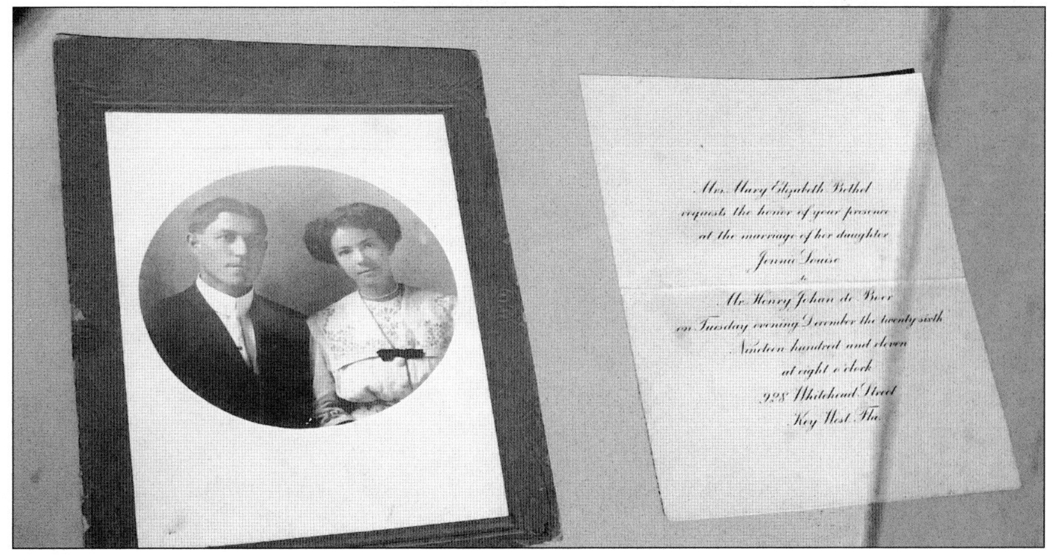

Mrs. Mary Elizabeth Bethel
requests the honor of your presence
at the marriage of her daughter
Jennie Louise
to
Mr. Henry Johan de Boer
on Tuesday evening December the twenty sixth
Nineteen hundred and eleven
at eight o'clock
928 Whitehead Street
Key West Fla.

Wednesday, October 8, 1952 THE KEY WEST CITIZEN

'igilant Sent...el Key West Light Stands Watch For Over Centur

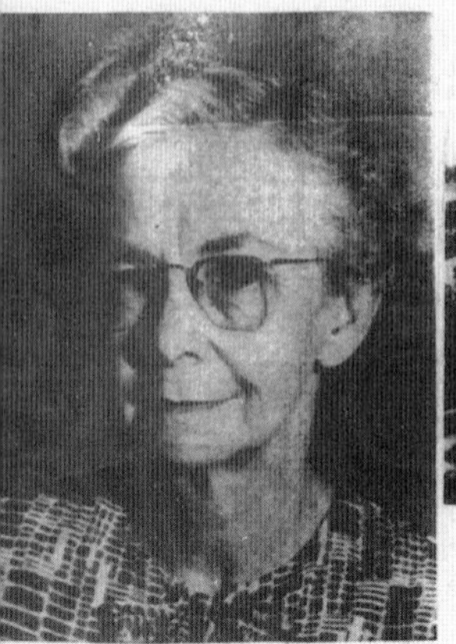

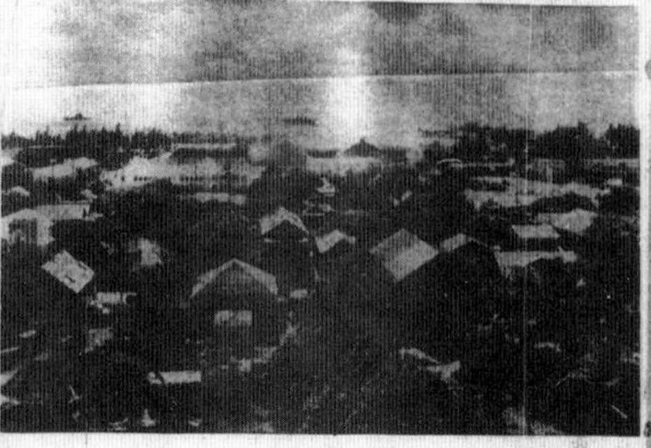

Citizen Staff Photo

PANORAMIC VIEW OF "THE OLD ROCK" looking toward the southwest was taken recently from the narrow balcony of the Key West Lighthouse which juts 115 feet high above the city. In the background are a cruiser and an aircraft carrier anchored off the huge Naval Station here. Left is Mrs. Jennie de Boer who remembers helping her father trim the kerosene wick in days before electricity was used for the beam. Right is Comdr. Henry B. Haskins, U.S. Coast Guard (retired) who spent 43 years in the lighthouse service of the southeast area and Key West.

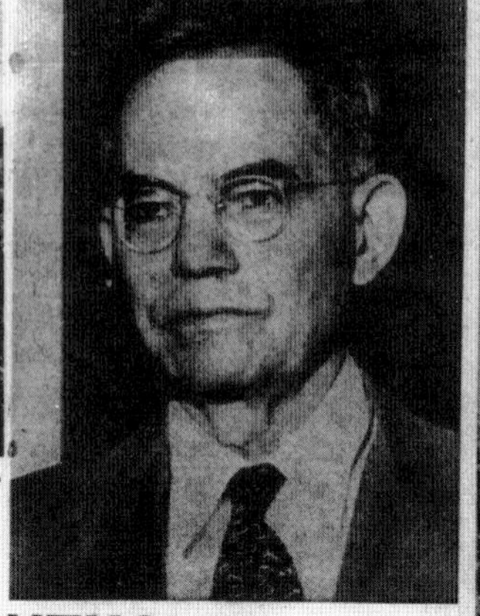

ISTORY OF 104 YEAR OLD ISLAND LIGHTHOUSE REVEALS STORY OF DEEP LOYALTY TO A SERVICE

By DOROTHY RAYMER

This newspaper article from the *Key West Citizen* commemorates the history of the Key West lighthouse and includes the memories of Jennie Bethel de Boer, who saw both her father, William, and her mother, Mary, tend the light. In the article, Jennie recalled, "I used to help my father trim those kerosene wicks." She also remembered taking refuge in the light with her mother and their neighbors during the hurricane of 1910: "we heard the glass break and the pieces of it came crashing down inside. . . . That was the first time the light ever failed." Not only was she married to Henry J. de Boer at the keeper's quarters, she also gave birth there to their first child, Anne Elizabeth. Her sister Lorena had her wedding reception on the lighthouse grounds, and her brother Merrill served as assistant keeper to their mother. Jennie Bethel de Boer, who worked for the *Key West Citizen* for many years, noted that "our family life centered around the lighthouse." (Courtesy of the Library of Congress.)

Eight

Lighthouses in the 20th Century

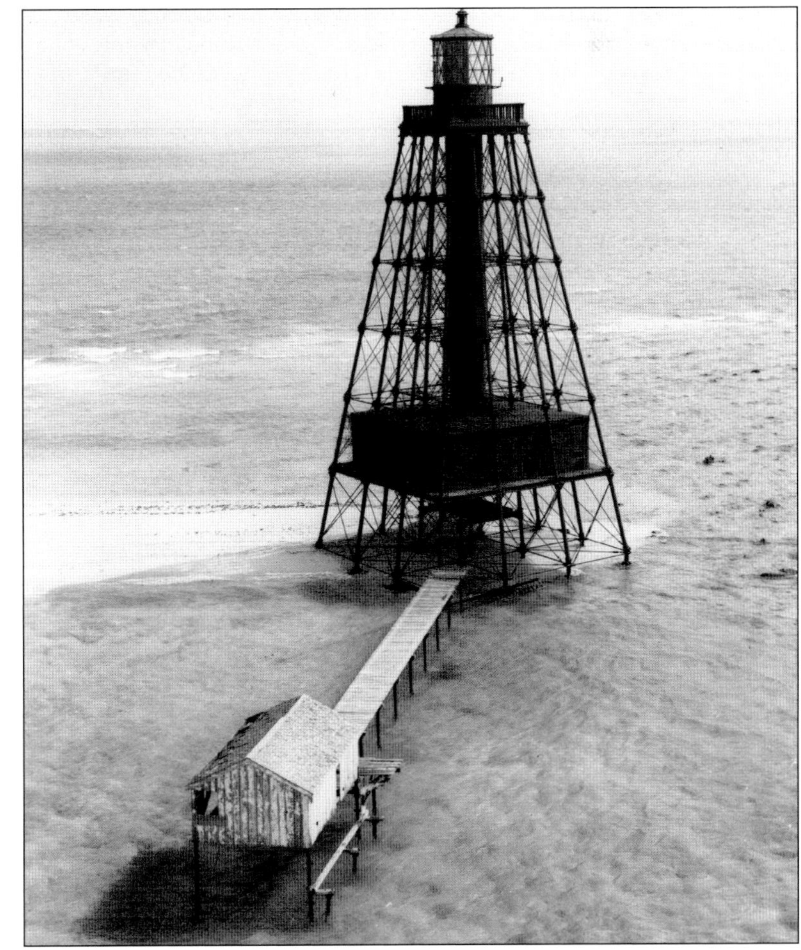

The 20th century brought with it tremendous change for the Florida Keys lighthouses. In fact, two of the light ceased to exist. The other nine survived, despite events such as the 1935 Labor Day hurricane and Hurricane Donna. Technology improved to the point that lighthouse keepers were retired as the lights were automated, one after another. (Courtesy of Monroe County Library, Key West.)

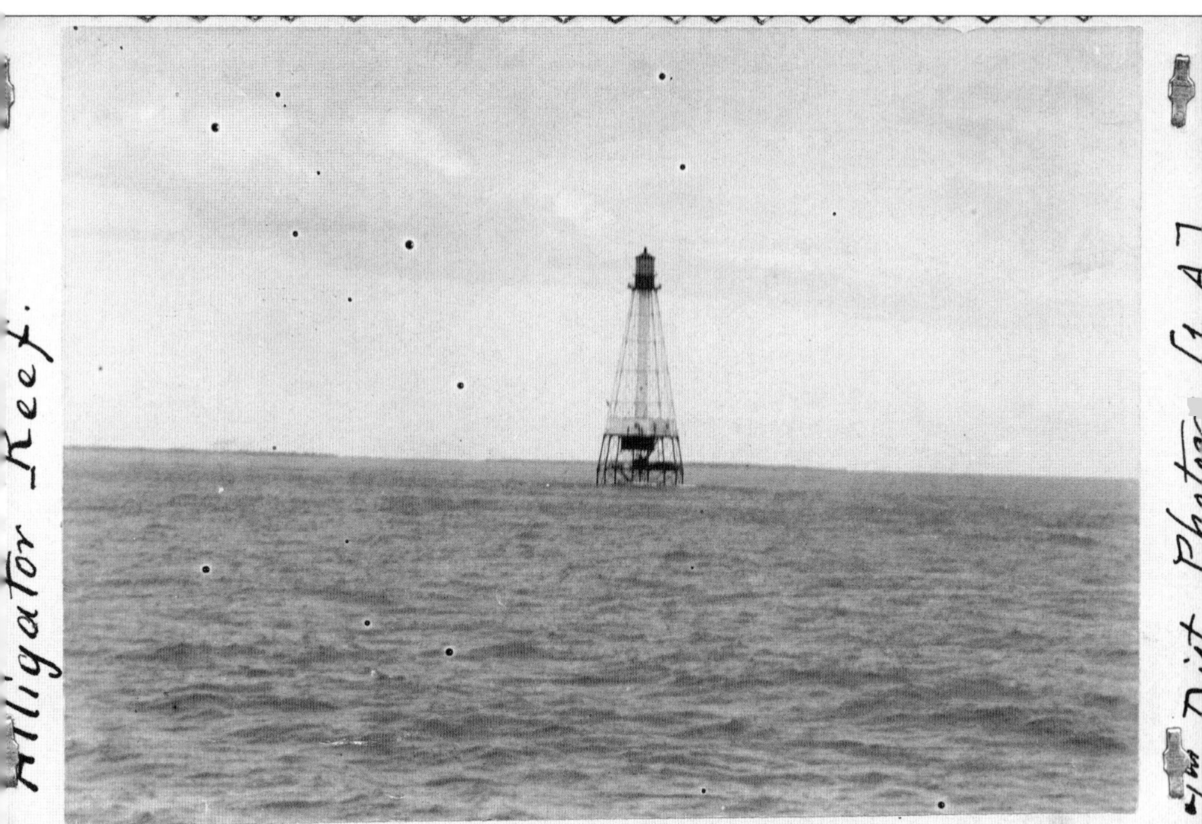

The Florida Keys lighthouses had distinctive signals or lights so that one could be distinguished from another. Starting with its lighting in 1873, Alligator Reef light's lantern once flashed "with five white flashes and the sixth, red," according to expert Tom Taylor. This iron pile lighthouse, off Islamorada in the Upper Keys, originally was outfitted with a first-order Fresnel lens, the largest type. Keeping the light, over four nautical miles from the Matecumbe Keys, could be quite dangerous. On Labor Day in 1935, a terrifying category-five hurricane with 180- to 200-mile-per-hour winds and 20-foot storm surge tore its way toward the islands. Keeper Jones Pervis later described in his log the wrecked landing platform and keeper's quarters. "Flying glass was danger to Life," he wrote soberly. (Courtesy of the National Archives.)

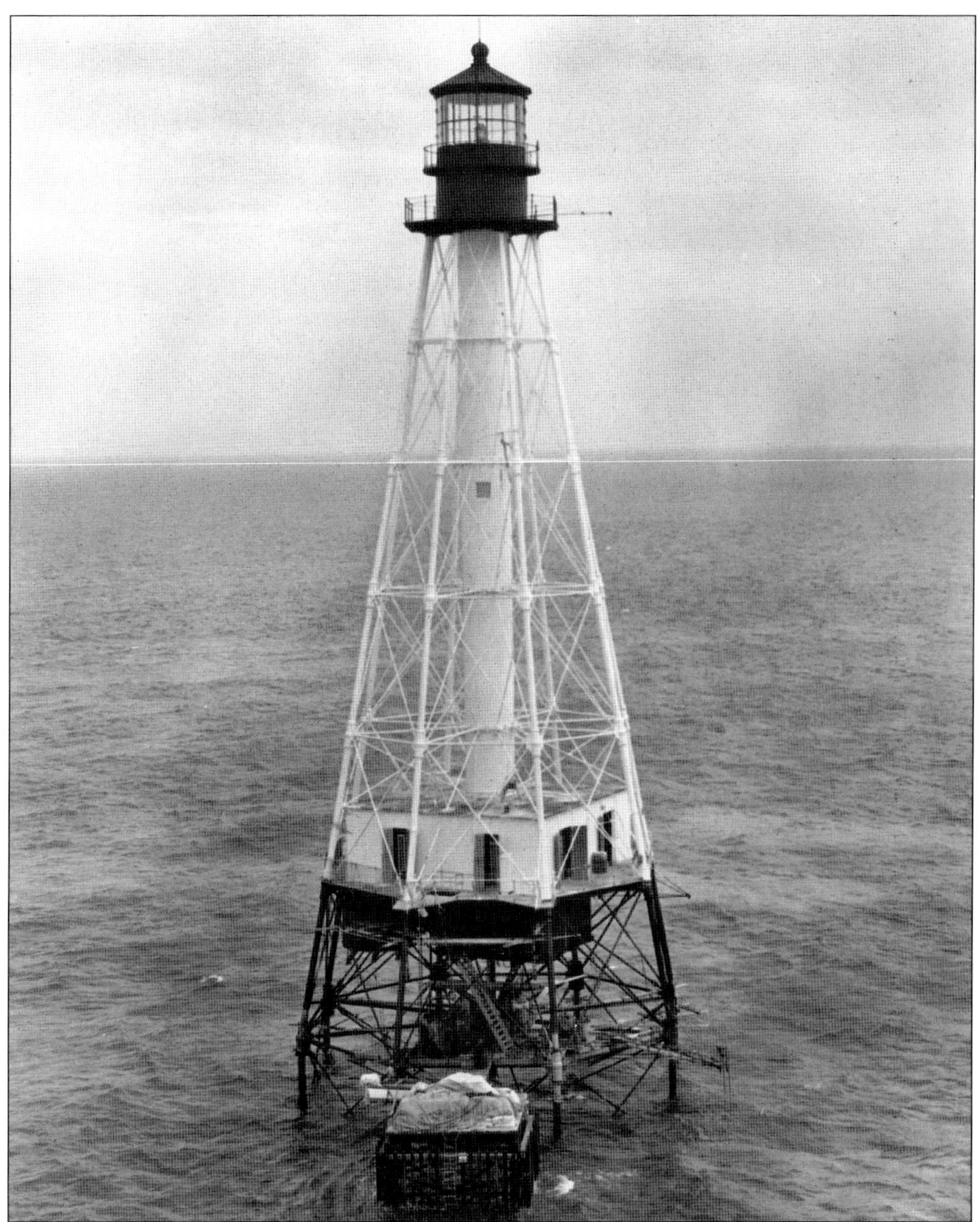

With its white and black paint, Alligator Reef lighthouse is a striking sight to behold. In the 1910s, its lantern was upgraded from an oil wick to an incandescent oil-vapor system. Another change occurred when the US Coast Guard took over the operation of all American lighthouses in 1939. After weathering Hurricane Donna in 1960, the Alligator Reef light was automated, and it later received a Vega VRB-25 beacon that rotated (and thus "flashed"). Following 141 years of operation, Alligator Reef lighthouse went dark in 2014. The light remains an attraction; boaters, snorkelers, and divers visit the reef here regularly. The National Park Service was looking for an organization to take ownership of the lighthouse, and in 2021, the US Department of the Interior awarded the Alligator Reef lighthouse to Islamorada nonprofit organization Friends of the Pool. (Courtesy of the US Lighthouse Society Archives.)

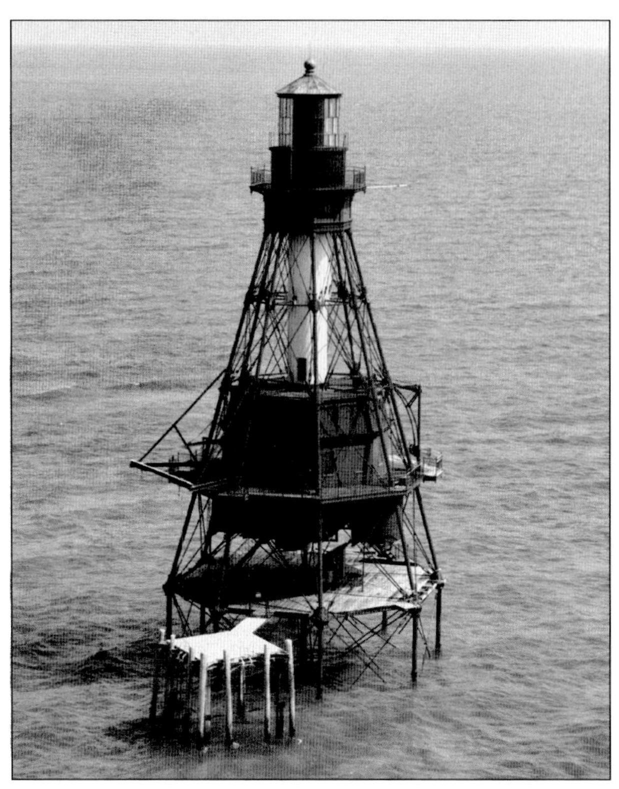

Located off the Lower Keys, American Shoal lighthouse emitted a light that flashed. After improvements in the late 19th century (addition of an oil house and two red panes to the lantern room), American Shoal was updated with an incandescent oil-vapor system in 1912. It was automated in 1963 with a solar-powered beacon. In 1990, the US Post Office issued a 25¢ stamp commemorating the American Shoal lighthouse with its name spelled "American Shoals." Although usually singular (American Shoal), on at least one 19th-century survey, "shoals" in the plural was used. The artist also took some license in depicting the US Coast Guard cutter cruising near the lighthouse, since the ocean there is only five feet deep. American Shoal was entirely deactivated in 2015. (Both, courtesy of Monroe County Library, Key West.)

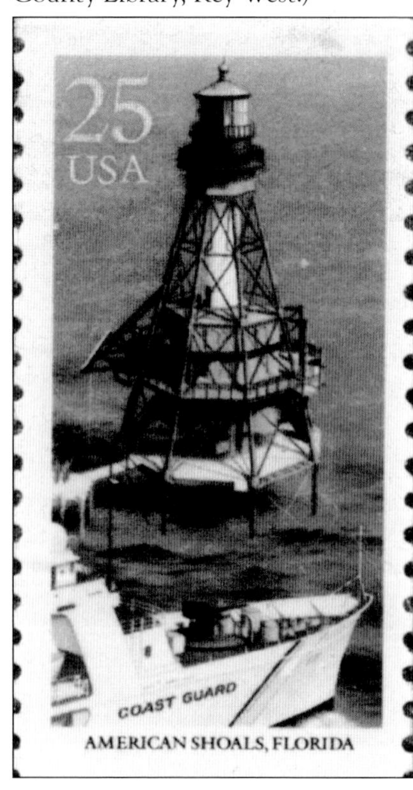

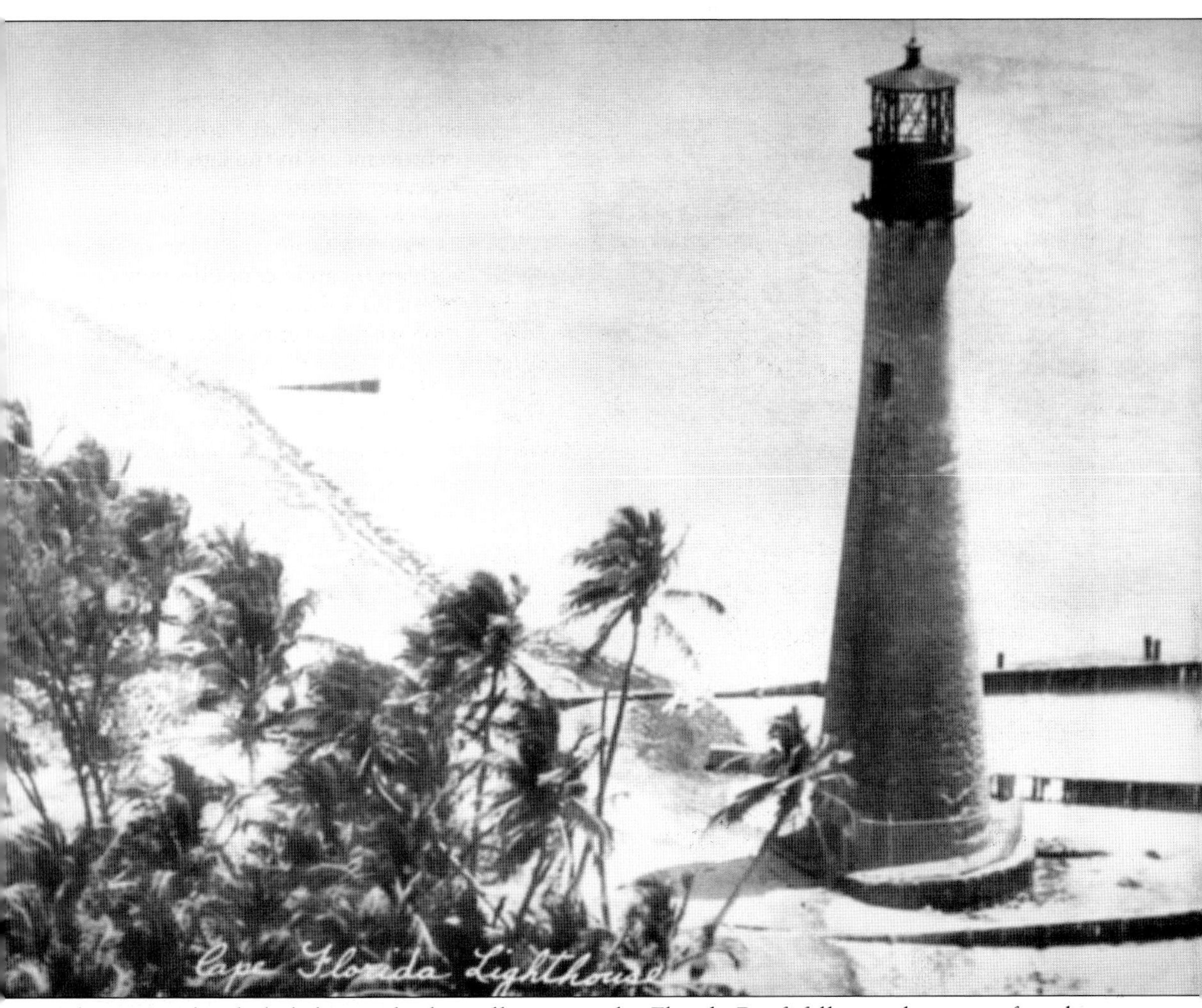

The Cape Florida lighthouse, built to illuminate the Florida Reef, fell into disrepair after the construction and lighting of Fowey Rocks lighthouse. The Cape Florida light had weathered a great many storms, some natural and some human-made: an attack by Seminoles in 1836, rebuilding in 1846, an attack and disablement by Confederates in 1861, repair in 1866, and de-activation in 1878. The lighthouse became, instead of a functional structure, a romantic landmark on Biscayne Bay. After a campaign to preserve the lighthouse and the surrounding land from development, the Cape Florida light became part of Bill Baggs Cape Florida State Park. Its outbuildings, including the keeper's quarters and an outhouse, were reconstructed and its lantern relit in 1978. Hurricane Andrew later inflicted serious damage, but the lighthouse was restored and has undergone additional restoration since. Today, the public can appreciate this historic structure, climb the tower, and join a park ranger's tour of the keeper's quarters. The shell of a 19th-century lantern room attributed to George Meade is on display on the grounds. (Courtesy of Jerry Wilkinson.)

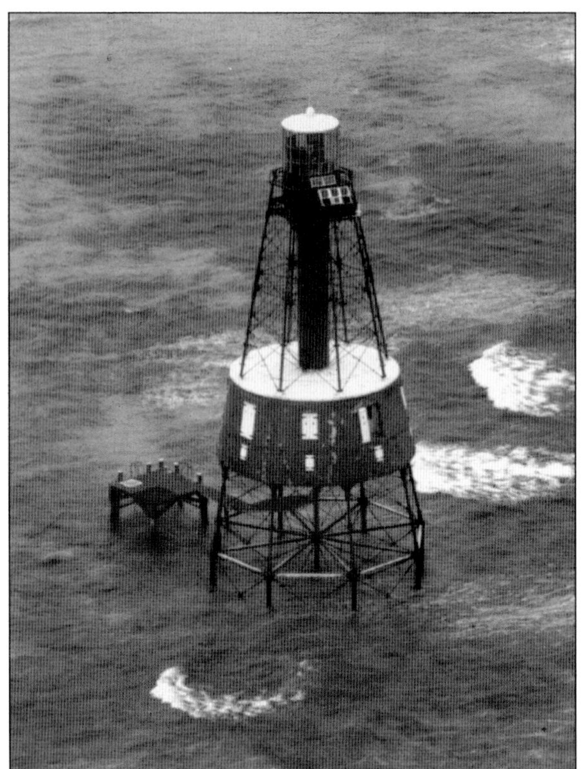

In 1913, Carysfort Reef lighthouse's oil wick lamps were updated to an incandescent oil-vapor system. In 1962, the light was automated and the revolving first-order Fresnel lens removed so that a third-order fixed lens could be installed. This lens was in turn replaced with a Vega VRB-25 rotating beacon. Then, in 2015, the light went dark. (Photograph by Mike and Carol McKinney, courtesy of the US Lighthouse Society Archives.)

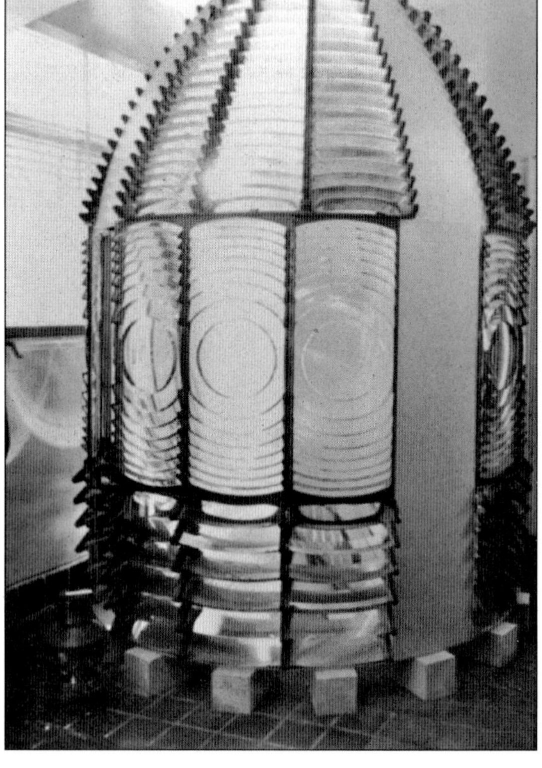

Carysfort Reef's first-order Fresnel lens was a work of art. Carysfort's lantern initially shone as a fixed light before being converted to one that flashed. Red panels were also placed in the lantern. Author Love Dean explained why: "The flashing white light identified the position of the light, and the flashing red sectors identified the position of the reefs." (Courtesy of Jerry Wilkinson.)

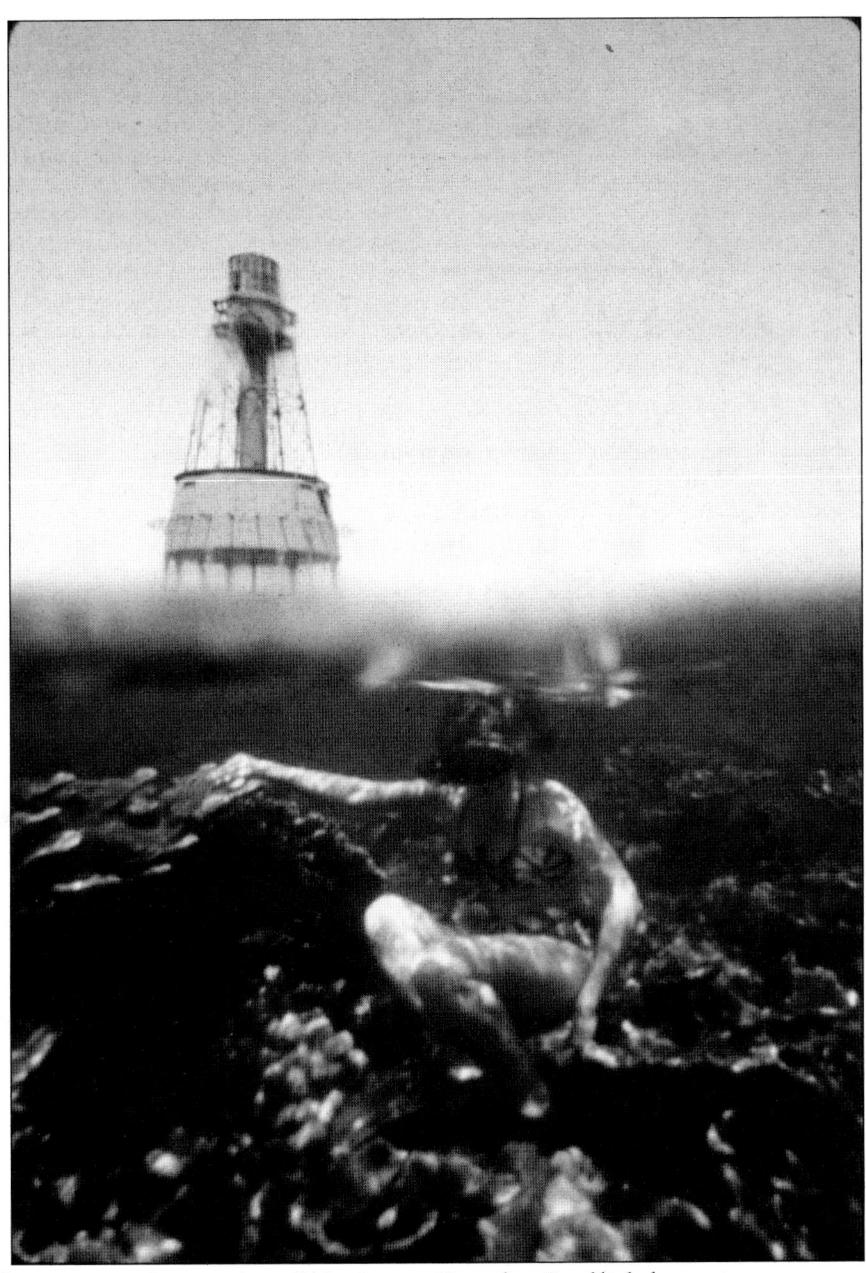

Located approximately six miles off Key Largo, Carysfort Reef lighthouse is not necessarily easy to reach for the general public. Yet the reef here can make for a gratifying snorkel, as the corals are less degraded than at certain other Florida Reef sites. To make the journey to the lighthouse is also an opportunity to observe an important piece of maritime history up close. George Gordon Meade predicted that the iron reef lights might last 200 years. Completed in 1852, the Carysfort Reef light has endured for over a century and a half. Even the terrible onslaught of the 1935 Labor Day hurricane could not dislodge the iron structure. Nonetheless, the function of lighthouses as aids to navigation has been superseded by Global Positioning Systems (GPS), and thus, even stalwart survivors such as the Carysfort Reef light have evolved into tourist attractions and historical monuments. (Courtesy of the State Archives of Florida.)

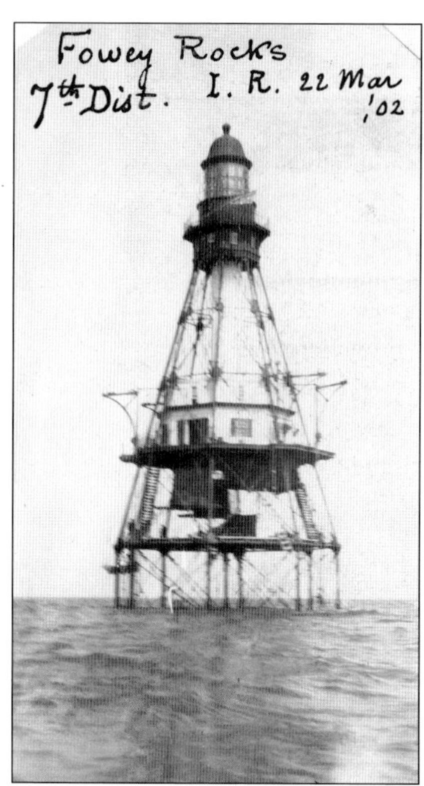

This photograph shows the Fowey Rocks lighthouse, the northernmost of the Keys lighthouses, in 1902. Like the other lighthouses previously mentioned in this chapter, the light's oil-wick lamps were changed out for an incandescent oil-vapor system. According to the late lighthouse expert Tom Taylor, by 1923, the 125-foot light was outfitted with a telephone thanks to a submarine cable from Miami. (Courtesy of the National Archives.)

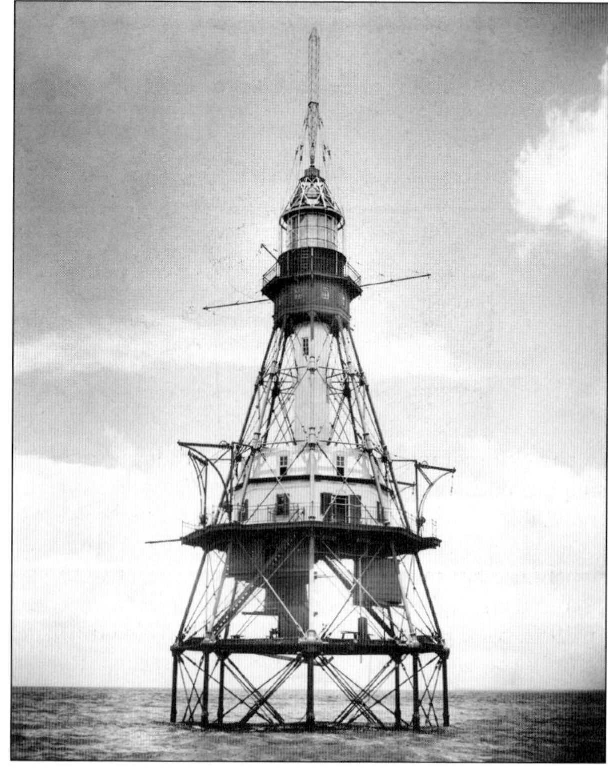

New technology came to the Fowey Rocks lighthouse in the 1930s, when the old incandescent oil-vapor system was removed in favor of modern electricity. In this case, generators supplied the electricity. In this photograph, one can see a radio beacon mounted on top of the lighthouse, another alteration in the 1930s. The 1935 Labor Day hurricane destroyed the light's bottom deck. (Courtesy of the US Coast Guard Historian's Office.)

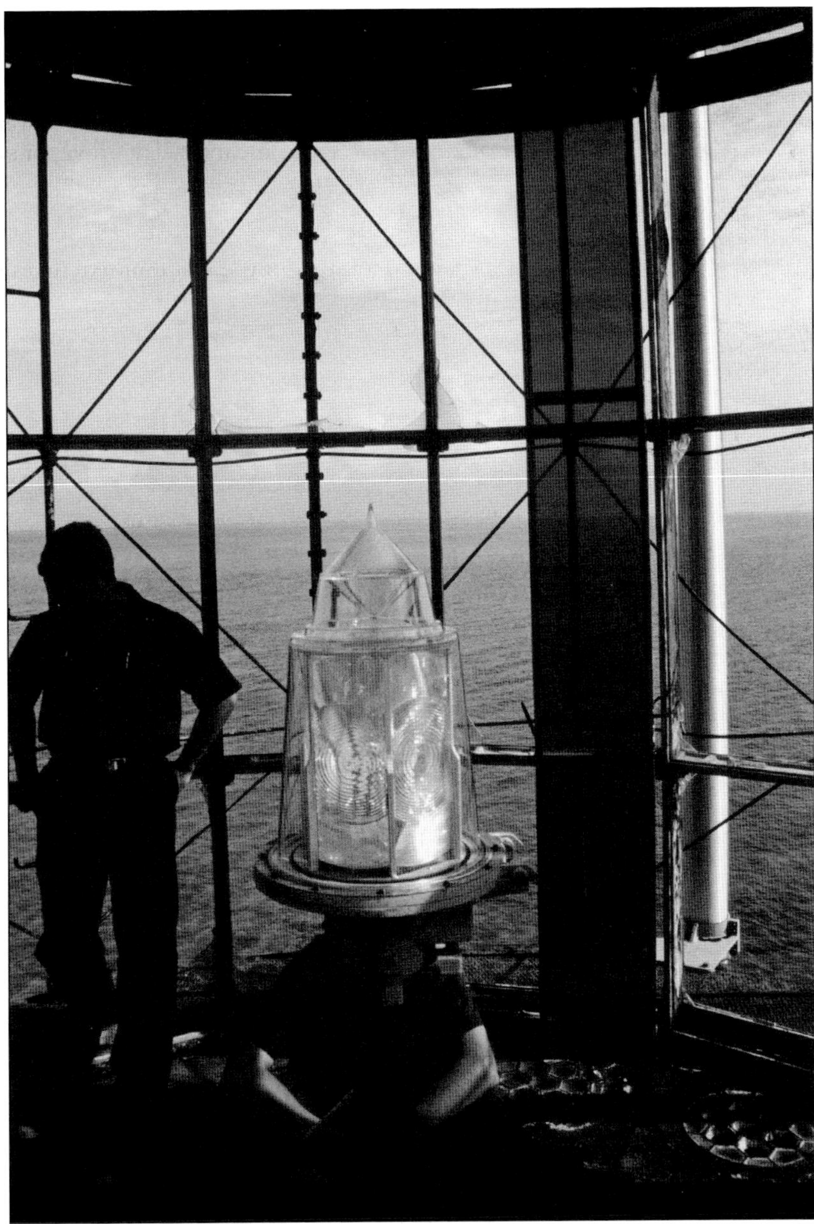

In this photograph, the original first-order Fresnel lens of the Fowey Rocks lighthouse has been supplanted by a much smaller plastic lens. Although embracing innovations in technology is inevitable, it is hard not to regret the removal of that beautiful and impressive lens. Happily, the Coast Guard National Aids to Navigation School in Virginia owns and exhibits this piece of lighthouse heritage. More changes were afoot in the second half of the 20th century: a windmill powered the light (although not very well) from 1975, a year after the light became automated. In 1982, solar power took its place. The following year, flash tube array lamps were installed but found to be unsatisfactory. Fowey Rocks received the same type of Vega VRB-25 rotating beacon installed at other reef lights. In 1992, Hurricane Andrew wiped out much of the lighthouse's glass, which was subsequently replaced. (Photograph by Ralph Eshelman, courtesy of the US Lighthouse Society Archives.)

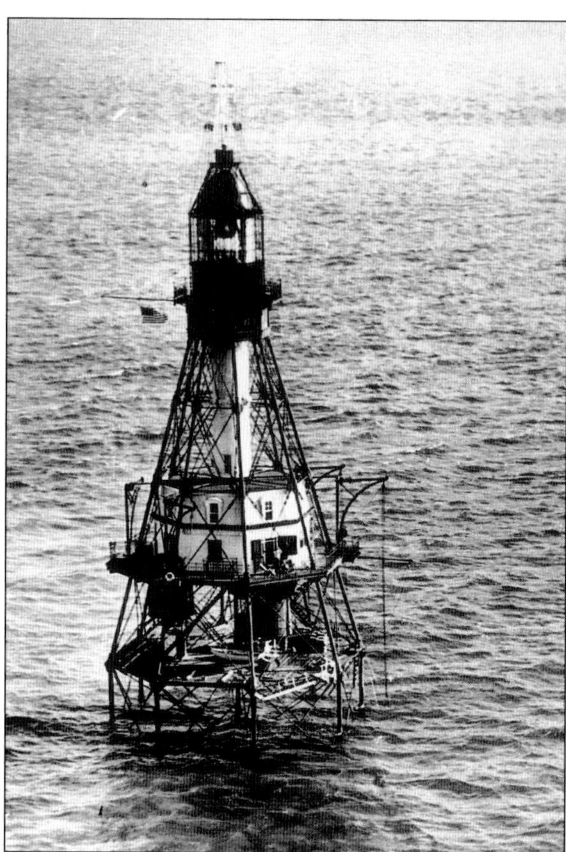

Since this photograph was taken, the radio beacon has been removed from atop Fowey Rocks lighthouse. With the creation of Biscayne National Park, Fowey Rocks fell under the aegis of the National Park Service. Unlike the lights mentioned previously in this chapter, Fowey Rocks lighthouse is still in operation. (Photograph by Ralph Eshelman, courtesy of the US Lighthouse Society Archives.)

After the military left Fort Jefferson in the 19th century, the fort was allowed to deteriorate. Neither it nor the lighthouse was maintained. In 1935, Pres. Franklin D. Roosevelt signed the Antiquities Act, which turned the fort into a national monument. In 1970, it joined the National Register of Historic Places, and in 1992, it became part of the Dry Tortugas National Park. (Courtesy of Monroe County Library, Key West.)

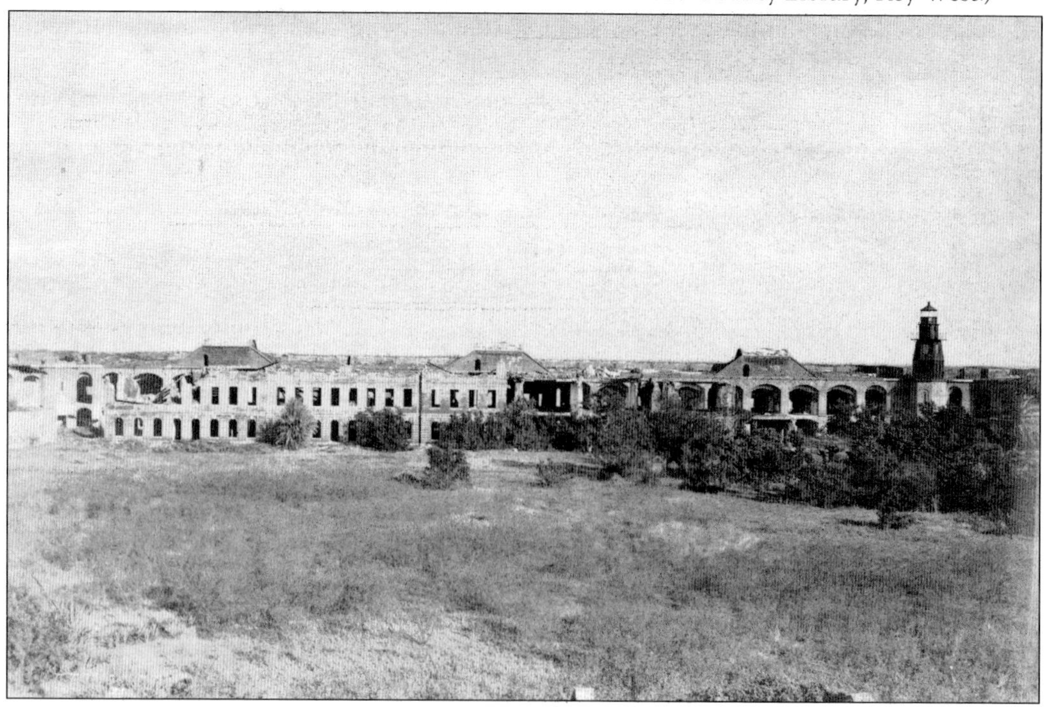

This photograph from the 1960s shows Garden Key's lighthouse at Fort Jefferson before the property became part of a national park. Since then, much has been done to stabilize the historic structures on the island. In 2020, a $4.5-million restoration was begun on the harbor light itself, which involved dismantling and removing it temporarily from the island. (Courtesy of Monroe County Library, Key West.)

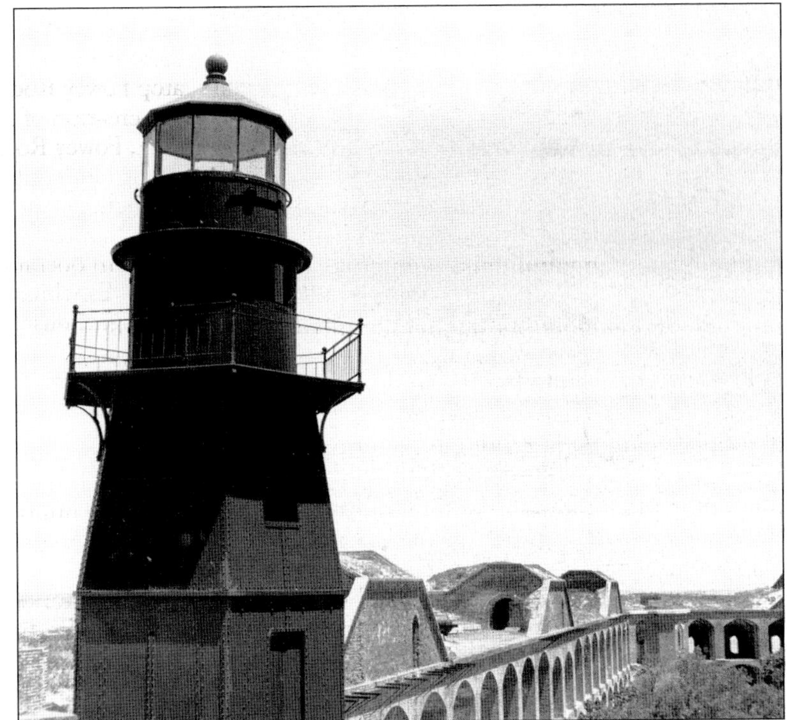

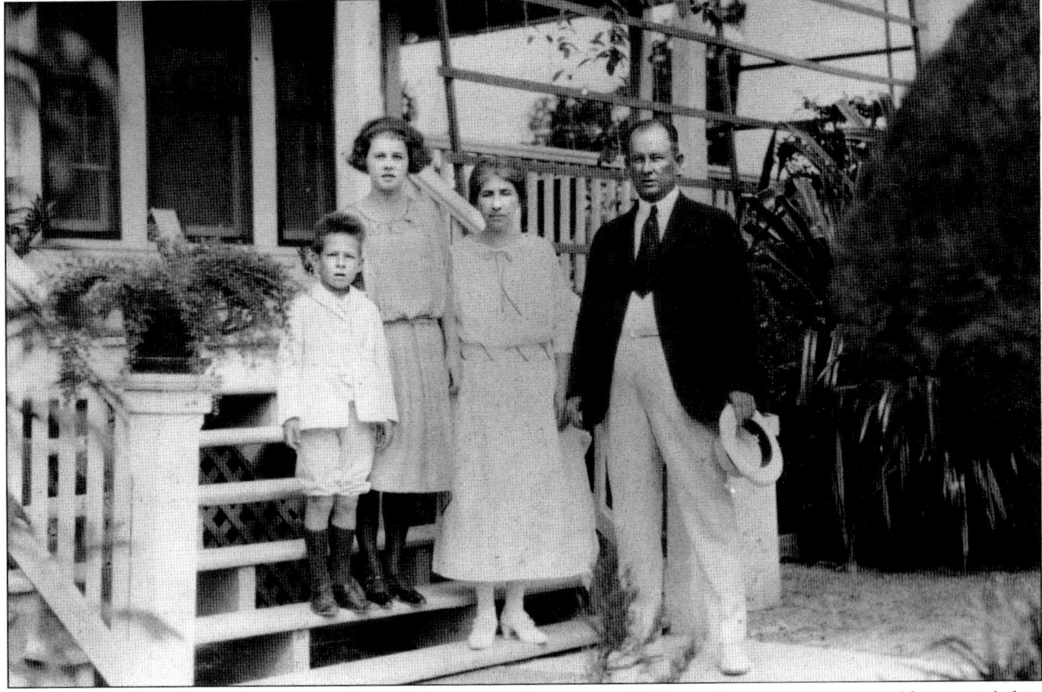

After the Key West lighthouse was automated in the 1910s, William Demeritt, pictured here with his wife, Kathleen Ackerman Demeritt, and their children, lived in the keeper's quarters. As lighthouse superintendent of the Seventh District, Demeritt made the case that the person holding that position should take up residence here. (Courtesy of Monroe County Library, Key West.)

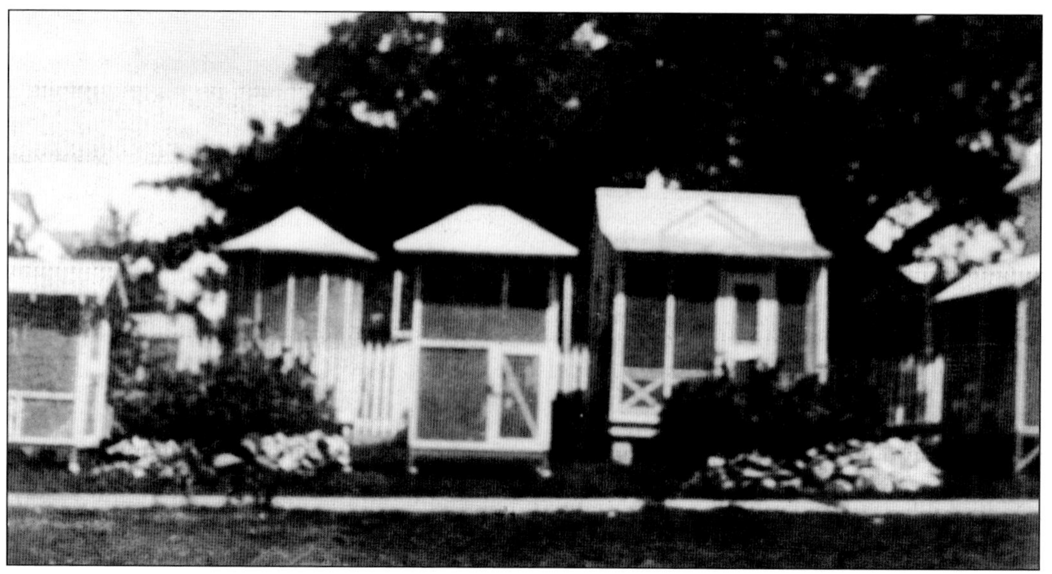

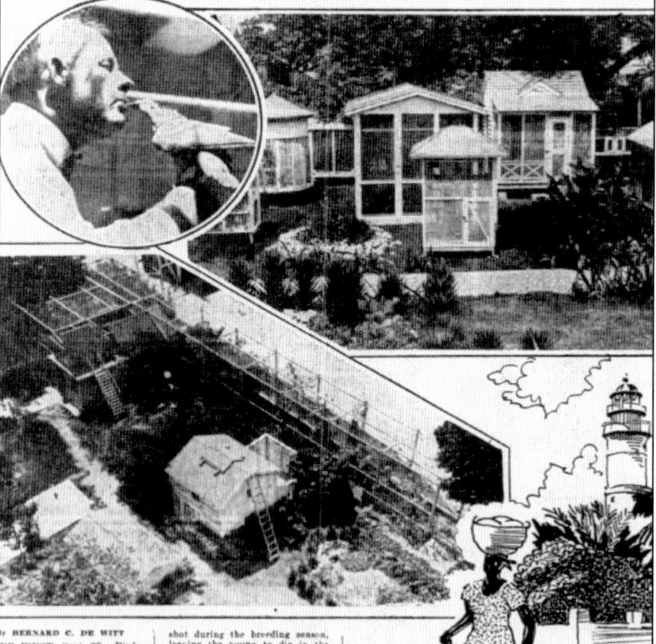

Lighthouse Official Has Large Private Aviary

Demeritt, Superintendent of Seventh District, Collects Birds at Key West Home for Unusual Hobby

Collection of birds in his private aviary at his home beside th lighthouse is the hobby of William W. Demeritt, superinte seventh lighthouse district, who is shown in the upper left kiss from Pete-E, his favorite white crowned pigeon. Upp several of the smaller aviaries while below is a corner of th reservation showing some of the aviaries.

y BERNARD C. DE WITT

EY WEST, Sept. 29.—Birds varying descriptions—love , canaries, foreign finches, e-crowned pigeons and other imens rare on the Florida —can be found in one spot ey West, where a small sanc- y and a number of aviaries been constructed and are g maintained as one man's y.

illiam W. Demeritt, superin- ent of the seventh lighthouse ict here, a native of this since a young boy has been ested in the birds found in easing numbers on the keys. e men have their golf, others s, some cards, some books, the greatest delight of the house superintendent in his s away from his office is ob-

shot during the breeding season, leaving the young to die in the nests. It has been said that on one small mangrove key alone over 40 nests, with dead squabs, were observed. It is not unusual for hunters from Key West to go to Sugar Loaf key, about 20 miles from Key West, and there slaughter birds when obtaining food, or when in flight between their feeding and nesting grounds," Mr. Demeritt says.

In addition to several aviaries, the largest of which is over 100 feet long, 12 feet high, and varying from eight to 24 feet in width, on the well-kept grounds of the lighthouse are several bird baths.

The baths have been placed within the grounds just to create a haven for migratory birds, and

shades—orange, blue, brilliant red, yellow, pure white, shades of gray, and others.

Their life, to the visitor, seems one of complete joy. Some sing, and others spend their days swinging back and forth on the trapeze-like furnishings within the aviaries. In the larger pens, many birds can be seen, and when they are stirred into action, their fluttering wings present a

houses that are locat end of the island t the tropical foliage o and, by looking di get a bird's-eye view house reservation, w ponds, bird baths, a and tropical plants a

While he is respo the lights in this superintendent of lighthouse district

A native Conch, William Demeritt made his home at the Key West lighthouse's keeper's quarters from 1917 to 1939. On the grounds he built a series of aviaries (pictured). Demeritt cultivated birds, including canaries and finches, out of concern for the dwindling number of birds in the Keys. He told the *Miami News* in 1934, "Unprotected, hundreds are shot during the breeding season, leaving the young to die in their nests." He built birdbaths and left food out for migrating fowl. At the time, visitors could tour the lighthouse and enjoy the tropical garden, with banana trees, date palms, cocoplums, seagrapes, and sugar cane. Reporter Bernard C. de Witt noted that "The lighthouse reservation, in the heart of the city, is considered one of the outstanding points of interest on the island." (Above, courtesy of Monroe County Library, Key West; left, courtesy of the University of Miami Library.)

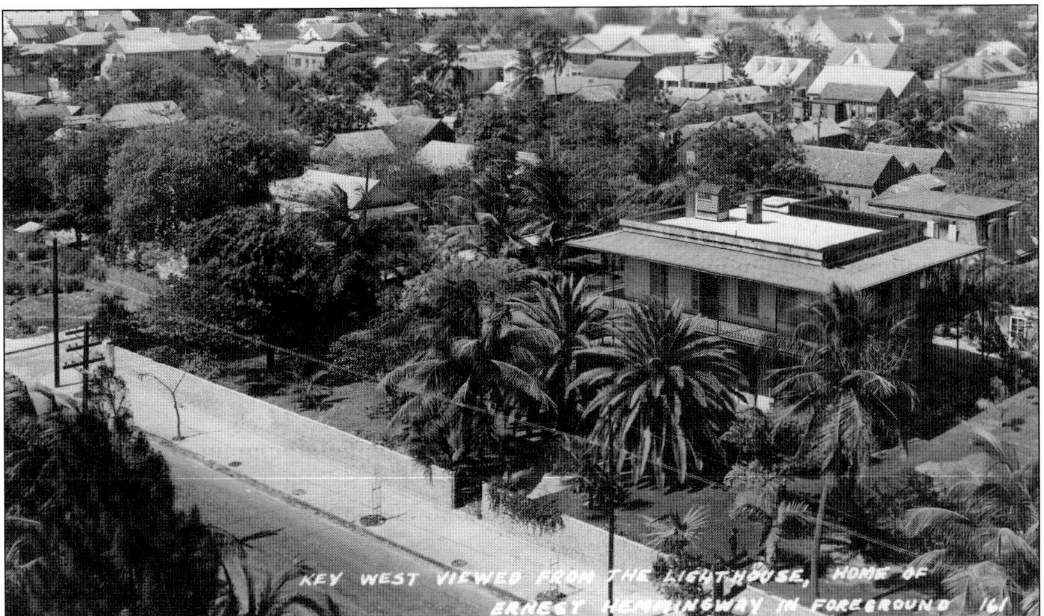

In the 1930s, Pauline and Ernest Hemingway resided in the former Asa Tift mansion on Whitehead Street, across from the lighthouse. Key West was increasingly promoted as a tourist destination to pull the city out of a grave economic spiral; tourists often tried to glimpse the island's most famous resident. Some say Hemingway had a brick wall built to keep out curious stares. However, visitors could peer from the top of the lighthouse into the author's garden. (On the other hand, the Hemingway family enjoyed one of the best views of Key West's lighthouse, as this photograph taken from their second-floor veranda indicates.) The growing popularity of Key West was reportedly one of the factors that drove Ernest Hemingway away. The start of his romance with Martha Gellhorn was another. (Both, courtesy of Monroe County Library, Key West.)

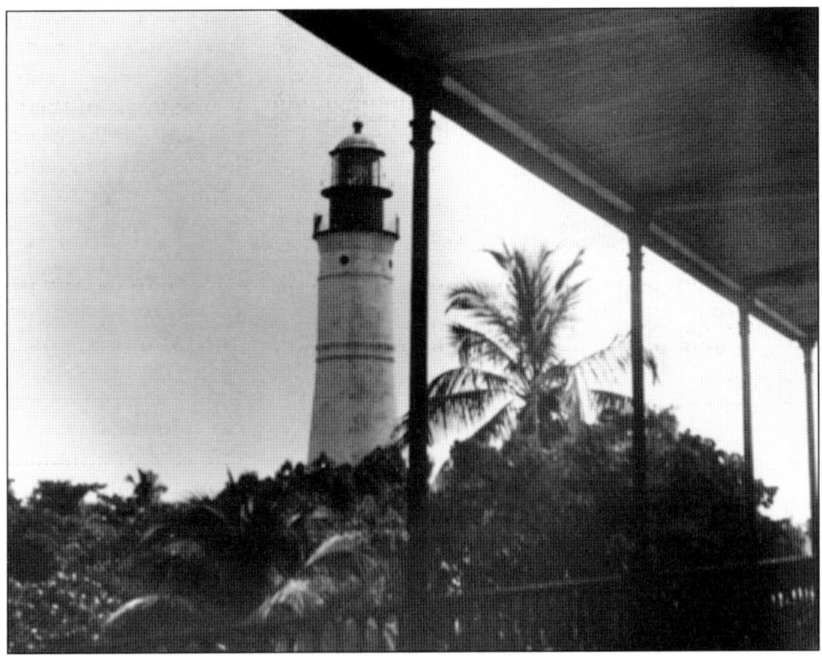

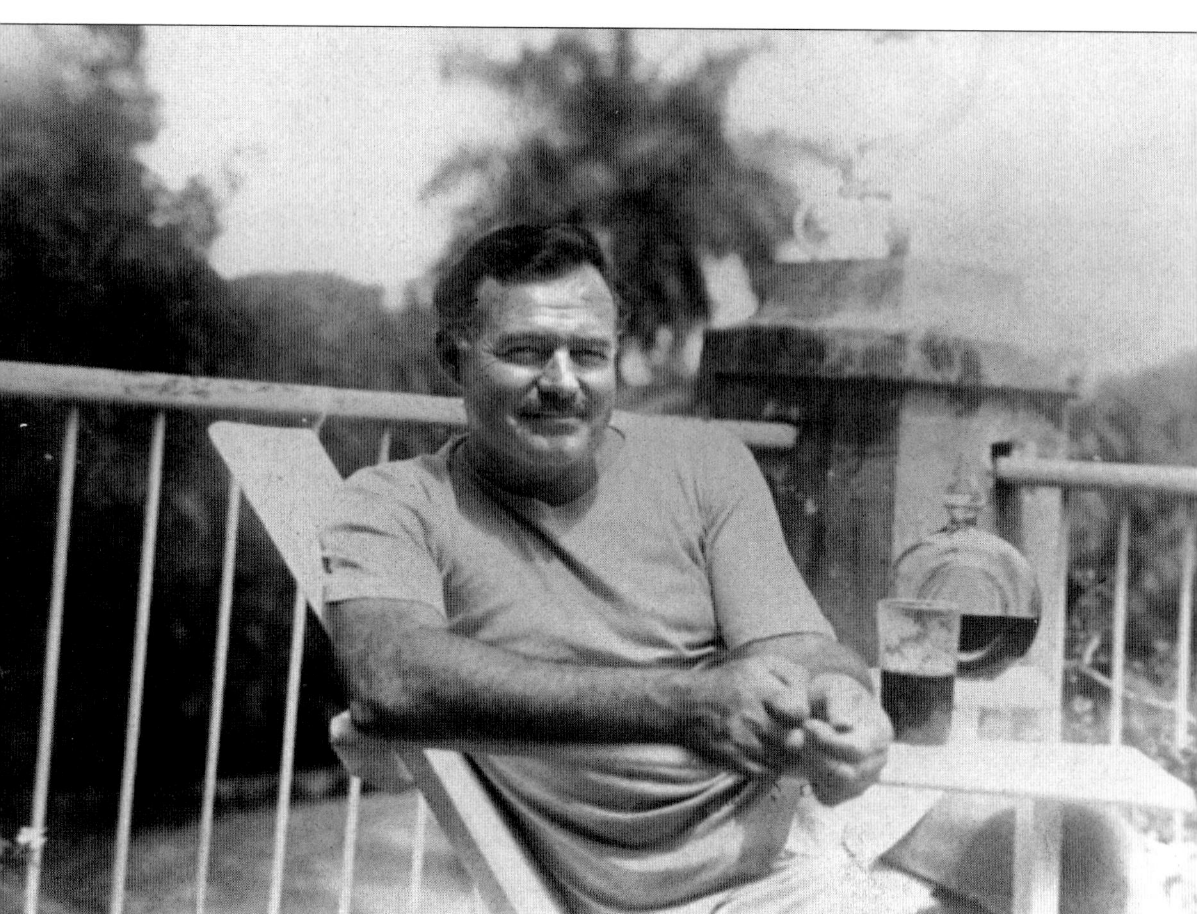

During his fishing trips on *Pilar* and his rum-running expeditions with Joe Russell (of Sloppy Joe's fame), Ernest Hemingway had grown closely acquainted with the Keys lights. References to Florida Keys lighthouses abound in Hemingway's novel *To Have and Have Not*. Capt. Harry Morgan mentions American Shoal lighthouse in chapter 6 as he tries to obtain his bearings. The Sand Key lighthouse is alluded to more than once; in chapter 18, Harry Morgan keeps "the rising, widening spire of Sand Key on his left." In chapter 23, the Coast Guard mate watches Sombrero Key's beam "starting to sweep out at sea." Both the islands of Loggerhead Key and Garden Key, where Hemingway was once stranded as a result of stormy weather, appear in the book. When bank robbers force Harry Morgan at gunpoint to take them aboard as they flee Key West, he makes note of the lighthouse rising above the other buildings. (Courtesy of Monroe County Library, Key West.)

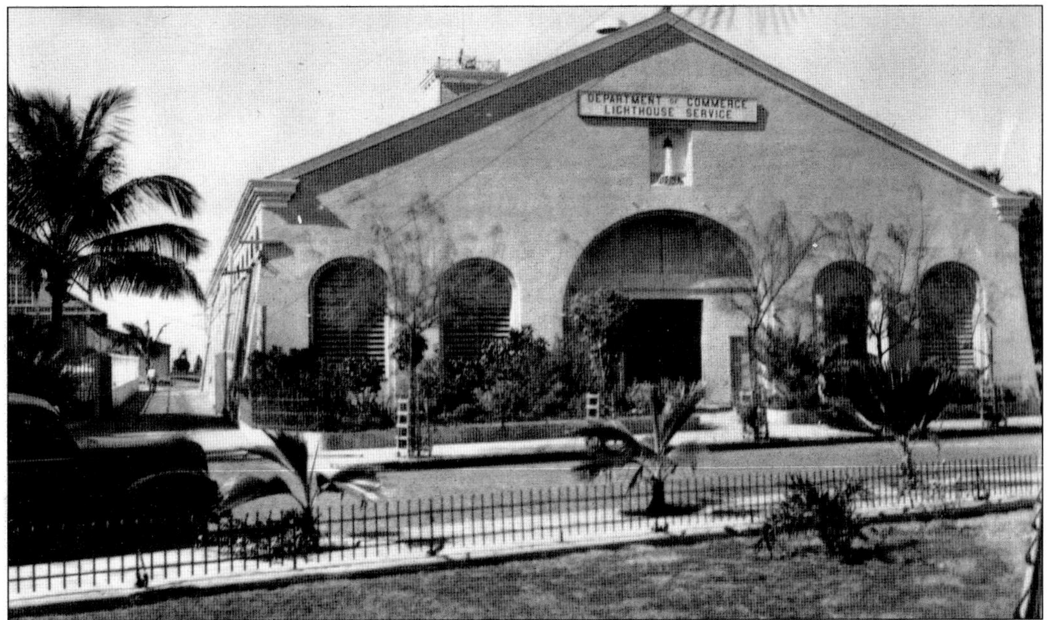

This distinctive 1861 Key West building stands on Front Street by the old customhouse. Originally constructed as a naval depot, it once served as the US Department of Commerce's Lighthouse Service office starting in 1932. A 1923 booklet explains that "In each district there is a central office at a location selected on account of either its maritime importance or its geographical position." (Courtesy of Monroe County Library, Key West.)

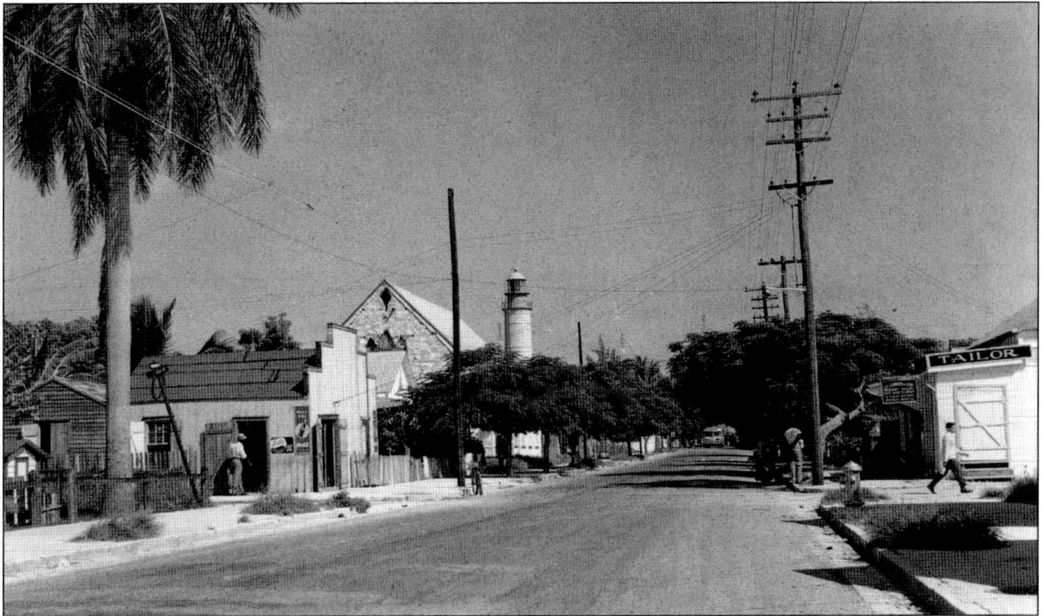

The Key West lighthouse rises above the tree line in this 1947 photograph. At this point, the US Coast Guard administered the US Lighthouse Service. During World War II, military personnel and the military's civilian employees thronged the streets. As the Navy's numbers began to decrease, with them went Key West's wartime economic boom. (Courtesy of Monroe County Library, Key West.)

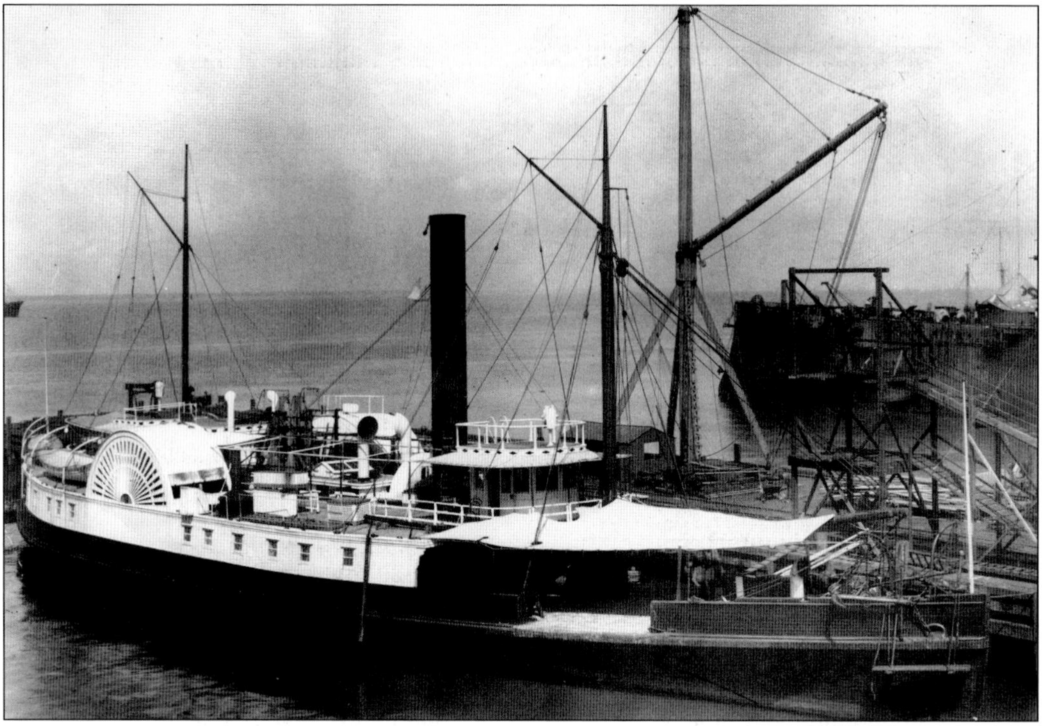

The US Lighthouse Service required tenders—vessels that could tend and maintain the lights. The tender *Wisteria* (or *Wistaria*), pictured here, had a dramatic end in the 1930s, when it burned to the waterline. It sank near an island off the north side of Key West; the island became known as Wisteria Island. (Courtesy of Monroe County Library, Key West.)

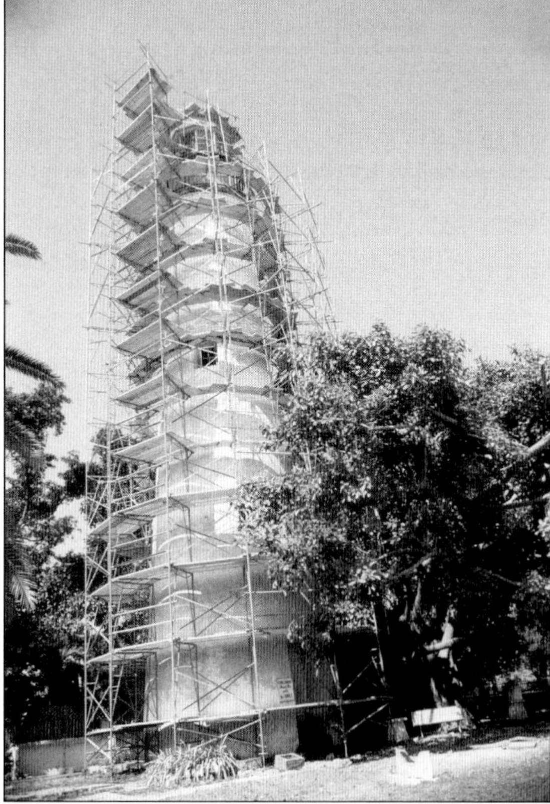

Lighthouses require consistent maintenance. In the 1980s, the Key West lighthouse needed major restoration due to damage to the bricks, water incursion, and cracking. Not only did the light undergo repair and replacement of degraded brick but it also saw its outbuildings (including the keeper's quarters) restored as well. The Key West Art & Historical Society maintains the property as a museum. (Courtesy of Monroe County Library, Key West.)

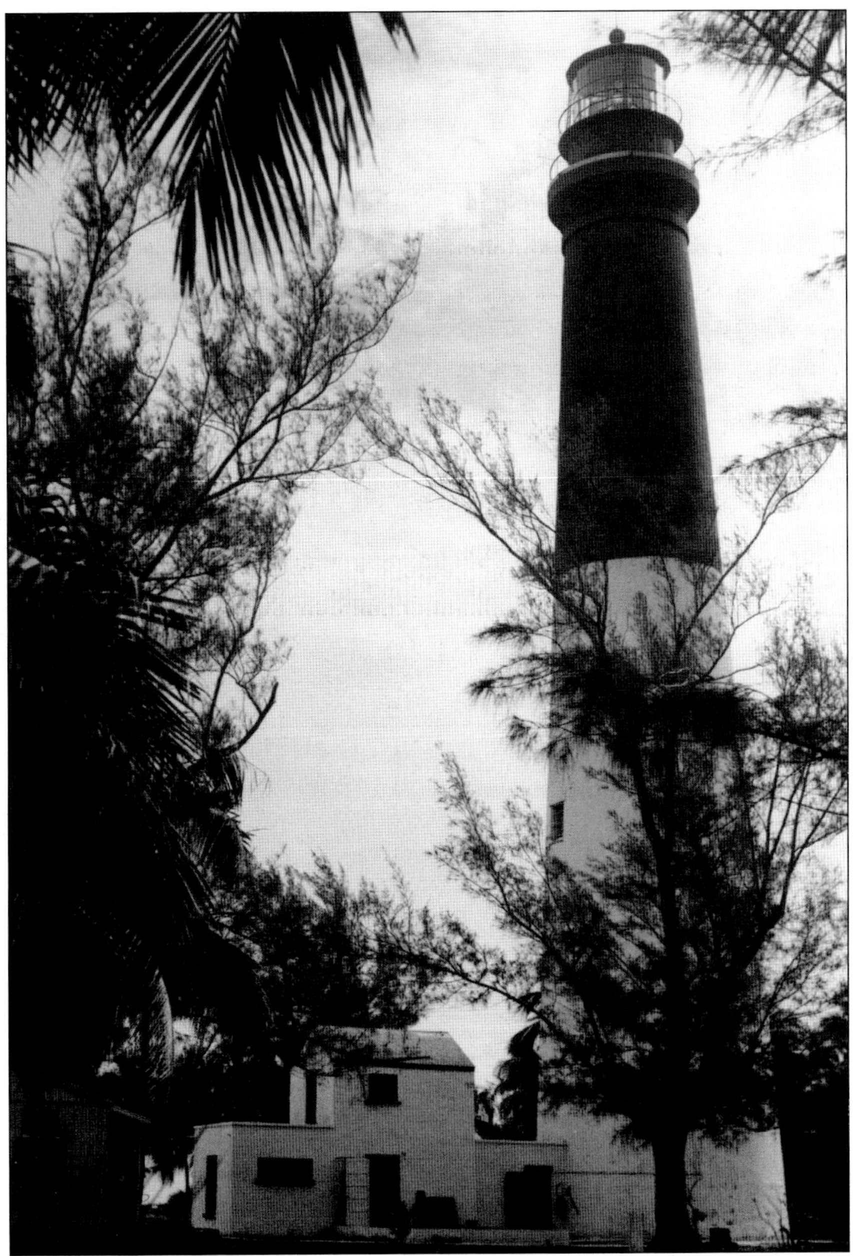

Loggerhead Key witnessed a number of developments in the first decade of the 20th century. In 1905, the Carnegie Institution of Washington established a marine biology lab on the northern side of the island; by 1908, the Dry Tortugas were designated a wildlife refuge, particularly to protect bird life. According to a 2009 historic structure report, a 1910 hurricane that swept across the Florida Keys damaged the light's lantern—as well as the lab and a wharf—and destroyed much of the vegetation. The Henry Lapaute company of France manufactured a new clamshell (or bivalve) lens for the Loggerhead Key lighthouse (officially known as the Dry Tortugas Light). The rotating lens created a white flash. The lens and lighthouse suffered damage from a hurricane in 1919 and from lightening in 1926. In the 1920s, lighthouse keepers, including those at Loggerhead Key, got their first radios. (Courtesy of Monroe County Library, Key West.)

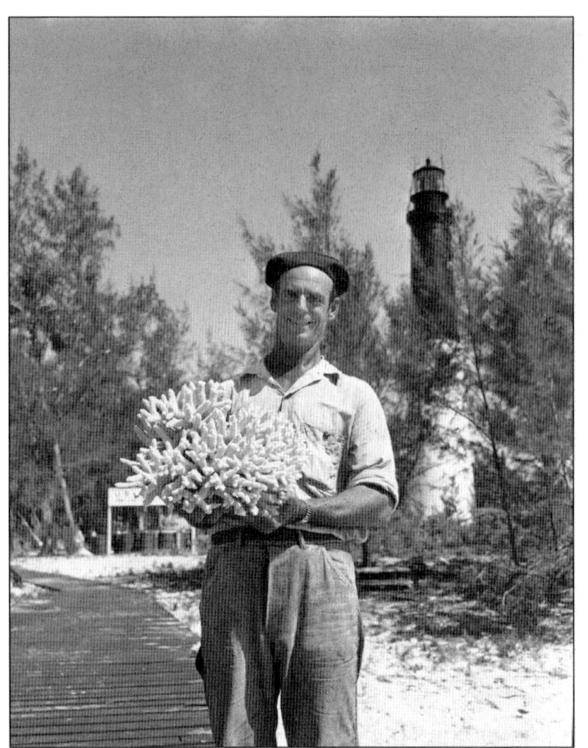

A Coast Guardsman poses in front of the Loggerhead Key lighthouse. Starting in 1939, the Coast Guard took over the US Lighthouse Service. During World War II, in order to frustrate Nazi U-boats, Florida Reef lights were dimmed, including Loggerhead Key's. In the 1980s, its clamshell lens was removed and replaced with a Directional Code Beacon DCB-24 that created a flashing light every 20 seconds. (Courtesy of the State Archives of Florida.)

This picture shows the keeper's quarters at Loggerhead Key. After the light's automation in 1987, volunteers and maintenance personnel continued to stay on the island to care for the light. In 1995, the old beacon was replaced with a Vega VRB-25 that created a flash every six seconds. The light went dark in 2014 and was decommissioned in 2015. (Courtesy of Monroe County Library, Key West.)

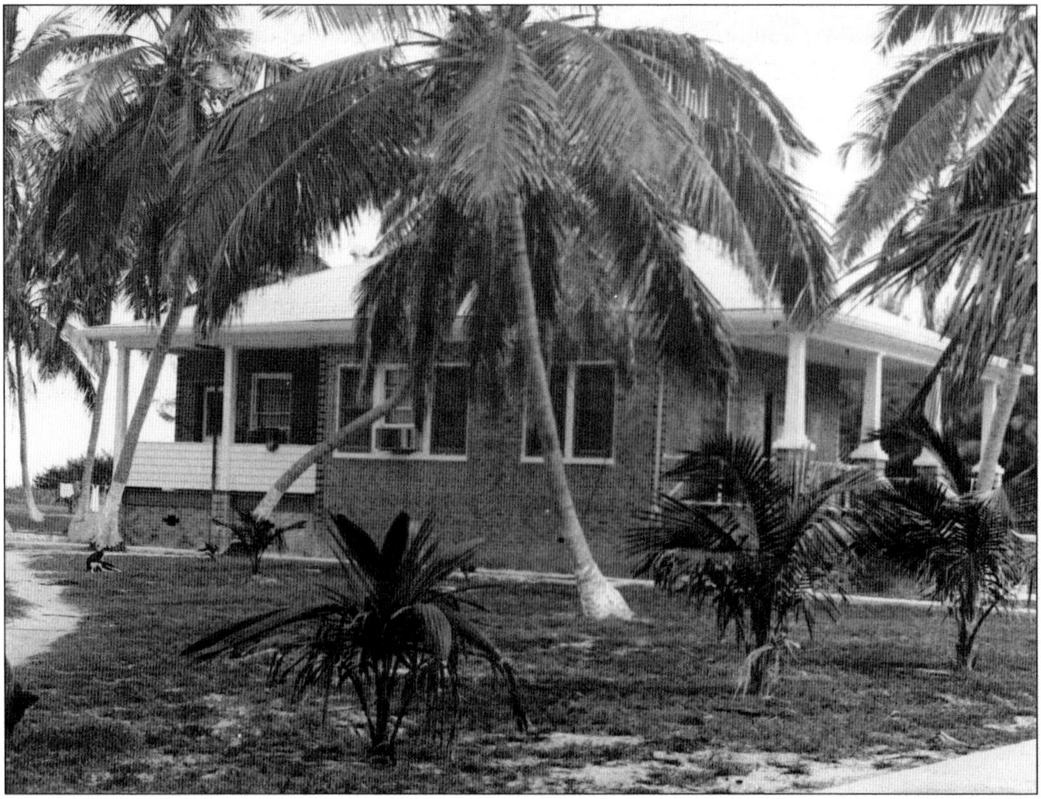

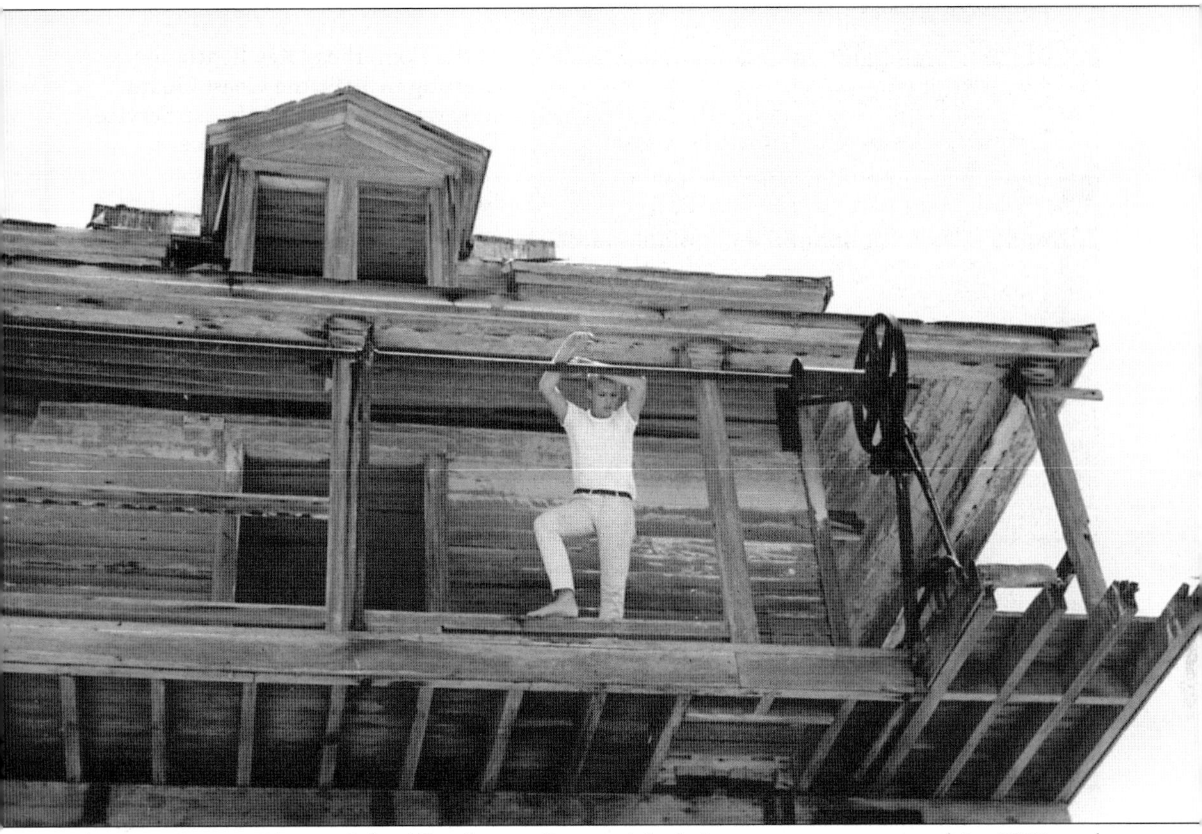

The Northwest Channel (or Northwest Passage) lighthouse was automated in 1913 and decommissioned in June 1921. Stories claim that Ernest Hemingway used the abandoned lighthouse as a writing retreat, but historian Tom Hambright doubts this was the case: "Hemingway was a very disciplined writer and would normally write the first thing in the morning." However, Hemingway knew the light from his many outings in *Pilar*. Over the decades, the wooden structure deteriorated, as its weathered appearance in this photograph attests. Traces of paint still cling to the timber; beams on the far right have broken off. In August 1971, the Coast Guard received a call about a fire in the Northwest Channel. By the time a 40-foot vessel arrived at the site, the lighthouse "was completely up in flames and out of control," according to a report in the *Key West Citizen*. The crew saw a small craft traveling away from the fiery scene. The boat was never located, and the cause of the fire remains a mystery. Only the lighthouse's supports and platform remained. (Courtesy of Monroe County Library, Key West.)

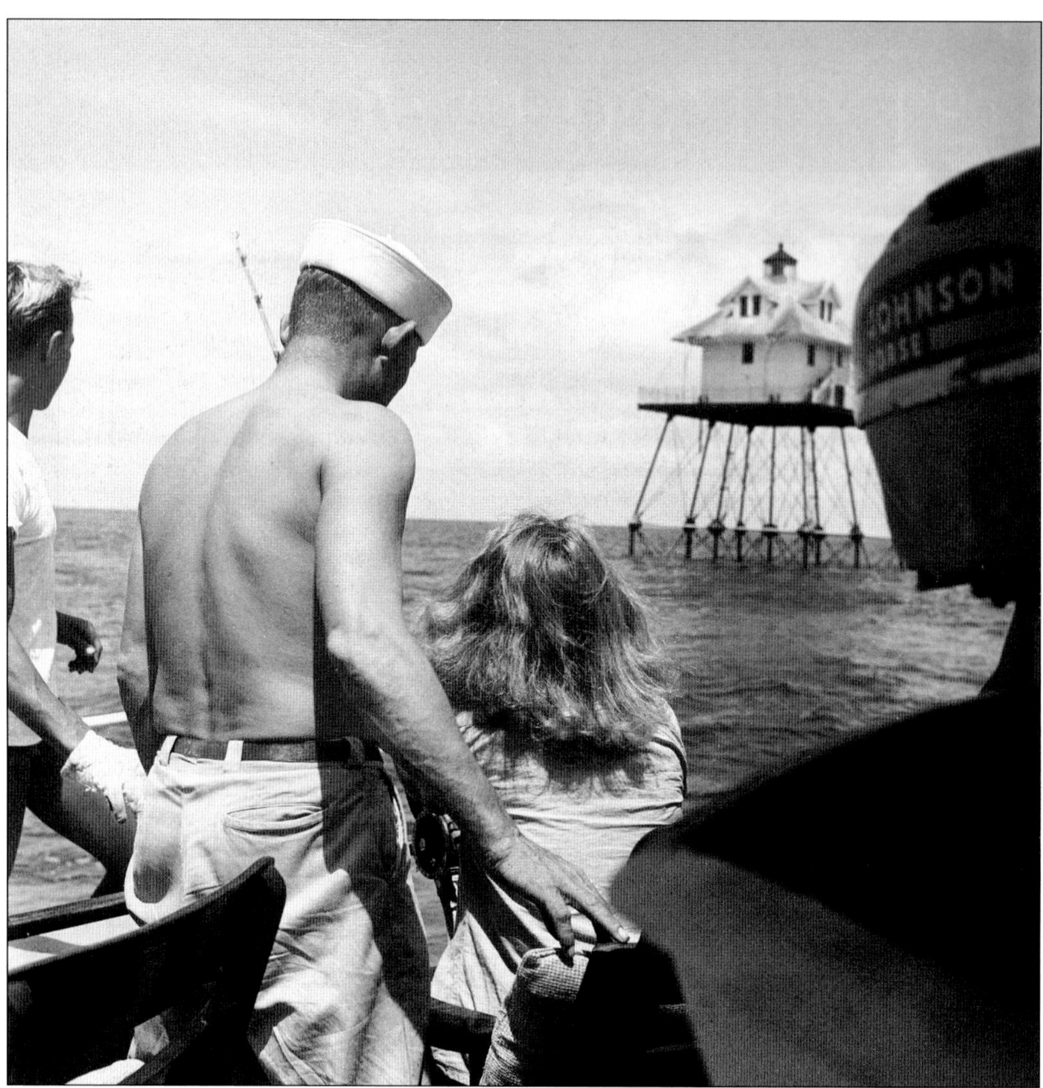

This photograph by Joseph Steinmetz shows his daughter fishing near the Rebecca Shoal lighthouse. The three-story cottage-style lighthouse endured intense weather from its first lighting in 1886. Located 43 miles west of Key West, the lighthouse was a challenging assignment; one assistant keeper died there in 1902, perhaps after a nervous breakdown, while another keeper met his death there in 1903. After automation in 1925, the lighthouse fell into disrepair and was further defaced by vandals. By 1953, the structure was considered a hazard and disassembled, with its lantern purchased by a scrap iron dealer. Incredibly, a resident of Key Largo later came across the Rebecca Shoal lantern and bought it. He had a decorative lighthouse constructed on his property to house the historic artifact. As for the original site, all the pilings there were removed and an automated beacon installed. (Courtesy of the State Archives of Florida.)

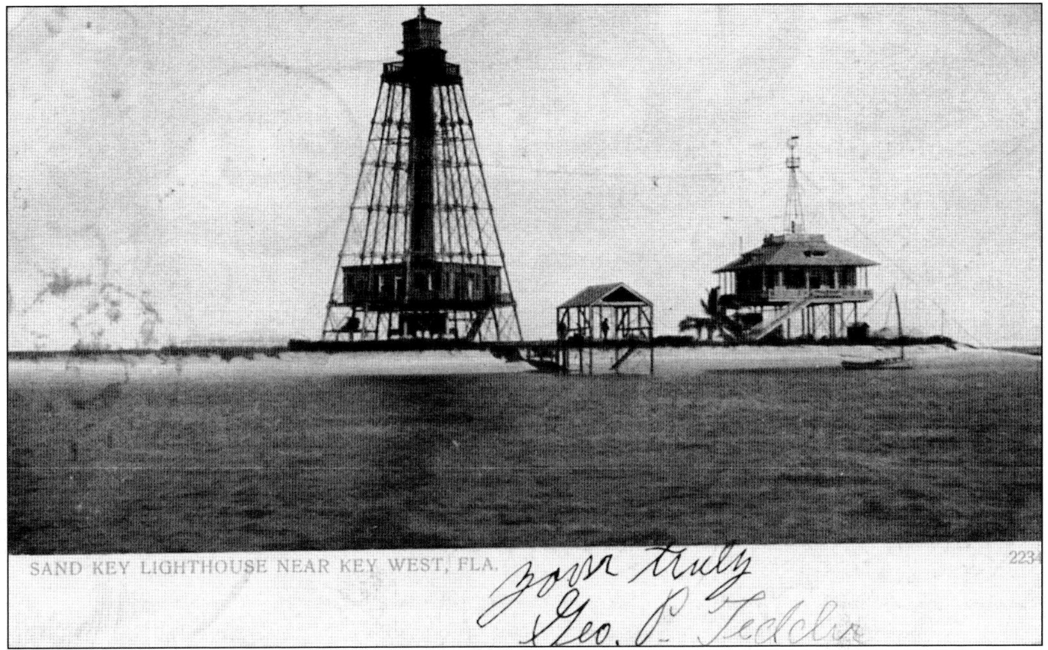

In the early 20th century, a weather station stood on Sand Key near the lighthouse. The station was enough of a technological novelty that this photograph was turned into a postcard that reads "Sand Key Near Key West, Fla." Also visible in the picture is a covered wharf. (Courtesy of Monroe County Library, Key West.)

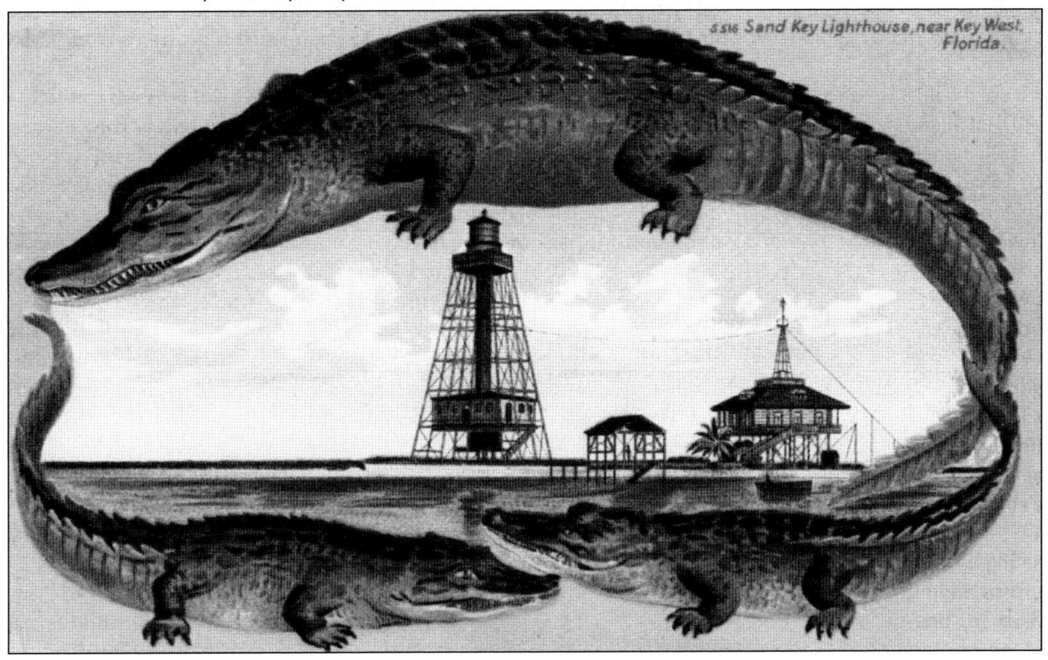

This souvenir postcard illustrates the Sand Key lighthouse, the weather station, the radio beacon, the wharf, and a small boat. Three alligators with sharp teeth and gleaming eyes surround the image. There were a number of alligator postcards issued for various Florida attractions, whether or not the locale had any gators. (Courtesy of Monroe County Library, Key West.)

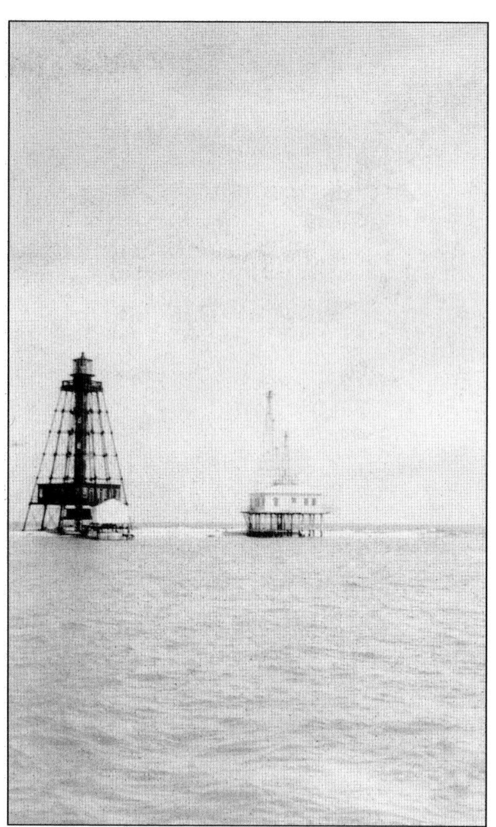

In 1909, Sand Key experienced a hurricane with a storm surge that rose 20 feet; winds and water destroyed all but the lighthouse itself. Structures must have been rebuilt quickly, because in 1910, yet another hurricane washed away an outhouse, a wharf, and a boathouse. One can also see that, compared to the previous photograph, the key itself has shrunk considerably. (Courtesy of the National Archives.)

In this photograph, Sand Key's weather station has been damaged by the 1919 hurricane and its tall antenna toppled. After hurricanes demolished it at least twice in the early 20th century, the weather station was rebuilt. Although the lighthouse suffered damage, including broken windowpanes and braces, the 19th-century light endured. (Courtesy of Jerry Wilkinson.)

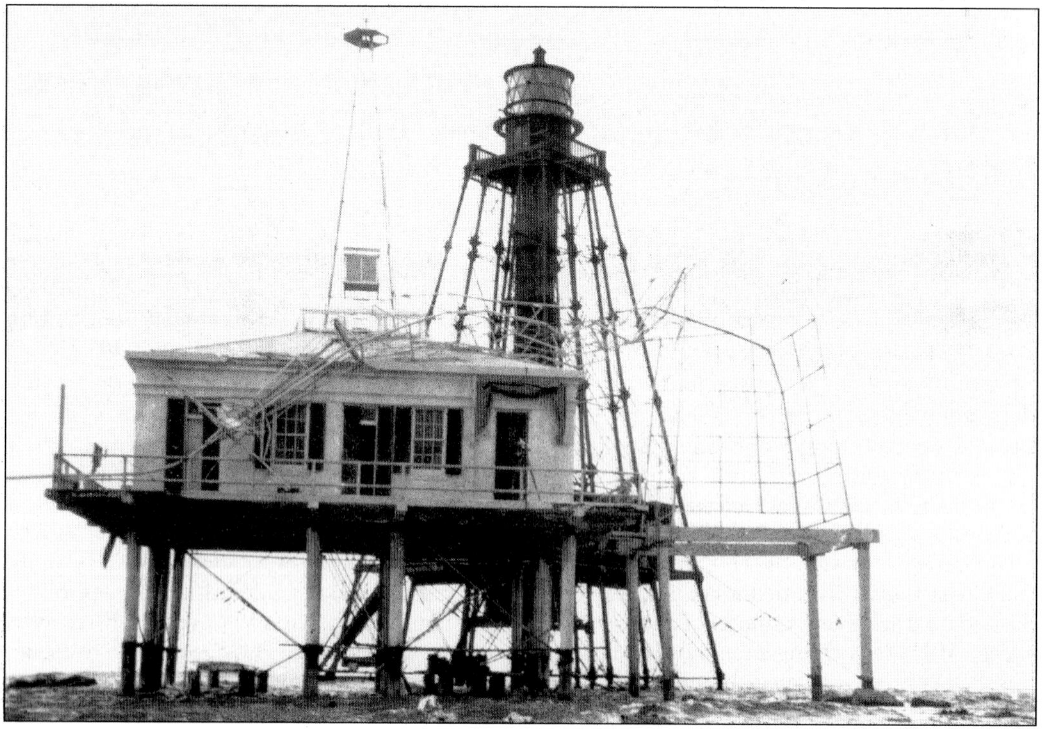

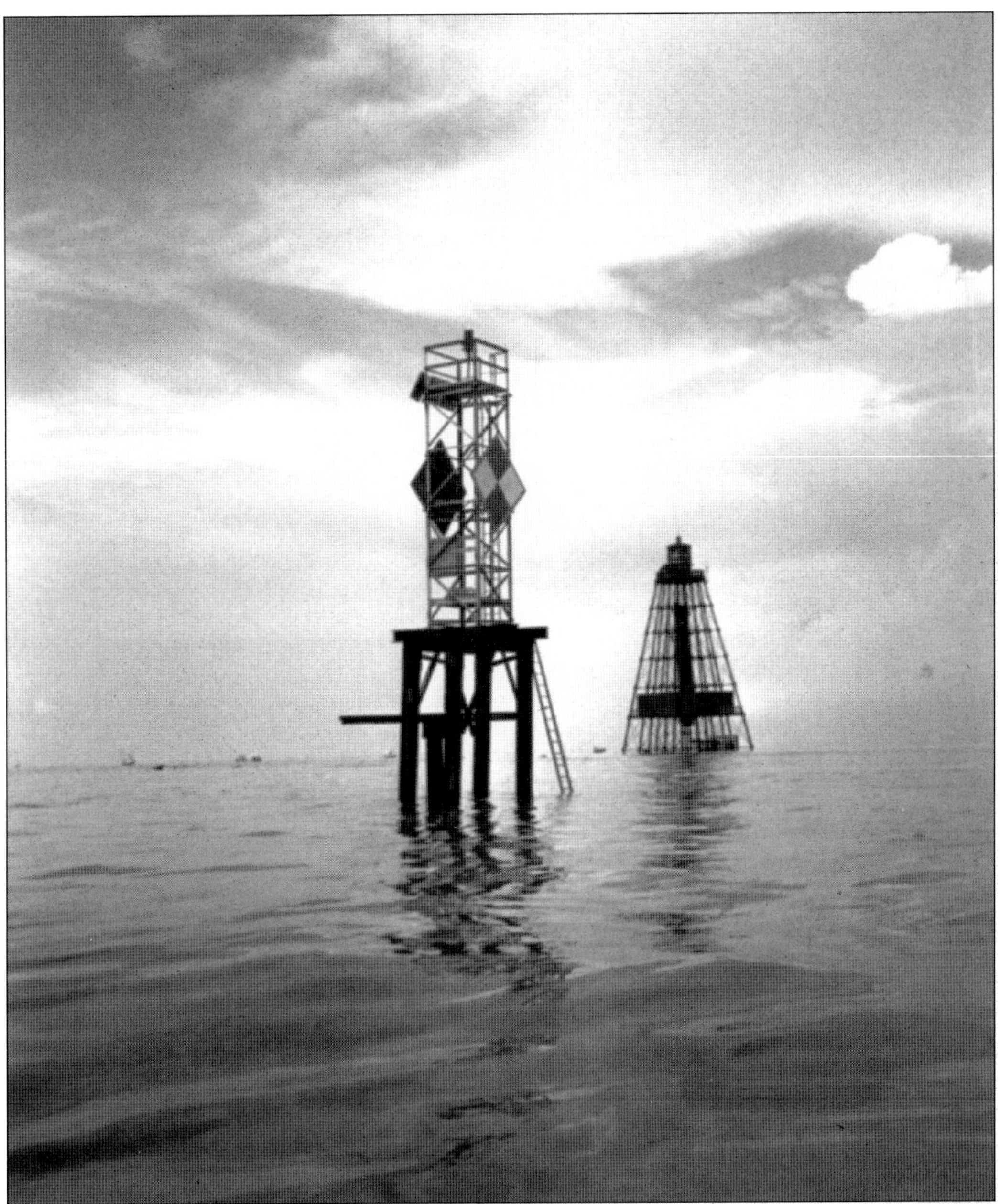

Keepers were no longer needed at Sand Key as of 1941, when the light was automated with a system that used acetylene gas. It kept its Fresnel lens until 1967, when it received a fourth-order lens. Then three different systems were installed over the years, including a flash tube array, a 300-millimeter flashing optic, and a 190-millimeter rotating lantern, all of which were powered by solar-charged batteries. In 1989, a fire decimated the lighthouse's quarters and stairwell. Afterwards, the Coast Guard installed a beacon (pictured here) near the light, a 300-millimeter optic that flashed 60 times every minute. Like other Florida Reef lighthouses, Sand Key eventually received a Vega VRB-25 rotating beacon; this flashed white every 15 seconds. The Sand Key lighthouse was ultimately deactivated in 2014, and the US government sold the light for $83,000 at auction in 2020. (Courtesy of Monroe County Library, Key West.)

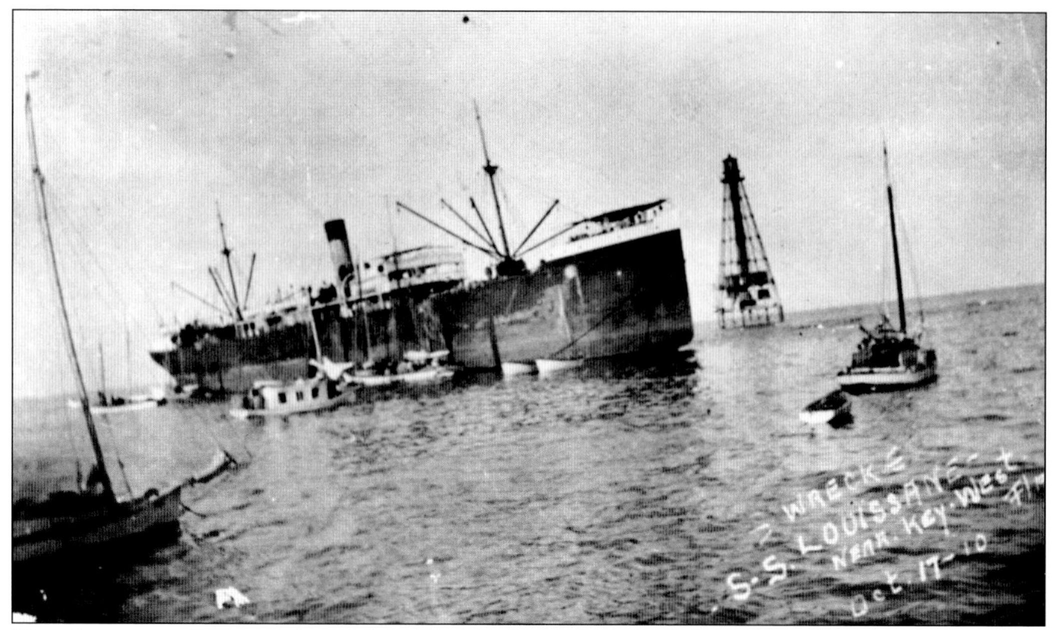

This dramatic 1910 image shows the French steamer *Louisiane* grounded 150 yards from Sombrero Key lighthouse. While en route to Havana, the ship was blown by hurricane-force winds onto the reef, "driven so high . . . that it will be impossible to float her until she has been stripped completely," according to the *Register and Defense Times*. Fortunately, the 548 passengers and the crew were rescued. (Courtesy of Monroe County Library, Key West.)

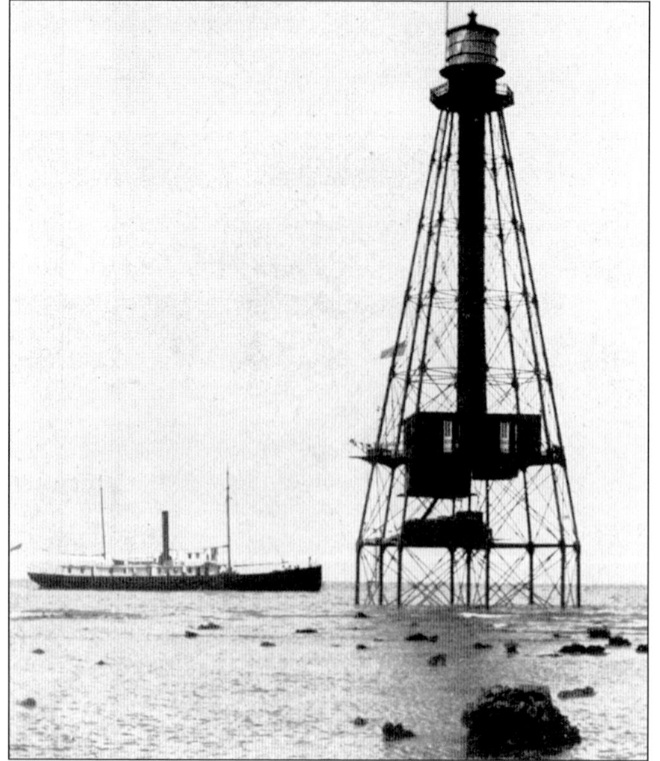

Here, a lighthouse tender (a vessel designed to maintain and supply lighthouses) approaches the Sombrero Key lighthouse in the Middle Keys. In 1912, the Lighthouse Board upgraded its oil-wick lamps with an incandescent oil-vapor system. As of 1939, Coast Guardsmen tended to the lighthouse, and they would do so until 1960. (Courtesy of Monroe County Library, Key West.)

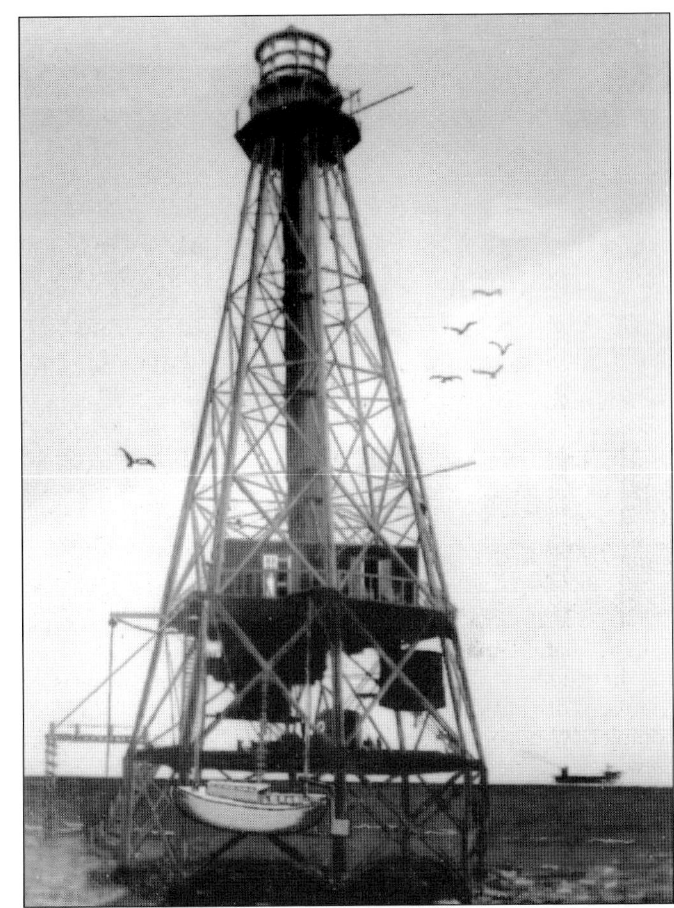

These images show the Sombrero Key lighthouse and its very small "double ender" craft. Keepers faced all kinds of dangers at Sombrero Key; some lost their lives while in service. In the 19th century, Richard White, Martin Weatherford, and Michael Eickoff died; in the 20th century, John Anderson and Willis Parker perished. Parker died in 1959, one year before the light's automation. Hurricane Donna crushed the Middle Keys in September 1960. Incredibly, the Coast Guardsmen kept the light lit; despite winds over 145 miles per hour and massive storm surge, the Sombrero Key lighthouse, its keepers, and the keepers' quarters survived. Fuel tanks and a platform were destroyed. According to author Love Dean, "Once onshore, the Coast Guardsmen swore they would never go back to the light and proceeded to get drunk." (Both, courtesy of Jerry Wilkinson.)

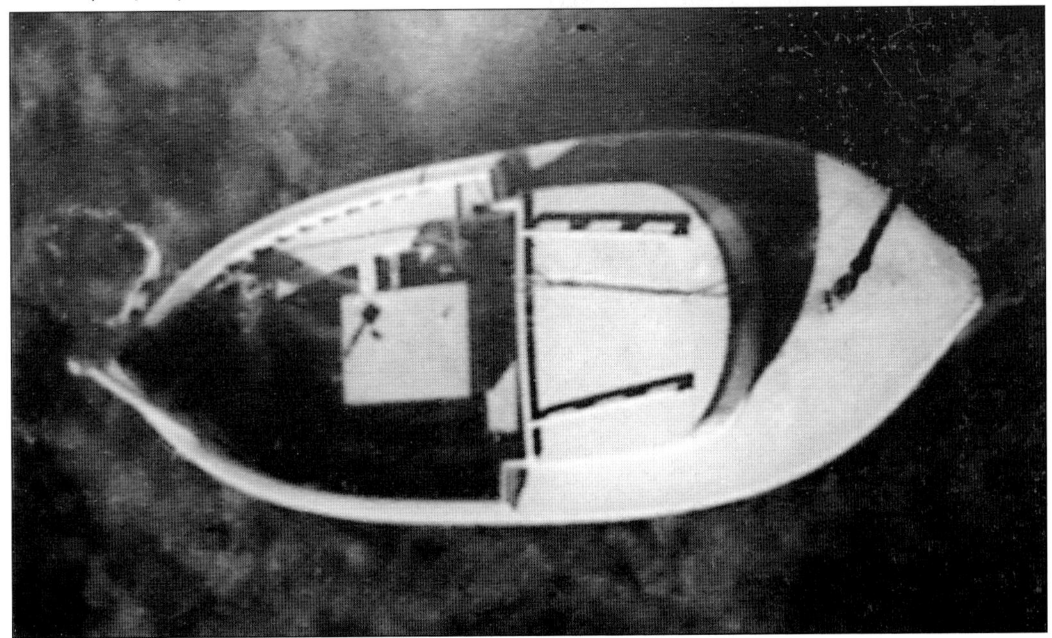

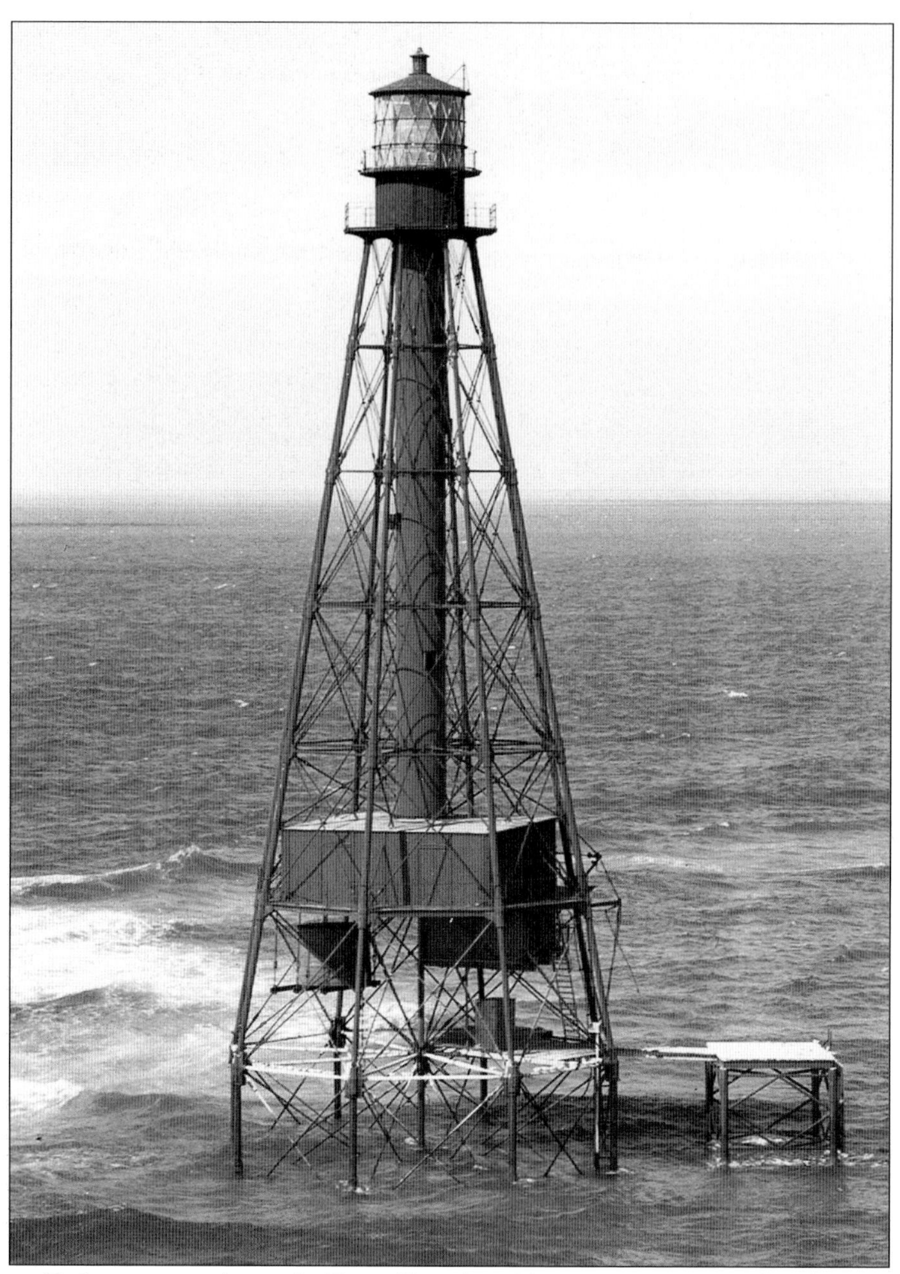

Sombrero Key's impressive first-order Fresnel lens from Henry Lapaute was replaced in 1982; flash tube arrays, then 300-millimeter lamps, and finally 190-millimeter optics were each tried in turn, similar to the pattern at Sand Key lighthouse. Then a Vega VRB-25 was installed. It featured five lights that flashed white every 60 seconds, with three red sectors. The 1858 lighthouse, whose construction was overseen by George Gordon Meade, was decommissioned and went dark in 2015. Although people are not permitted to climb onto the light, divers, snorkelers, and boaters regularly visit Sombrero Key to appreciate the corals and one of the most impressive lights constructed to protect mariners along the Florida Reef. It stands within the Sombrero Key Sanctuary Preservation Area, where fishing, anchoring, and touching the corals are strictly prohibited. (Courtesy of the US Lighthouse Society Archives.)

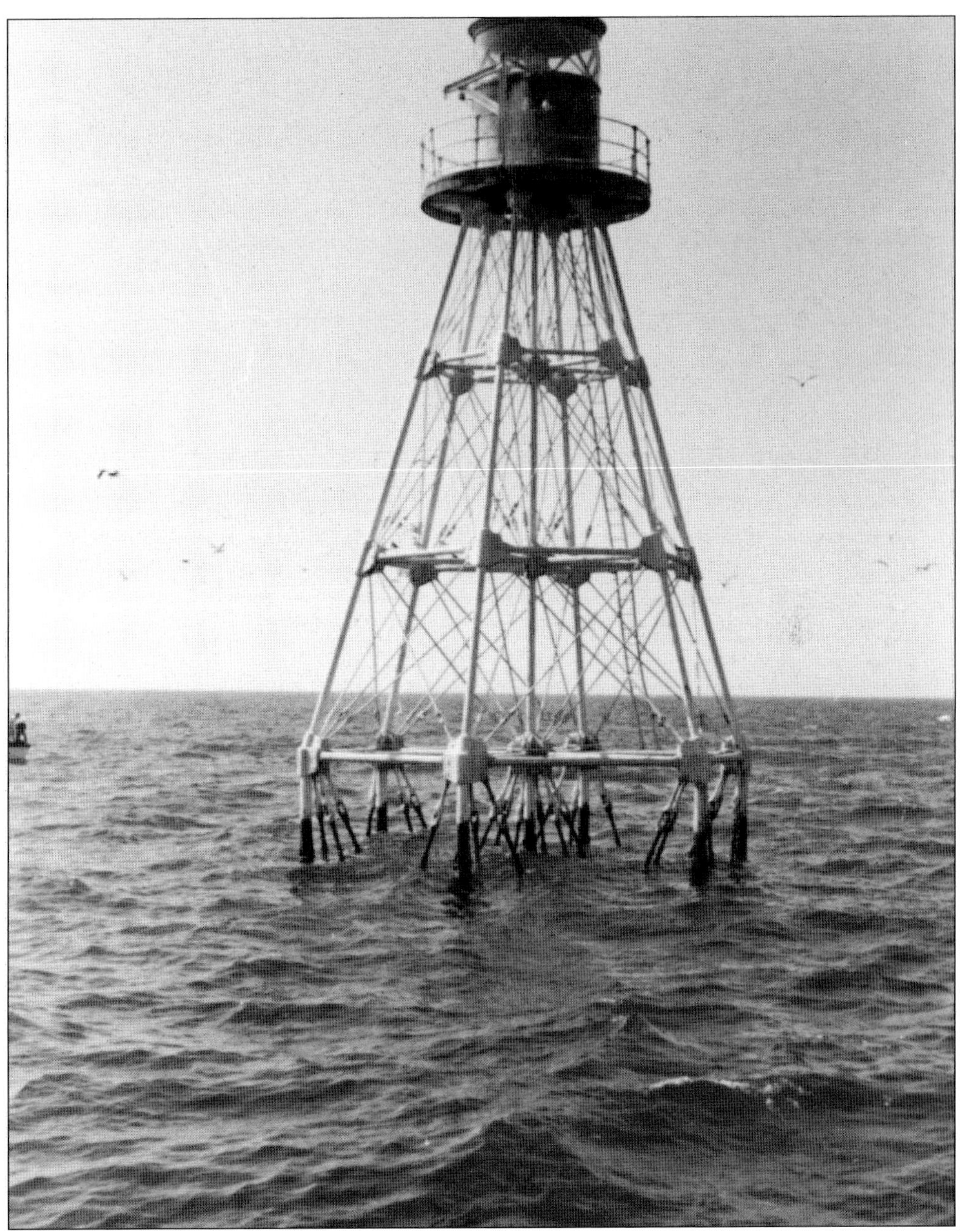

Between 1921 and 1935, the Lighthouse Board installed a series of automated lights in the Florida Keys. These were not lighthouses, although their form does bear a strong resemblance to some of the Florida Reef lights; they were secured with screwpiles as well. The first two were erected at Molasses Reef and Pacific Reef. (The Pacific Reef lantern is today on display in Islamorada at Founders Park.) Another was placed at Hens and Chickens Shoal in 1929, and in 1933, one placed at Smith Shoal (pictured here). The Smith Shoal tower has been removed. In 1933, a light was installed at Tennessee Reef, and two more were built in 1935, one at Cosgrove Shoal and one at Pulaski Shoal. They were shorter than the lighthouses (approximately 35 to 49 feet) and had a smaller range. The development of these lights reflects that era's greater trend toward automation. (Courtesy of Monroe County Library, Key West.)

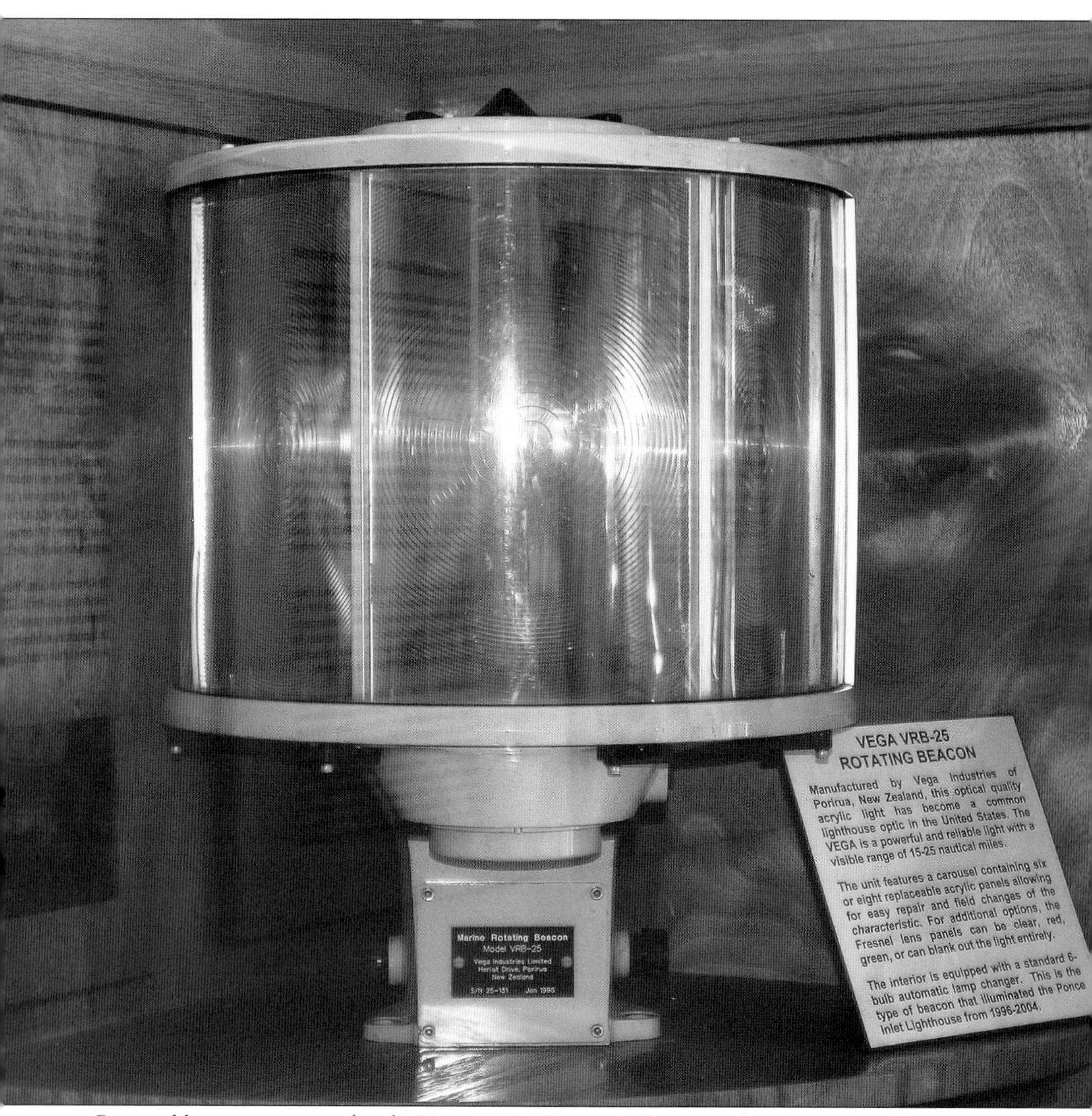

Pictured here is an example of a Vega VRB-25 rotating beacon; these automated beacons were installed at a number of Florida Keys lighthouses in the 20th century. This one came from the Ponce Inlet lighthouse in Florida, where it operated from 1996 to 2004. The beacons were developed and manufactured by the Vega company of New Zealand. As the display explains, "The VEGA is a powerful and reliable light with a visible range of 15–25 nautical miles. The unit features a carousel containing six or eight replaceable acrylic panels allowing for easy repair and field changes of the characteristic. For additional options, the Fresnel lens panels can be clear, red, green, or can blank out the light entirely. The interior is equipped with a standard 6-bulb automatic lamp charger." (Photograph by Tom Tag, courtesy of the US Lighthouse Society Archives.)

Nine

Lighthouses as Destinations

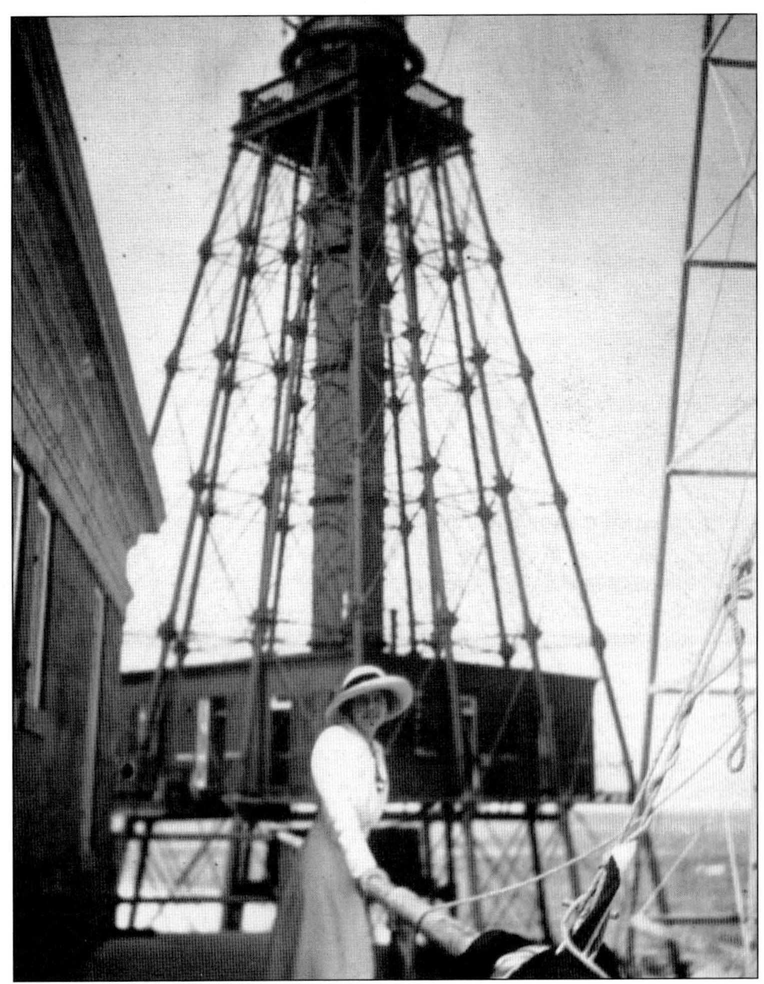

Even when the Florida Reef lighthouses still functioned as active aids to navigation, certain of the lights became destinations or attractions for visitors. People were and are fascinated by the immensity of the structures, their often remote locations, their beauty, and their history. Tourists and locals have been especially drawn to the lighthouses at Sand Key, Fort Jefferson, and Key West. (Courtesy of Monroe County Library, Key West.)

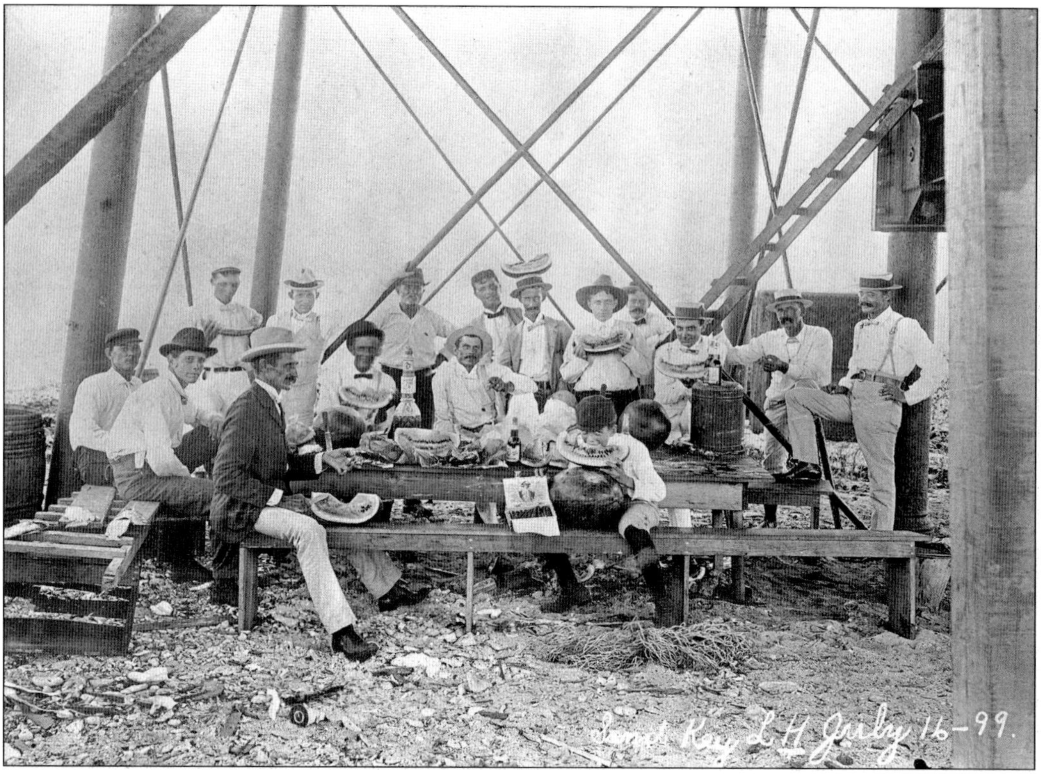

Sand Key L.H. July 16-99.

In 1899, when casual photographs were not as ubiquitous as they are today, people still hammed it up for the camera. Here a group of men and a boy appear to be eating giant slices of melon under the Sand Key lighthouse. One man even manages to balance a slice on his hat. There are also bottles of liquid refreshment and cigars. (Courtesy of the State Archives of Florida.)

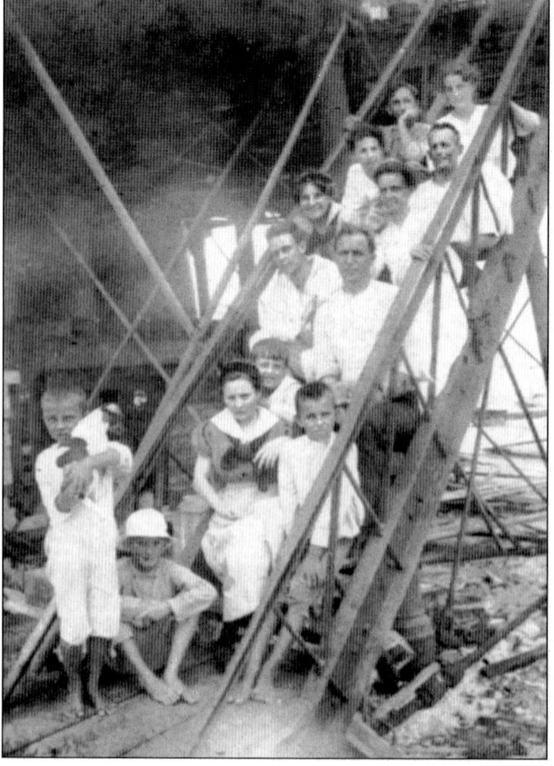

Located six nautical miles from Key West, Sand Key made for an exciting outing for Key Westers. The lighthouse keepers welcomed the company and the possibility of fresh supplies. Children, men, women, and a family pet pose on the lower staircase in the early 1900s. (Courtesy of Monroe County Library, Key West.)

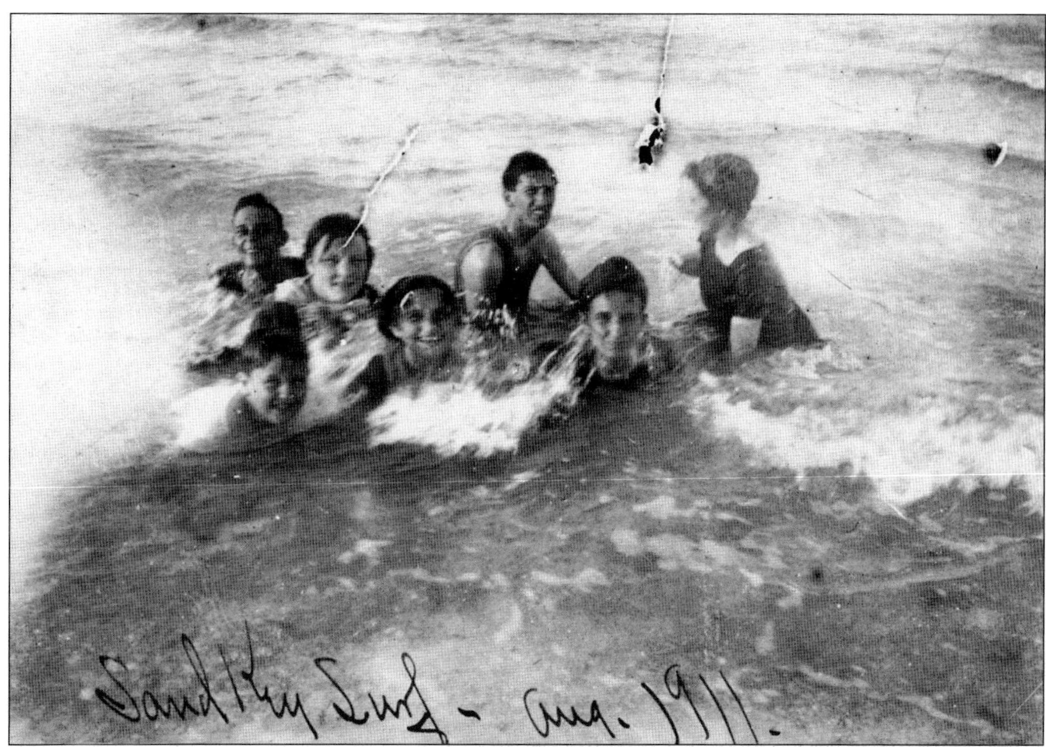

In 1911, swimmers grin for the camera in the surf off Sand Key. An outing to the island might involve visiting the lighthouse, enjoying a packed lunch, and cooling off in the ocean. Swimming was becoming increasingly popular in America; Key West had its own athletic club on the beach. (Courtesy of Monroe County Library, Key West.)

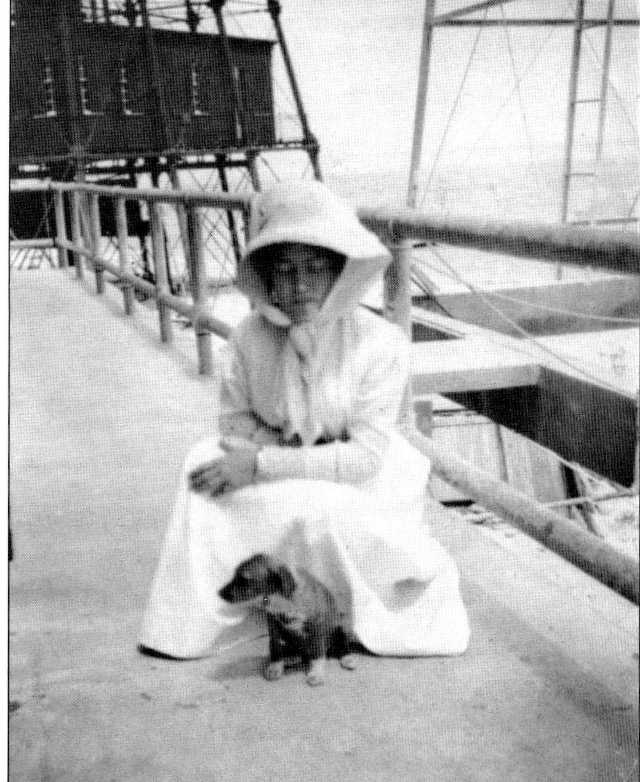

In this 1912 photograph, a visitor from Key West sits with a puppy; in the background are the cross-braces and keeper's quarters of the Sand Key lighthouse. The young woman may be posing at the weather station. Two years earlier, everything on the island except the lighthouse itself had been washed away during twin hurricanes, but structures were quickly rebuilt. (Courtesy of Monroe County Library, Key West.)

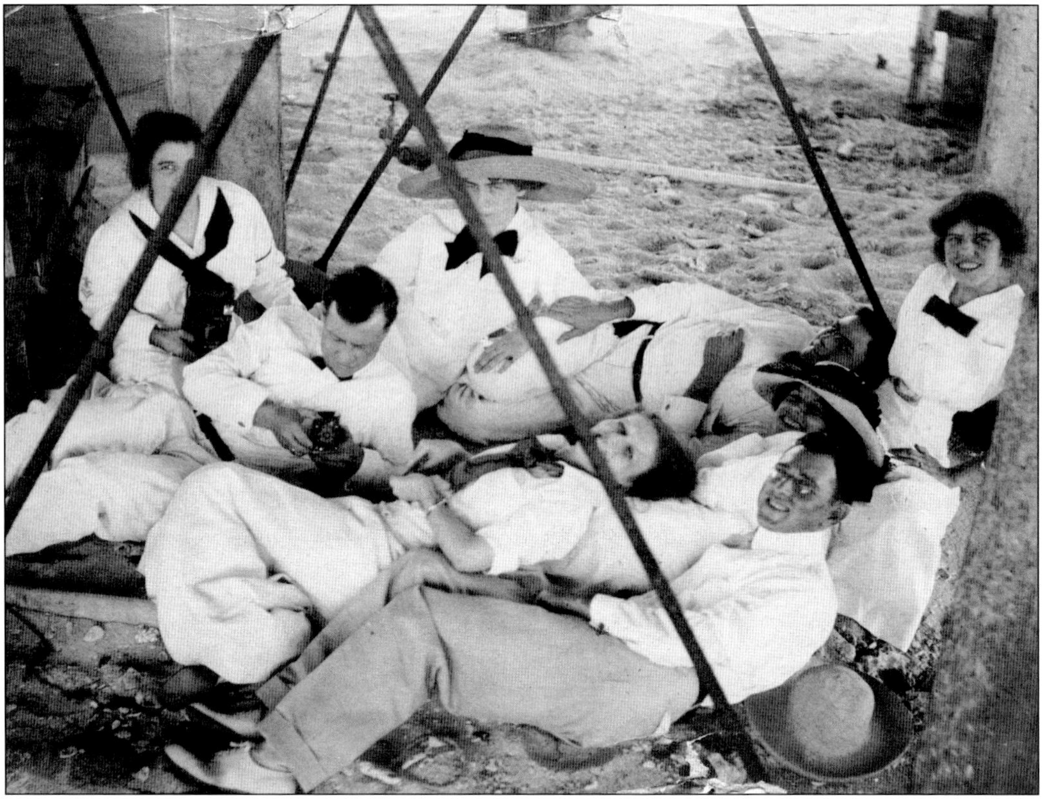

Another 1912 image was taken of young men and women collapsing with giggles under the Sand Key light. They are all dressed in white for the tropics, and a few have straw hats. It is a photography excursion? Both the man and woman on the far left hold cameras, and perhaps they are posing for a friend of theirs. (Courtesy of Monroe County Library, Key West.)

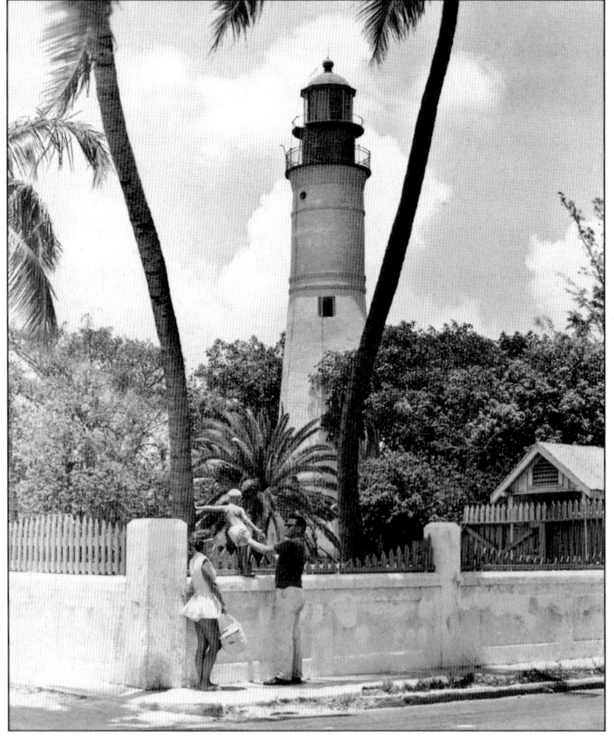

A family stands before the Key West lighthouse, the mother holding a picnic basket. Given the careful composition of the photograph, it may well have been taken as part of a tourism campaign to promote Key West. The lighthouse continued to be an island attraction and offered visitors a chance to explore an accessible, inland light. (Courtesy of the State Archives of Florida.)

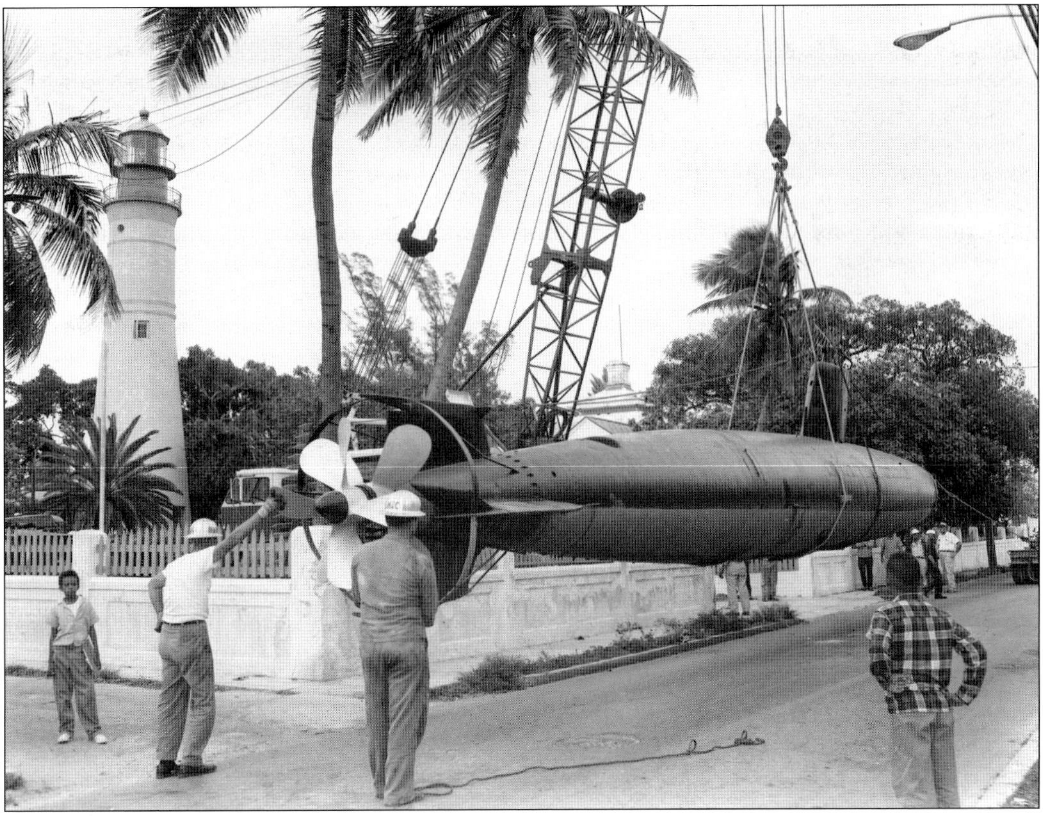

With the Coast Guard taking over the administration of American lighthouses, the Key West keeper's quarters ceased to be a family residence. The question then arose: what to do with the premises? The Coast Guard arranged for the Key West Art & Historical Society to rent the house, which became a military museum. One of the items on display was a miniature submarine, pictured here. (Courtesy of Monroe County Library, Key West.)

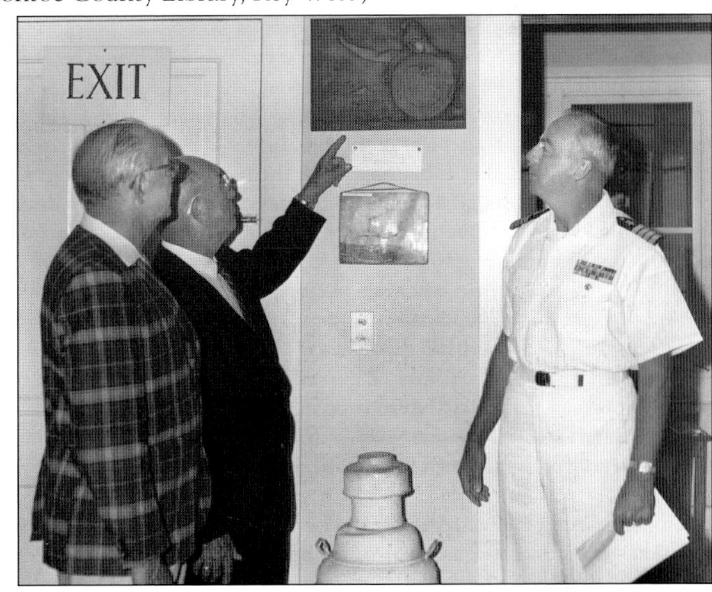

Colonel Stokes (left) and Capt. Francis Smith (center) inspect part of an exhibition inside the military museum, housed within the Key West lighthouse's keeper's quarters. Standing beside them is Capt. John Higgins, commanding officer of Key West's naval station from 1966 to 1968. A greater interest in historic preservation and the island's history began to take root in the late 1950s and 1960s. (Courtesy of Monroe County Library, Key West.)

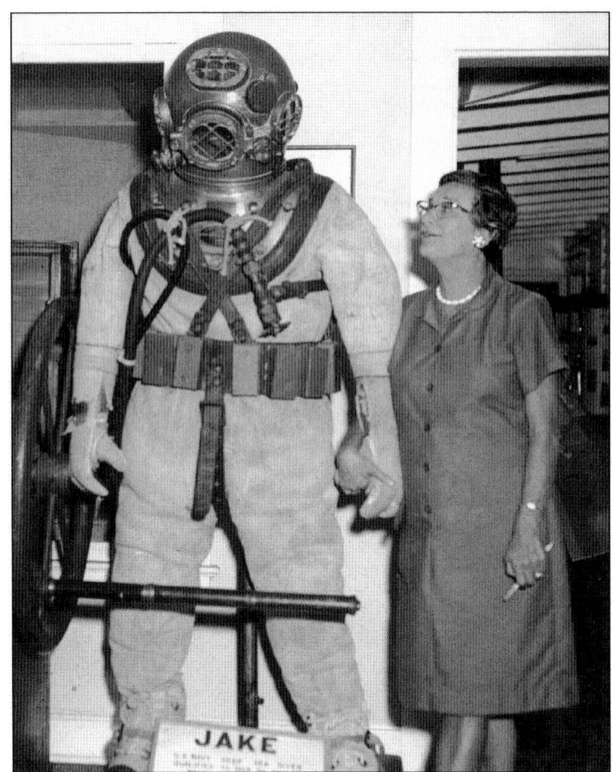

The military museum's curator, Francis Fuller, comically holds hands with "Jake," a diving suit and helmet displayed inside the former keeper's quarters at the Key West lighthouse. The museum also exhibited a jet fighter, models of aircraft, and photographs of Florida Keys lighthouses. (Courtesy of Monroe County Library, Key West.)

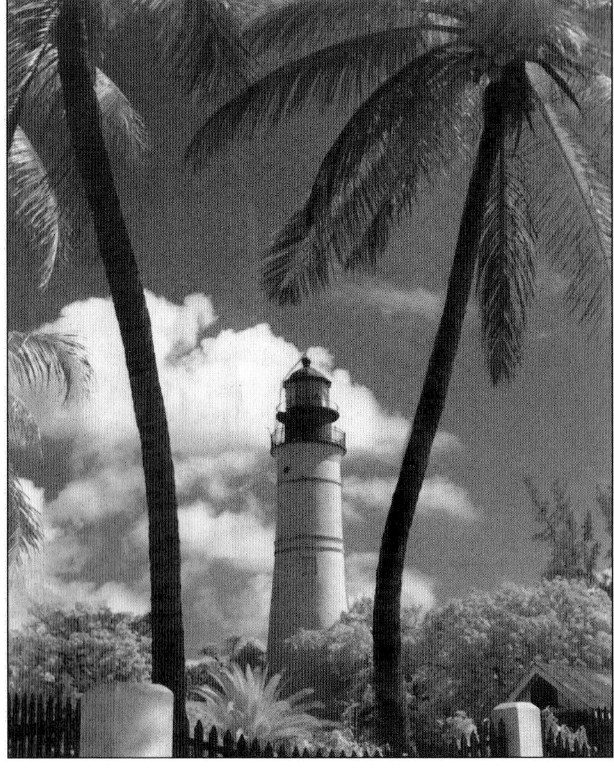

Once the Coast Guard decommissioned the Key West lighthouse in 1969, the tower itself became part of the military museum experience. In the 1980s, the lighthouse and quarters were restored, and the Key West Art & Historical Society reorganized the museum so that its focus was the history of the lighthouse and its keepers. Today, the museum continues to offer a fascinating glimpse into the past. (Courtesy of Monroe County Library, Key West.)

Sarasota photographer Joseph Steinmetz and Lois Foley Steinmetz pose in front of the Tortugas harbor light at Fort Jefferson in the Dry Tortugas. The island's diminutive size, the fort's distinctive brick arches, the tropical waters, and the unusual lighthouse make Garden Key an ideal spot for photography. (Courtesy of the State Archives of Florida.)

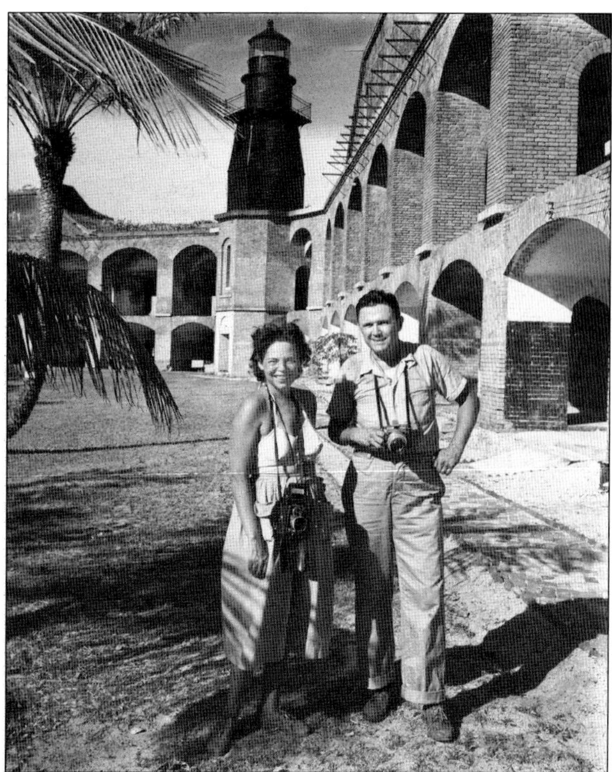

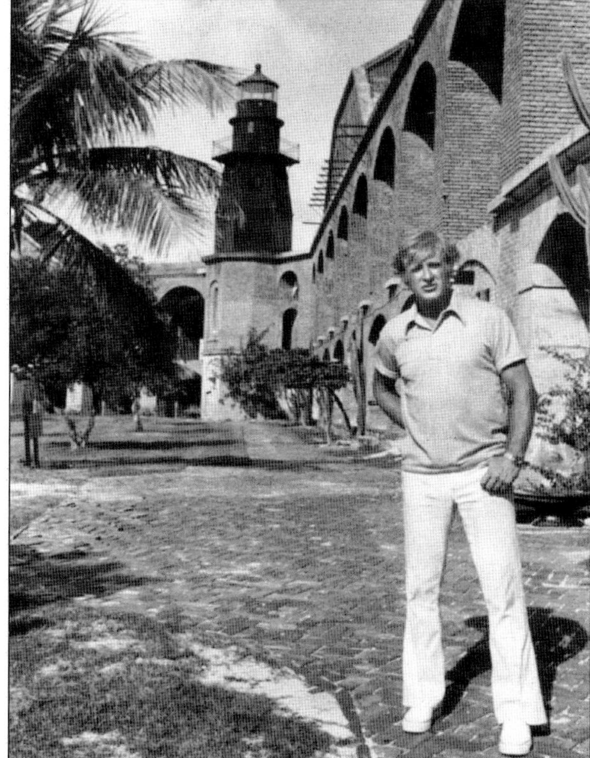

Actor Lloyd Bridges has posed in a similar location to the Steinmetzes in this 1970s photograph. As of 1970, Fort Jefferson was included in the National Register of Historic Places. Although Garden Key lies approximately 68 miles from Key West, it gradually became a popular tourism destination. (Courtesy of Monroe County Library, Key West.)

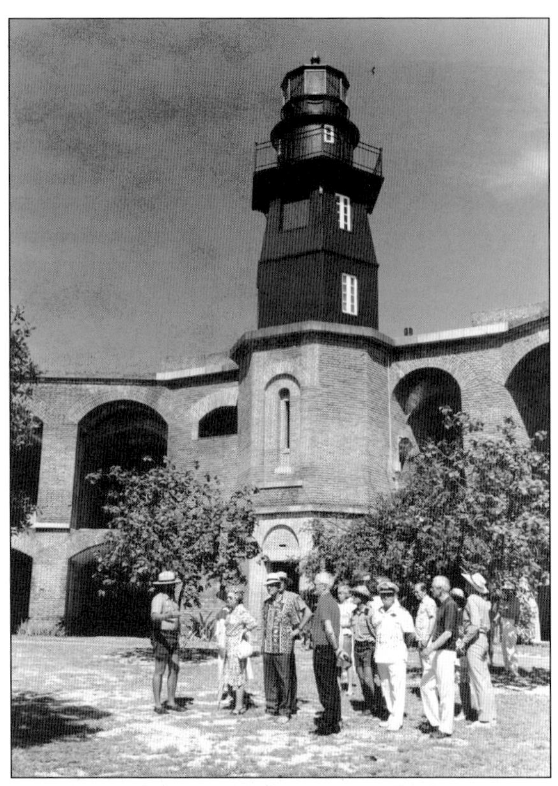

The harbor lighthouse at Fort Jefferson holds a special distinction: it has been visited by the Queen of England. In this 1991 photograph, park ranger Matt Fagan guides Queen Elizabeth II and Prince Philip through the historic property. On this intensely sunny May day, the Duke of Edinburgh wears a panama hat, and Her Majesty carries a parasol. (Courtesy of Monroe County Library, Key West.)

Queen Elizabeth and Prince Philip stand under the harbor light. The couple arrived at Fort Jefferson aboard the Royal Yacht *Britannia*. Behind the queen, barely visible, is a woman in a red shawl: Wilhelmina Harvey, the first female mayor of Monroe County. Harvey was known as the "Queen of the Conch Republic" and appropriately presented the English queen with a conch shell. (Courtesy of Monroe County Library, Key West.)

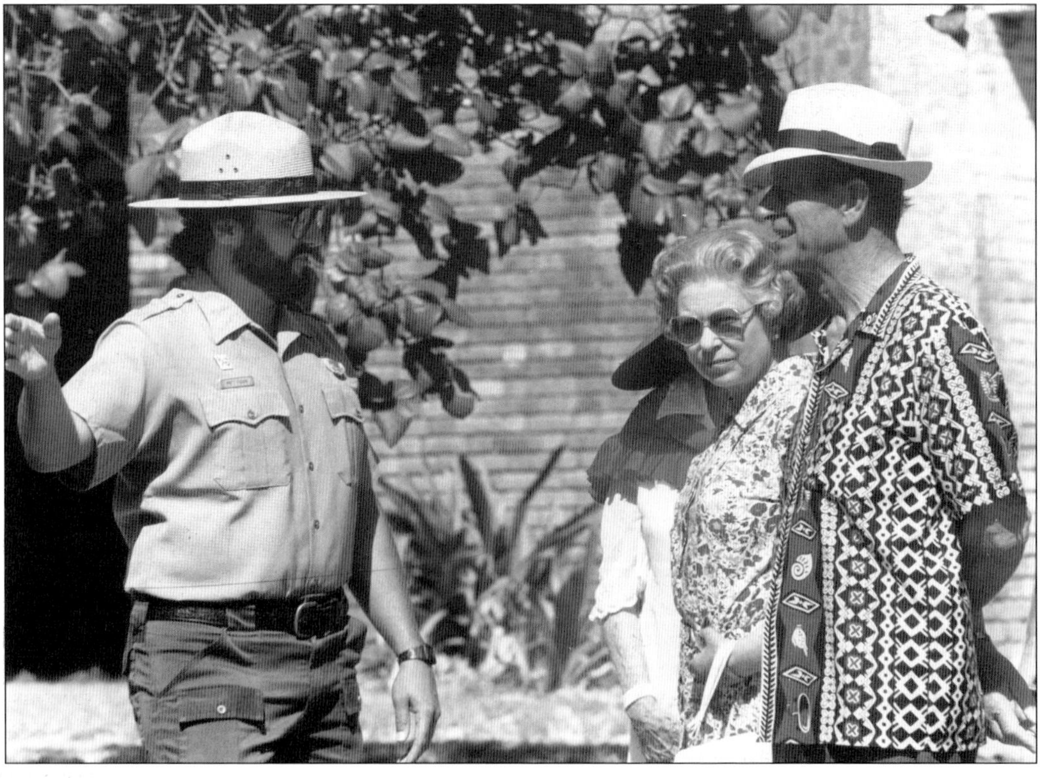

Ten

Private and Decorative Lighthouses

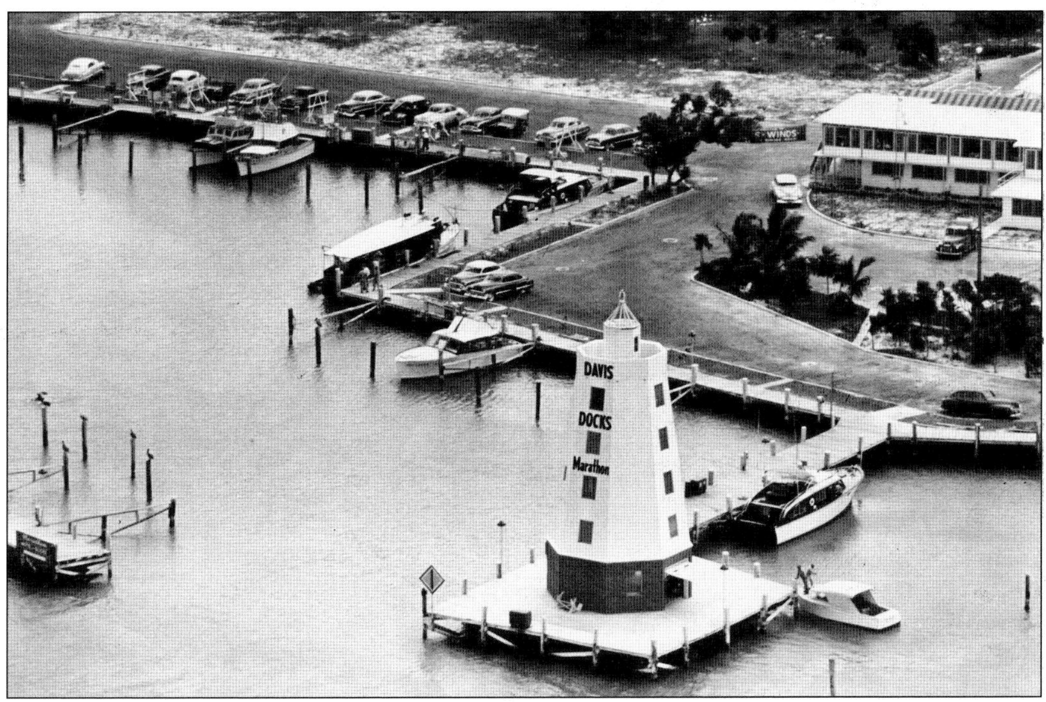

The US government built the Florida Keys lighthouses, from the Dry Tortugas to north of Key Largo. Yet private citizens have also erected their own lights. Sometimes these function as private aids to navigation; other structures were constructed as whimsical tributes to treasured Keys icons. The light pictured here illuminates the dockage at a resort in Marathon. (Courtesy of Monroe County Library, Key West.)

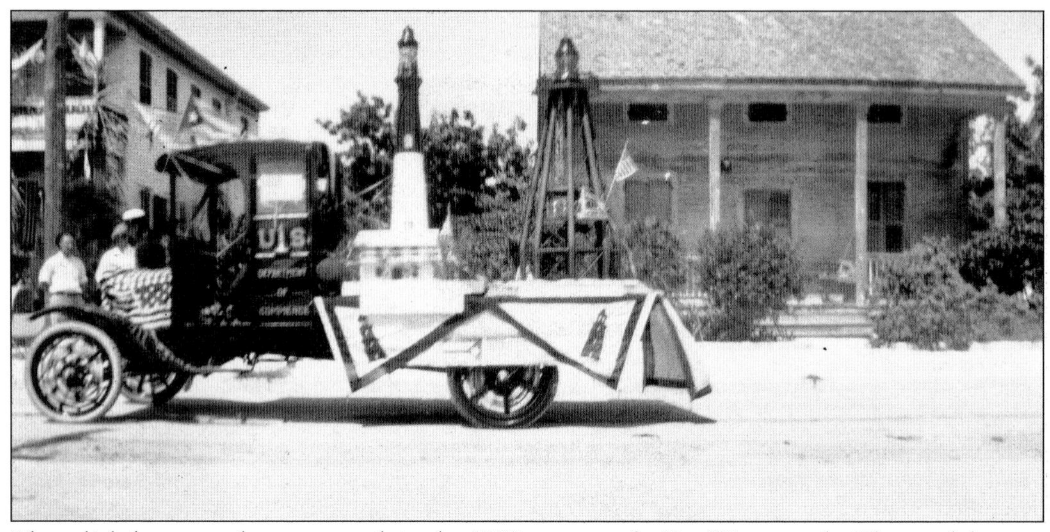

These lighthouses rode atop a truck in the 1920s as part of a Key West parade. The truck bears a lighthouse logo and the words "Department of Commerce," because at that time, the Lighthouse Board fell under that department's auspices. On the left is a model of Loggerhead Key's lighthouse in the Dry Tortugas and on the right the Sand Key light. (Courtesy of Monroe County Library, Key West.)

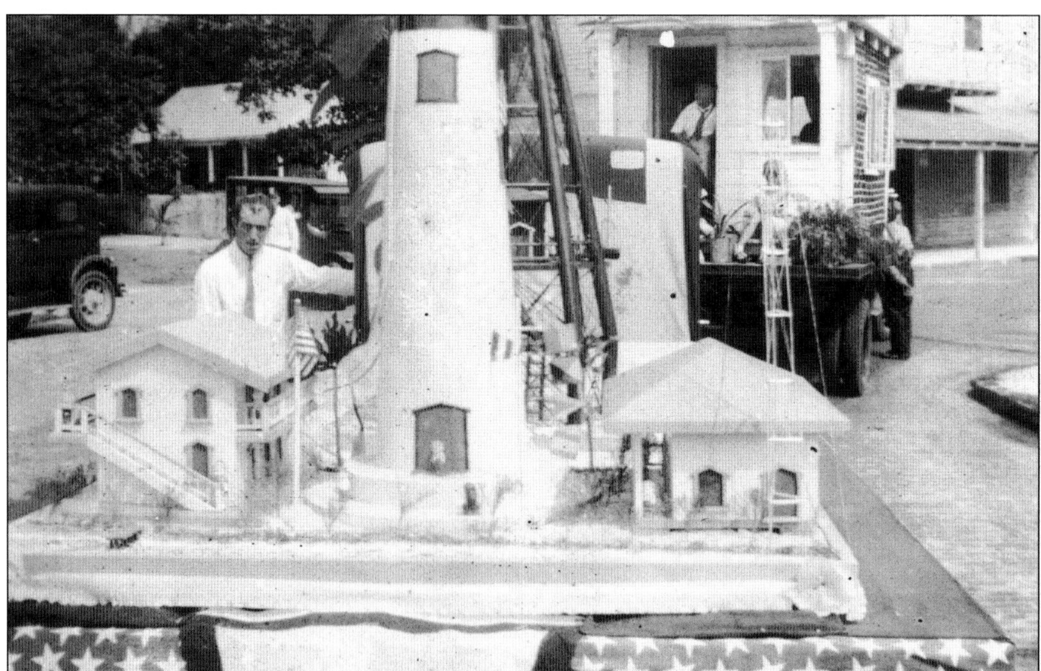

A rather harried-looking driver (left) warily surveys the tall lighthouse float on the back of the Department of Commerce truck. Here one can see the Loggerhead light's keeper's quarters to the left of the model. Judging from the photograph, the models stood approximately five to six feet tall. (Courtesy of Monroe County Library, Key West.)

In 1921, an automated lighthouse was installed on Pacific Reef in Biscayne Bay, approximately three miles southeast of Elliott Key. Pacific Reef was a screwpile light with a pyramidal, skeletal tower. The light's lantern was eventually removed and put on display in Founders Park in Islamorada. (Courtesy of Jerry Wilkinson.)

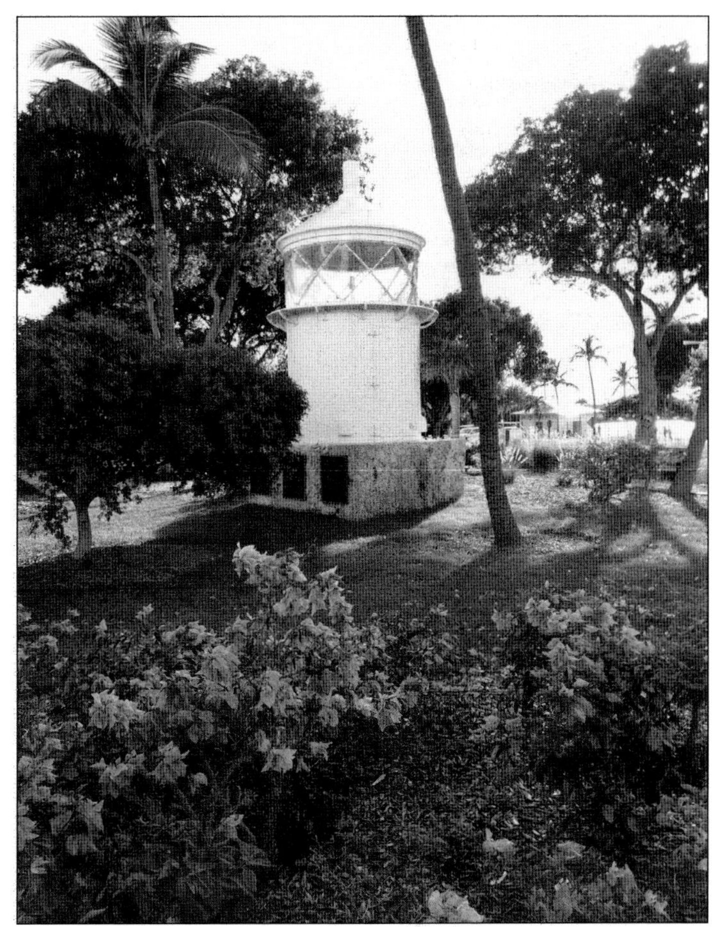

Floyd and Iva Storm Davis purchased property in Marathon in 1949 and constructed a resort, the Marathon Motel and Docks or, later, Davis Docks. Their lighthouse was completed in 1951. Later, the Davises sold the resort, and the new owners called the property Faro Blanco ("white lighthouse"). The lighthouse still exists and is a familiar sight to Middle Keys boaters. (Courtesy of Jerry Wilkinson.)

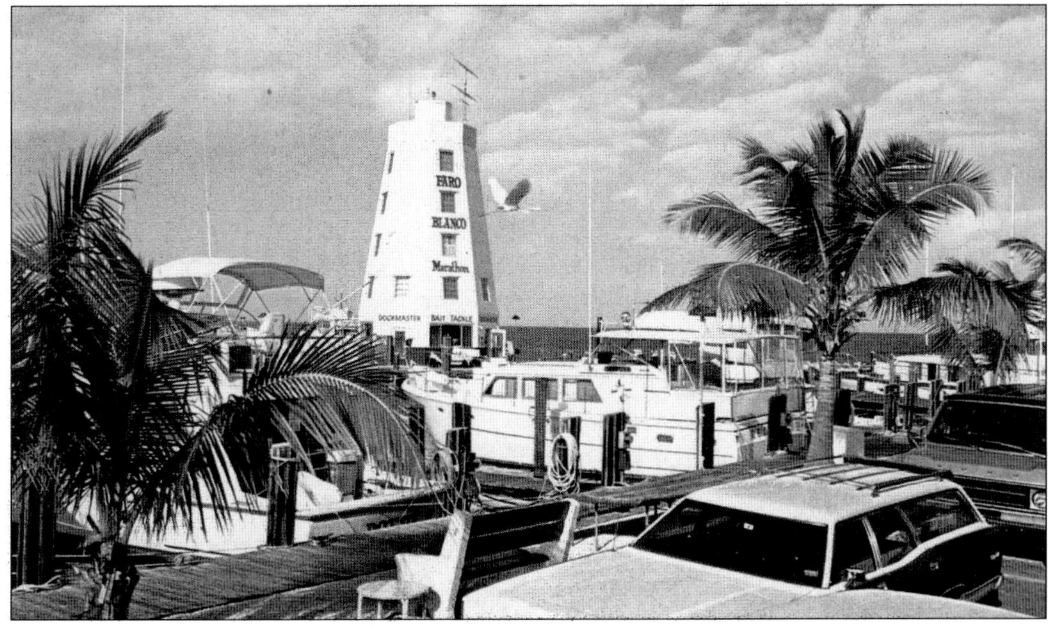

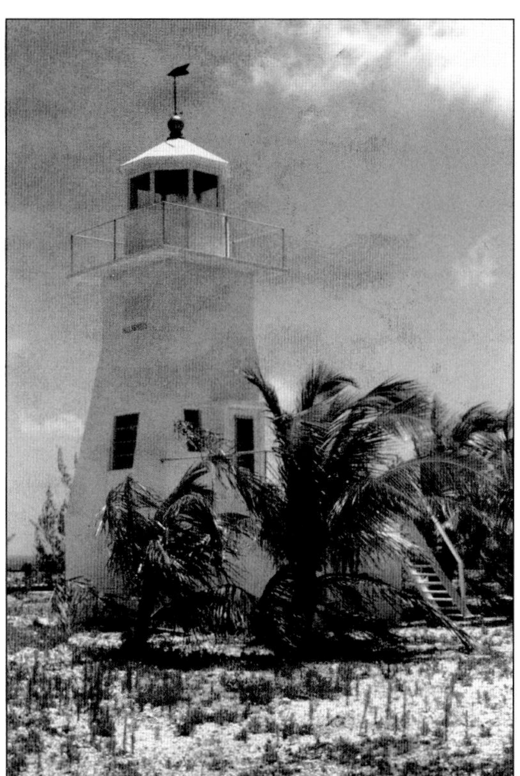

In 1959, a Key Largo property owner discovered the original lighthouse lantern for Rebecca Shoal at a scrap metal dealer in Ocala. After purchasing it, he hired contractor Ralph Smith to construct a base and tower for the lantern. When David and Mariana McGraw bought the property, they refurbished the lighthouse and added two guest rooms. (Courtesy of Jerry Wilkinson.)

Helene "Mama" Baur, Ray Baur Jr., his sister, Gloryanne Baur Sandrey, and her husband, Alexander "Sandy" Sandrey, established a branch of the family restaurant, Chesapeake House, at Mile Marker 83.4 by Whale Harbor. Chesapeake House opened in early 1960, and its steel-reenforced masonry lighthouse became a Keys landmark. (Courtesy of Monroe County Library, Key West.)

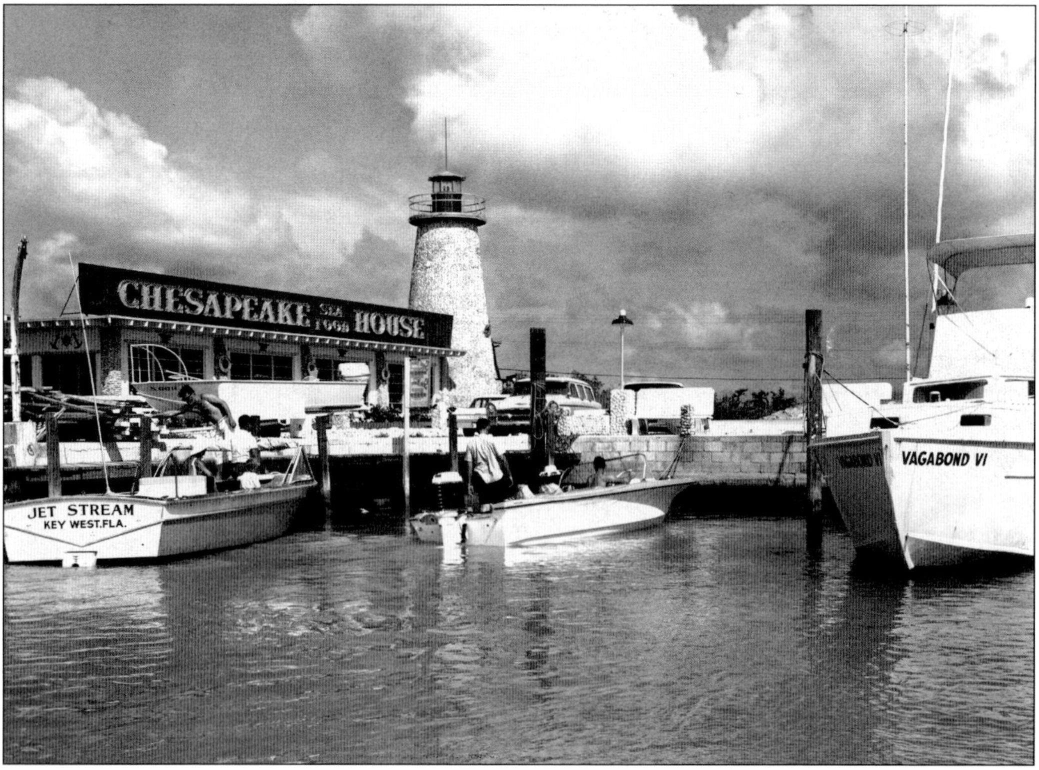

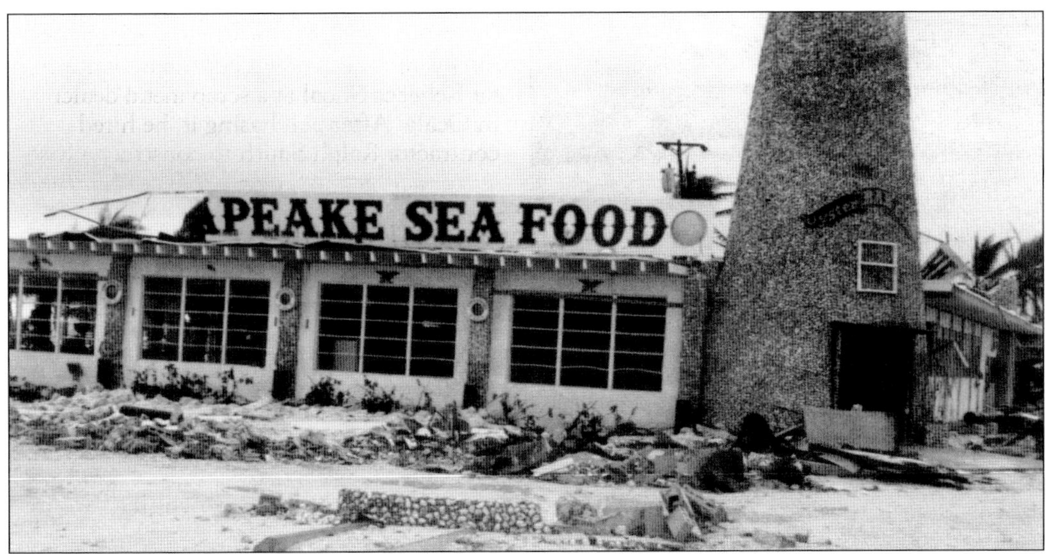

When Hurricane Donna arrived in 1960, packing 140- to 155-mile-per-hour winds, Ray Jr., Sandy, Charlie Beaman, and three Chesapeake House employees sought refuge inside the lighthouse. Although the restaurant itself sustained major damage, the lighthouse survived—as did the six who rode out the storm inside. The family rebuilt the restaurant by February 1961. (Courtesy of Monroe County Library, Key West.)

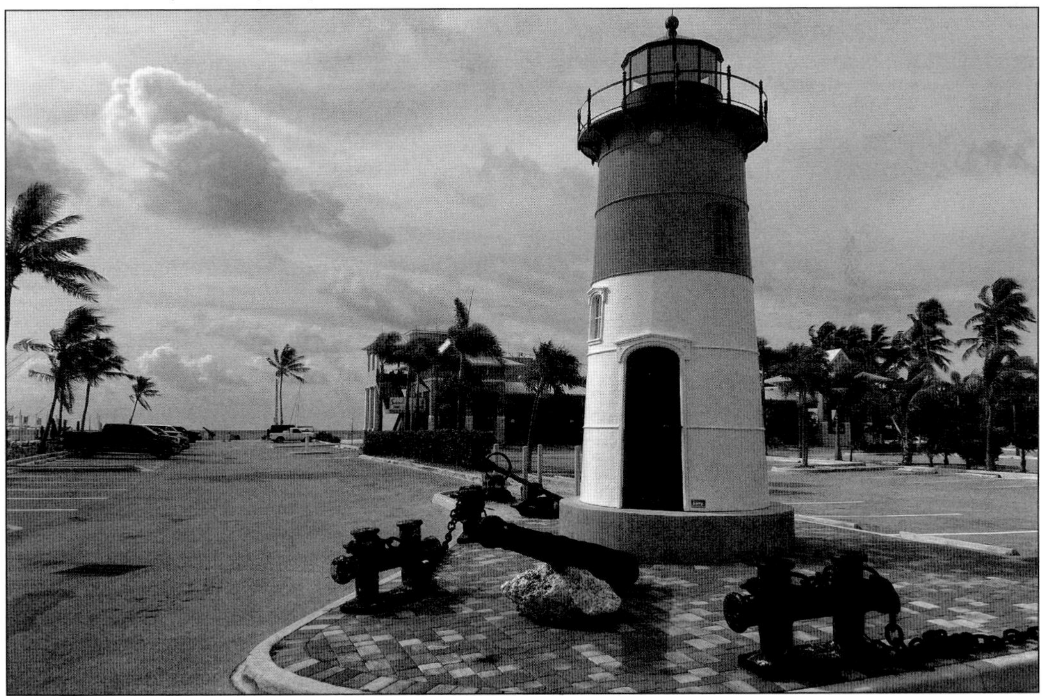

Chesapeake House evolved into the Whale Harbor restaurant, famous for its seafood buffet. In 2013, an electrical fire caused extensive damage; the property was rebuilt and redeveloped as both Whale Harbor Restaurant & Marina and Wahoo Restaurant. In 2017, lighthouse enthusiast Larry Herlth, also known as "Lighthouse Larry," constructed the new lighthouse (pictured here) and installed it in the parking lot. The lantern does illuminate at night. (Courtesy of Zickie Allgrove.)

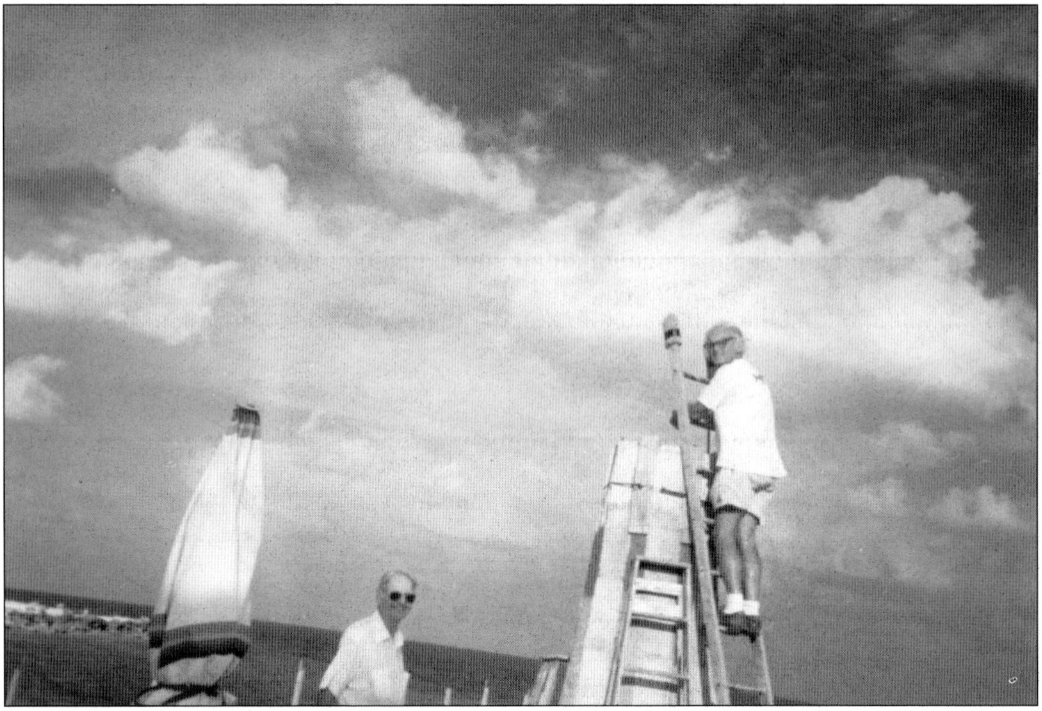

Florida Keys historian Jerry Wilkinson works on a private lighthouse with his father-in-law, John Pierce, in 1993. The light stands behind his home in Tavernier on Key Largo. Jerry is president of the Historical Preservation Society of the Upper Keys and served on the board of the Florida Keys Reef Lights Foundation in its early days. (Courtesy of Mary Lou Wilkinson.)

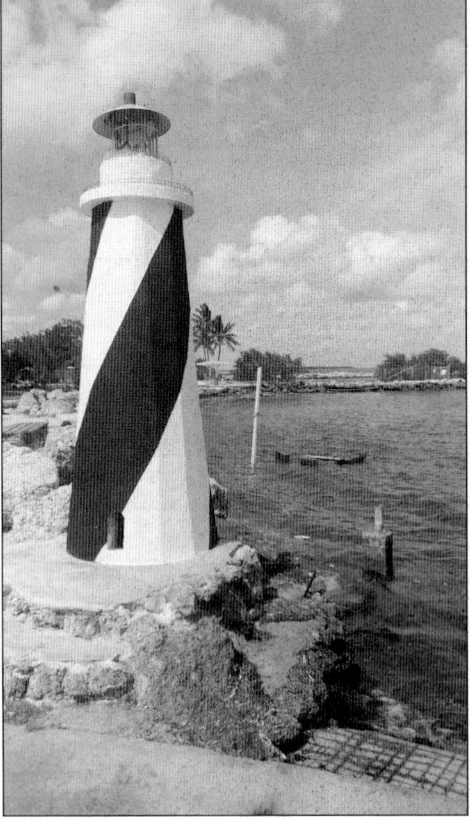

The private white-and-black striped lighthouse belonging to Jerry and Mary Lou Wilkinson survived Hurricane Irma in 2017, although it sustained some damage to its lantern. The light has since been repaired and continues to serve as a local landmark for boaters off the island of Key Largo. (Courtesy of Zickie Allgrove.)

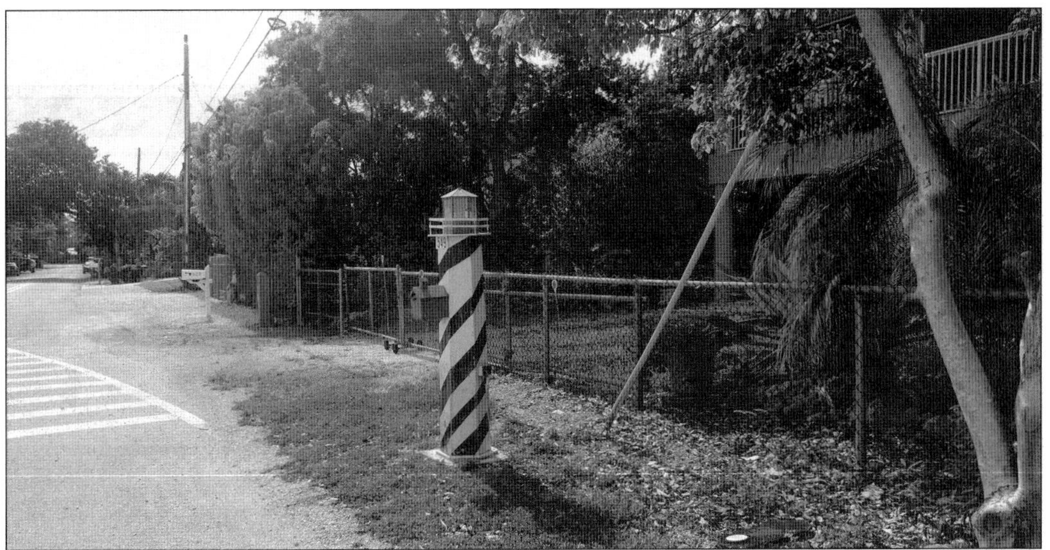

A much smaller white-and-black striped lighthouse can also be found in Tavernier: this one is part of a mailbox at a home not far from Harry Harris Park. A number of Florida Keys residents have installed whimsical lighthouse mailboxes as well as manatee and sailboat mailboxes. (Courtesy of Laura Albritton.)

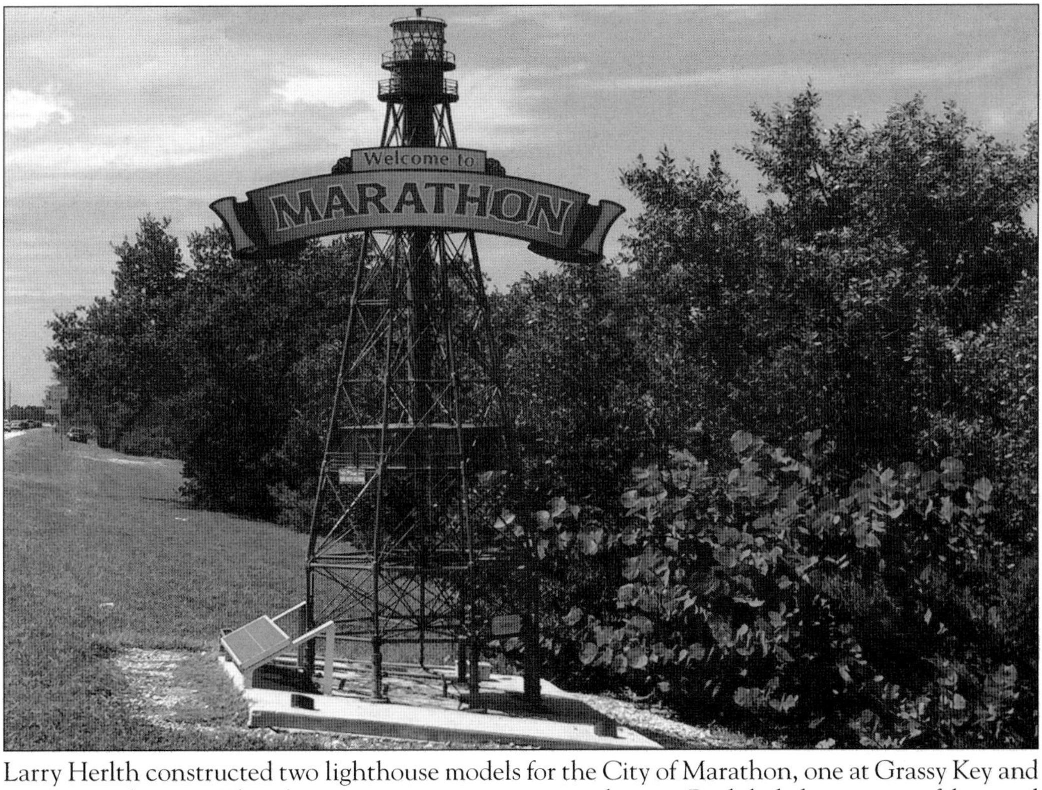

Larry Herlth constructed two lighthouse models for the City of Marathon, one at Grassy Key and one at Knights Key. They function as entrance signs to the city. Both lighthouses were fabricated and installed at a total cost of $41,160. The lighthouse (Grassy Key pictured here) is a model of the Sombrero Key light, which lies off the Middle Keys. (Courtesy of Zickie Allgrove.)

Bibliography

Dean, Love. *Lighthouses of the Florida Keys*. Sarasota, FL: Pineapple Press, 1998.

De Witt, Bernard C. "Lighthouse Official Has Large Private Aviary." *Miami News*, September 30, 1934.

Hailey, Charlie. *Spoil Island: Reading the Makeshift Archipelago*. Plymouth, UK: Lexington Books, 2013.

Hambright, Tom. "Northwest Channel Lighthouse." *Florida Keys Sea Heritage Journal* 21, no. 1 (Fall 2010).

Hurley, Neil E. *Lighthouses of the Dry Tortugas*. Aiea, HI: Historic Lighthouse Publishers, 2002.

Liller, Josh. "Bright Ideas #2: George Meade." *US Lighthouse Society News*, July 15, 2020.

Malcolm, Corey. "Understanding the Key West Hurricane of 1846." *Florida Keys Sea Heritage Journal* 20, no. 4 (Summer 2010).

Mirsky, Steve. "Key West Lighthouse and Keeper's Quarters Museum." *Lighthouse Digest Magazine*, August 2006.

"Mystery of the Lighthouse at Key Largo." *Lighthouse Digest Magazine*, June 2004.

Swanson, Gail. *Sombrero Key Lighthouse at the Florida Keys*. Orlando, FL: Florida Keys Reef Lights Foundation, 2014.

Taylor, Thomas W. *Florida's Territorial Lighthouses, 1821–1845*. Allandale, FL: Thomas W. Taylor, 1995.

———. *Lore of the Reef Lights: Life in the Florida Keys*. West Conshohocken, PA: Infinity Publishing, 2006.

Thiesen, William H. "The Long Blue Line: Barbara Mabrity—Long-time Lighthouse Keeper and Hurricane Heroine." My CG, March 26, 2021.

Wilkinson, Jerry. "Chesapeake Sea Food House." *History Talk from the Upper Florida Keys* 49 (Fall 2009).

———. "Lighthouse Display Case." Florida Keys History Museum. www.keyshistory.org/caselighthousespage2.html.

About the Historical Preservation Society of the Upper Keys

The Historical Preservation Society of the Upper Keys (HPSUK) is a nonprofit organization dedicated to preserving the area's rich cultural heritage in order to pass it on to future generations. The purpose of the society is to preserve prehistoric and historic sites and artifacts located in the Upper Keys and the surrounding territorial waters and to collect and preserve memorabilia related to the early residents. The society works to preserve drawings, pictures, photographs, and films related to Upper Keys history and to write, record, and collect pertinent interviews. HPSUK maintains an extensive website at keyshistory.org and endeavors to disseminate knowledge of Upper Keys history and culture through meetings and more.